An Enemy Such as This

An Enemy Such as This

Larry Casuse and the Struggle for Native Liberation
in One Family on Two Continents
across Three Centuries

David Correia

With a Foreword by Melanie K. Yazzie

Haymarket Books
Chicago, IL

Published in 2022 by
Haymarket Books
P.O. Box 180165
Chicago, IL 60618
773-583-7884
www.haymarketbooks.org
info@haymarketbooks.org

ISBN: 978-1-64259-737-0

Distributed to the trade in the US through Consortium Book Sales
and Distribution (www.cbsd.com) and internationally through Ingram
Publisher Services International (www.ingramcontent.com).

This book was published with the generous support of Lannan Foundation
and Wallace Action Fund.

Special discounts are available for bulk purchases by organizations and institutions. Please email orders@haymarketbooks.org for more information.

Cover and interior design by Eric Kerl.
Cover photo by Anthony Louderbough.

Printed in Canada by union labor.

Library of Congress Cataloging-in-Publication data is available.

10 9 8 7 6 5 4 3 2 1

They brought disease, raped our women, killed our brothers—the animals, murdered our elders, leveled out the vast forests, polluted our rivers, filled our air with chemicals, called us savage, pagans, Indians. . . Never before had we ever had an enemy such as this.
—**Larry Casuse**, February 13, 1973

Their evil is mighty
but it can't stand up to our stories.
So they try to destroy the stories
let the stories be forgotten.
They would like that
They would be happy
Because we would be defenseless then.
—**Leslie Marmon Silko**, "Ceremony," March 1977

Contents

Foreword

Melanie K. Yazzie

The night of June 1, 2020, about twenty comrades from The Red Nation were walking back to our Albuquerque, New Mexico, office after a five-hour Black Lives Matter march. The march would have lasted longer—and taken us into the heart of downtown—had a large group of heavily armed militiamen not stormed the crowd at Walter Street and Central Avenue twenty minutes prior, causing confusion and panic.

In a public interview that aired the following day, I said we were being hunted the entire night. Many of the Native people who attended the march assembled around a large American Indian Movement flag so we wouldn't lose one another in the large crowd of thousands. I don't remember when I noticed two men—both white, both dressed in camouflage—following us. When we sped up, so did they. When we slowed down, so did they. At times, they would duck into dark alleyways only to reappear further down the block. They stayed about ten yards away from us, watching, keeping pace, tracking.

The march leaders ended the protest not long after the militiamen appeared, likely to ensure everyone's safety. People began the two-mile trek back up Central Avenue to their parked cars to call it a night. As we approached our office amid this stream of protesters, two figures came out of the shadows: the two white men who had been following us earlier in the night. Many of our comrades had already reached the office, and a few were out front on the sidewalk. The two men reached them first, claiming they were protecting businesses from looters and demanding to know the comrades' affiliation with our office. The larger one moved to pull a pistol out of his belt. The move was short lived. For security reasons, we had kept the lights off in the office. The two men didn't realize that some twenty Native people were inside—with half a dozen more approaching, me included.

As swiftly as the militiamen stormed the protest twenty minutes earlier, twenty Native people heard the commotion and came streaming out of the dark office, quickly confronting the two men. Realizing immediately their miscalculation, they mumbled an apology and retreated, running across the street and into the darkness. We never saw them again.

As I stated in my interview the next day, it was clear they followed us because we were Native. To be Native in a bordertown like Albuquerque— whether at a protest or walking down the street—is to be a threat. Suspicious. Criminal.

To be Native in these spaces is to be hunted.

◄·······►

David Correia begins *An Enemy Such as This* by detailing the history of scalp hunting that originated in Mexico's genocidal nineteenth-century campaign to exterminate the Apache. The practice became so prevalent that an entire regional economy developed around it. Apache scalps outpaced beaver pelts as the most valuable commodity on the frontier.

Mexican politicians and American and French businessmen subsidized this lucrative enterprise. Often politicians and businessmen were the same people, as the story of Santa Rita mine owner Steven Curcier demonstrates, a story Correia documents to tell the colonial history of Santa Rita copper mine where Larry Casuse's father, Louis, worked, and where Larry was born. Soldiers, mercenaries, and trappers became entrepreneurs, skilled in the art of the hunt.

Indian killing became a profession.

Fast forward to 1973. Larry is fed up with the politicians and businessmen in Gallup, New Mexico. For the previous decade, Gallup's local elite owned and operated the Navajo Inn, perhaps the most notorious liquor establishment in Gallup's history. By the late 1960s, it was the most profitable bar in the state of New Mexico. Located mere yards from the boundary of the Navajo Nation, the bar represented misery and death for Navajo people, who frequently died along Highway 264 from exposure or car-related accidents. By the mid-1970s, McKinley County—with Gallup as its county seat—had the highest alcohol-related mortality rate in the nation.

As Correia notes, "Larry would have pointed out that Navajo misery in Gallup was not an aberration or product of past colonial conquest. Navajo immiseration produced the conditions that made the Gallup economy possible in the first place." Once hunted for their scalps, Indians were now hunted according to the cruel calculations of the bordertown's predatory economy. The trade was still their death, their flesh. The profession had been replenished with a new generation of Indian killers: pawnbrokers, liquor store owners, and traders.

These were the conditions on March 1, 1973, when the foot soldiers—cops—of Gallup's elite murdered Larry. As Correia writes, Larry's mother Lillian, who was across the street in Gallup's welfare office, recalls someone storming into the office yelling, "That Larry Casuse finally got what he deserved." Reporters from the town's newspaper took photos of Gallup police posing with Larry's body—a souvenir from their kill.

Like many Native people before him, Larry had been deemed a threat. Suspicious. Criminal. Hunted and then killed, his love for his people all the more reason to celebrate his death.

The Red Nation formed in 2014 in the bordertowns of the Southwest, the same geographies of violence that ignited in Larry (and many others) the spirit of Indigenous resistance in the 1970s. We talked frequently of Larry in those days—in fact, we still do. We collaborated closely with KIVA Club, the Native student organization at the University of New Mexico Larry helped lead forty years earlier. When we would protest bordertown violence (a term we, along with Correia and Dr. Jennifer Nez Denetdale, coined to capture the brutality Native people experience in these spaces) in the streets of Albuquerque and Gallup, many of us would wear KIVA Club T-shirts with Larry's face on the front, the back stating, "The Indian Movement was then born . . . it was born because we must once again regain the balance between good and evil." Larry said these words a little over two weeks before he died. We knew from the beginning that the evil of which he spoke was the evil of settler colonialism, possessively and feverishly defended by settler men—the hunters, the killers of Native people and the anticolonial political and social orders we carry in our souls. Like Larry, we were fed up with seeing our Indigenous relatives brutalized by these modern-day Indian killers. Sometimes at our protests we would chant, "What would Larry do?" Just as often, we would be sitting around a table or a fire plotting our next protest or event, quietly asking ourselves and each other, "What would Larry do?" It was never a rhetorical question, nor was it said in jest. It was always serious, and we already knew the answer. Of course, we knew what Larry had done. We knew what he sacrificed. And we knew we could never turn away from our people, from the flame of Native liberation that Larry and so many other ancestors in the Indian movement tended to so that our generation—indeed, all future generations—could pick up the torch and carry their prayer, their story, forward.

In this way, "What would Larry do?" is the essence of The Red Nation. He lives on in each of us. He was alive on June 3, 2020, when a group of Native organizers from The Red Nation—all of whom were women and LGBTQ2+, myself included—drove into Gallup to protect Navajo women and youth participating in a Diné-led solidarity march with Black Lives Matter. Gallup's wealthy downtown business owners were literally up in arms, calling on citizens from across the region to join them in armed protection of their businesses from would-be looters. As a small march of mostly Diné youth and women passed through downtown, white and Hispano men stood at business doors like sentinels protecting the Native flesh bounty hoarded inside. Cops perched atop roofs tracking the marchers' movements. United in their hunt, these Indian killers circled the wagons against the Indian hordes, salivating at the possibility of a good kill.

While they didn't get their trophy that day, I'm sure they enjoyed their hunt. A notorious motorcycle gang casually lounged outside of Camille's Sidewalk Café, keeping tabs on the marchers as they held a rally in front of the courthouse a dozen yards away. The café's owner, himself a wealthy and influential white businessman in the region, had offered refuge and service to those helping with the armed protection of local businesses. Camille's was the temporary hunting lodge where this generation of Indian killers fortified their settler masculinity by tracking Native women and youth.

While this display of unadulterated hatred might seem remarkable, I want to point out that those men were afraid of our security team. They did not expect Indigenous people—let alone women—to organize protection for the marchers, to display such unadulterated love for our people that we would stand between them—and their guns—and the women and youth of our nations. That we would look them in the eye and show no fear. Unlike the day Larry was killed, there was no bloodshed that day. I believe this is because we prevented it; yes, by our presence, but more so because of the prayer we carried in our hearts, the same prayer Larry carried. We made sure Gallup knew we weren't afraid to be Indigenous in our own homelands (despite its obsessively greedy claims otherwise), and we sure as hell weren't going to tolerate any more Indian killing.

I think that is what Larry would have done.

◄■■■■■►

Oftentimes the violence of colonialism seems impossible. Impossible to wrap our heads around. Impossible to stop. Impossible to endure. I can't guess at Larry's thoughts, but I imagine he felt all of this, as many Native people do. *An Enemy Such as This* doesn't attempt to capture Larry's thoughts. In fact, the book doesn't focus much on the now infamous circumstances of Larry's death. Instead, it documents Larry's history, and that of his family, through a heart-wrenching arc of violence and war across two continents. It pulls no punches about this violence, something Larry never turned away from, either.

But violence wasn't the only story for Larry. While the hunt may seem a forever war with no end, and Indian killers tense with anticipation for the kill at every turn, the Indigenous refusal to disappear is, I would argue, far more enduring. Like his Apache forbearers, Larry represents an undeniable reality, an unshakeable strength. "Their evil is mighty / but it can't stand up to our stories," writes Leslie Marmon Silko. These words open *An Enemy Such as This*. Like all Indigenous freedom fighters, Larry is a story. As long as this story continues, so too will Indigenous life. Settler colonialism is the negation of life, held together through violence. You can't forge a future out of negation. Indigenous resistance is a story of affirmation.

Larry is an affirmation. The Red Nation is an affirmation.

"We are all Larry," a crowd chanted in downtown Gallup the morning of September 8, 2019. The Red Nation was about to conclude our third annual Native Liberation Conference at the El Morro Theater, just one block from where Larry was killed forty-six years earlier. Conference-goers were wrapping up a radical-history walking tour of downtown Gallup by circling around to do some chants. In that moment, those relatives became a part of Larry's story, the story of liberation. This book, too, is now a part of this story, a part of the prayer and the long struggle for freedom that Larry carried in his heart, and that we in The Red Nation carry in ours.

As we say in The Red Nation, "Long live Larry Casuse! Long live Indigenous liberation!" Nizhoni.

Delbert Rudy, March 1, 1973

He'd never told anybody the story of his kidnapping before. That's the first thing he says when we sit down. His wife corrects him. No, that's not quite true, she says. Oh right, he says. Once, at a church picnic, he found himself in a get-to-know-you game where you introduce yourself by saying something true about yourself that no one will believe.

"Hi, I'm Delbert Rudy, and I was kidnapped by Indians."

◄•••••►

On the morning of his death, Larry Casuse walks into a branch of the American Bank of Commerce in Albuquerque, New Mexico, and withdraws his last $63.39, closing his account.

At the same time, Delbert Rudy, a junior premed major at the University of New Mexico, plays pick-up basketball after a morning of class. He walks back to his car after the game to head home. He'd parked that day in a student lot at the far southeast corner of campus. "That corner was all dirt," he tells me. "That whole corner was all dirt; that was all student parking. And so, that's where my car was parked. So, I was walking back. I think I must have. . . I'd go to the gym a lot; I was walking back, and I think I was carrying my cowboy boots and I was in my tennis shoes. And the cars are all parked real close and I'm just walking back, and I get to my car, and I put my boots down and I get my keys out. And the guy comes up and says, 'Don't move.'"[1]

Rudy looks up and a man is standing in front of him holding a pistol. "And I'm fumbling with my keys," he explains. "And just out of the blue.

'What?' I think I said. I look up and here's Casuse with this automatic pistol. He's a great big guy."

Larry Casuse wears steel-rimmed glasses and a rolled, red bandanna around back hair that drops just above his collar. Delbert looks behind him and sees another man. Robert Nakaidinae, skinny with long hair in a ponytail, holds a hunting knife. He doesn't know either of them, had never seen them before. He does the math in his head. Larry's "a big guy so I didn't think I was going to knock him down with a punch or something. I thought about running. I was pretty fast, and I could have knocked Nakaidinae down easily."

Casuse can tell Rudy is considering running. "Hold it or I'll shoot you," he tells him calmly. He tells Delbert they need his car, a blue 1969 Chevy Nova. "OK, here's the keys." "No," Larry replies, "we're taking you too."

Nakaidinae puts his knife in his bag and walks toward Rudy. "They handcuff me behind my back and put me in the back seat. I remember being concerned because we drove off and my boots were still on the ground back there."

Casuse drives to a gas station south of campus. Rudy lies in the back seat, arms bound at the wrists. "They covered me up with a blanket. That's when I started to get nervous."

They get gas. Casuse drives. Nakaidinae sits in the passenger seat with his bag in his lap.

"I started talking to these guys. Probably because nothing else to do and probably because it was rational to assess what the risk was for me. If I thought it was going to go south. Like if they decided to get off the highway and go down a back road I was going to try to crash the car."

Casuse never pulls off the highway.

"We started talking," Rudy says. "We talked the whole way. Just so you know, my mindset—I'm conservative, I'm not a John Bircher or anything. You know the land grant stuff up north, the T.A, raid, I didn't have any sympathy for the minorities for that, none.[2] So that's my mindset. That may be useful when you look at what I finally thought of Casuse."

"They said the plan was to go to Gallup," Rudy explains, a reservation bordertown two hours west of Albuquerque and just southeast of the Navajo Nation, "and kidnap the mayor and go up into the mountains. They never stressed any intent to kill him. They just wanted to kidnap him. They wanted attention to what they couldn't get anyone to pay attention to."

What did they want attention to?

"The whole thing was about the bar. I remember Rainbow, or maybe Navajo Inn. As I recall there were seven guys who owned this, and one was the mayor of Gallup. The basic problem was that this was close enough that the Indians would walk to it, and they'd get drunk in the wintertime, and they'd get kicked out of the bar, and they'd pass out on the way home, and they'd freeze to death. This still happens today," he says.

"They'd gone to the mayor, the owners. All the levels of politics," he says. "City, county, and state and nobody would address it. So, they went through, and I don't remember all the things they did, but their sole purpose was to move the bar far enough away that you needed a car to get to it and so if you left you'd have a car, you'd be OK because you'd be sheltered. It sounded like this had been going on for quite a while. And my impression was that he had tried to follow the rules. He'd tried to do everything legitimately. It wasn't working. You read the newspapers. It was all in the newspaper about Indians found frozen dead. I knew what he was telling me was true."

Delbert emphasizes Larry's politeness. He asked questions and Larry patiently answered them, all the way to Gallup. "I didn't think that what they were doing was illogical," he says. "Because again they didn't say they were going to kill the guy. Their plan was to kidnap him, get off up into the mountains, hold him hostage until everybody agreed to move the bar."

Did you say anything to them about their plans?

"I don't remember exactly what I said but I wasn't arguing against. What they said sounded reasonable. Think about it. If you have a cause that's a real cause and you've done everything you can do legitimately, and you can't effect the change. What's your next step?"

"There was no 'I hate the US government,' there was no 'the Indians are downtrodden.' This was a very focused individual. He wanted that bar moved so people would not freeze to death in the wintertime. And that was it."

Delbert continues: "Casuse was a smart guy. He was not stupid. The way he talked was smart. His thought process was clear. He was focused, logical.

I think he understood that what he was doing was a big deal. I suspect he understood the ramifications and possibilities. Well, he obviously did."

"Do you know what his biggest miscalculation was, in his plan?" he asks me. I start to answer but he interrupts. "We got there, I don't remember the exact time, this all happened right around five. It's rush hour. They couldn't get [the mayor] to the car because it was bumper to bumper [in Gallup]. Everybody was getting off work. You could have walked and kept up with [traffic] and they knew they couldn't have gotten away from the cops."

City hall lies just south of Route 66, and Larry parks in a lot near the building. The three of them, Larry, Robert, and Delbert, get out of the car, and Robert takes the handcuffs off Delbert. "They needed them for the mayor," Delbert tells me. As Larry and Robert turn to walk toward city hall, Delbert starts to follow behind them until, suddenly, he realizes they're done with him. "It's over," he thinks. He turns and runs into an office building across the street. Insurance office, or something, people sitting behind desks, talking on phones. Delbert bursts in and they give him strange looks. He expects Larry and Robert to emerge any minute with the mayor in handcuffs, so he half-hides in the office. "I was sitting inside the building," he says, and peeking out the window looking for Larry and Robert. Every now and then he'd briefly walk out of the office to look around. "I was out wandering around because the people were looking at me funny, pointing at me."

Larry and Robert never reappear. "After a while a police or sheriff guy, older guy, picked me up," Delbert says. "I remember he was a big guy, older guy. He got me in the car and we started talking and he drove me to the police station." Delbert didn't know it at the time, but police initially thought he was an accomplice. "As it turned out, their initial concern was [making certain] that I wasn't a part of it. So, I got in a car, and we went to the police station." The questioning at the station is brief. "They were asking me, and I was telling them the sequence of events." They didn't seem all that interested in Delbert. This is thirty minutes or so after arriving in Gallup. He asks the cops about Larry and Robert. He wants to know what happened and the cop tells him. "When they went out the front" with the mayor, Delbert says, "I guess, the cops were out there already. And [Larry and Robert] end up getting into a sporting goods store, I guess, to try to get weapons or something, and they had the mayor with them. And there was shooting, and Larry got wounded at some point, and at some point the mayor ran through the window. He ran through the plate glass window." The cop tells Delbert that Larry's dead. "I have not a clue how fast that happened. I don't remember hearing any gunshots." The cop says, "Casuse killed himself and Robert gave up." What the cop didn't tell Delbert was that after the cops killed Larry they dragged his body out of the sporting goods store and onto the sidewalk and left him there while cops, in groups, posed with rifles over Larry's dead body. A reporter for the *Gallup Independent* took photograph after photograph of the smiling cops.

"Once the sheriff was done with me, once they finished with me, 'Go sit in a chair,'" the cop says. "And then they ignored me." He can't remember how long he sat there or what he was thinking. Eventually a tall white guy in a black suit sits down next to him. An "FBI guy was talking to me. The thing that I remember," Delbert says, is that "he didn't spend a long time talking to me." Delbert's watching the commotion in the police station. It was full of people, he tells me, and "they were setting up cots in the police station and people were carrying M16s. I said, 'What's going on?' They said they had reports that busloads of Indians were on their way to Gallup, and they were getting ready for a war."

This is when the FBI agent tells him he can leave. "And I went." The cop who brought him to the station drives him to his car, still parked where Larry left it. Delbert doesn't remember how he got his keys, or if he got gas, or what time he left Gallup.

They just let you take it?

"Yeah, I just drove home." He calls his mother first and tells her what happened and that he's in Gallup. "What are you doing there, dum-dum?" she asks him.

You told your mother you were kidnapped, and she called you "dum-dum?"

He smirks and explains. "Have you ever read much about Victorian attitudes?" he asks. "The most common expression I heard was that 'Children are seen, not heard.'" Toughen up and get your work done. Don't worry about the past. Don't fret about the future. Rudy explains to his mom what happened. "I told her the story and said, 'I'll be home sometime.'" When he got home, his "dad was asleep, he had to go to work the next day." His mom was up but they only "talked about it for a few minutes." They went to bed and that was it.

"I woke up the next morning, late, and my mom said, 'The newspapers are calling,' and I said, 'I'm not talking to anybody.' At that point I felt sympathy for what [Casuse had] done, and I didn't think this needed to be sensationalized. He never espoused violence against anyone. He was trying to stop violence. People were dying and nobody was doing anything. What option did he have? He just didn't think it out. You can argue right or wrong, but there was a logic to it. If you believe in the cause, you do what he did."

KIVA Club members hold signs and march down Central Avenue in Albuquerque in protest of the police killing of Larry Casuse. Photo by Anthony Louderbough. Courtesy of Special Collections/Center for Southwest Research (UNM Libraries), 000-954(4)-0001.

The next day, as young Native activists prepare to march in Albuquerque and Gallup in protest over Larry's killing—protests that would last a month and shut down the city—a reporter asks Victor Cutnose, an American Indian Movement organizer, why Larry did it. What? You still don't understand, huh? It's simple, he says.

"This town wants blood—Indian blood."[3]

Their Evil Is Mighty

"We here at Wounded Knee realize that our fight is the
same fight that Larry Wayne Casuse fought so bravely.
At Wounded Knee we'll honor him, our spiritual
leaders will have special ceremonies for him. In this
Indian way, we'll find unity with him and all of you."
—**Dennis Banks, Russell Means, Carter Camps**,
and **Clyde Bettencourt**, March 2, 1973

Larry's brother Donald tried to make sense of his older brother's death and
thought immediately of Gallup, New Mexico. "You didn't talk about the
Gallup that everyone saw, the Gallup of the drinking and the violence
and the poverty. You didn't talk about it because it just was. It was just how
it was. And Lillian [their mother] accepted it, most everyone accepted that,
in a way that Larry never could. Lillian accepted that the drinking was an
Indian problem, not a political problem. The violence was an Indian problem, not a problem that had something to do with poverty or with misery. Larry made a commitment to be part of making life better for Navajo
people in Gallup. Who does that? Who does that? How many people are
willing to give their life to help people they don't know?"[1]

In the weeks after Larry's death, amid the protests, the marches, the
student walkouts, and the demands for investigations, Larry's friends and
family offered possible answers to Donald's question. Some blamed Larry's
legal troubles. Less than a year earlier he'd hit and accidentally killed a young
Navajo woman while driving on the road to Gamerco, north of Gallup. He

7

A line of protesters marching from the campus of the University of New Mexico to downtown Albuquerque following the police killing of Larry Casuse. Photo by Anthony Louderbough. Courtesy of Special Collections/ Center for Southwest Research (UNM Libraries), 000-954(4)-0003.

felt profound guilt and it made him "excitable and high strung," they said.[2] He couldn't talk about it without breaking down in tears. Others suspected that he'd grown discouraged in his failure to shut down the Navajo Inn and stop the suffering and misery the bar produced. Larry was part of a group formed in Gallup years earlier called Indians Against Exploitation that organized protests and petitions and worked to end the violence against Native people in Gallup, but some wondered if maybe he'd stopped seeing organizing as an answer. Maybe he'd decided he needed different tactics. "He thought he would have to utilize the white man's way of doing things to get anything done—just to shake people up enough to get a few lines in the paper, to grab people in midair and say, 'Wait a minute! Listen to me!'"[3]

Maybe an answer could be found in the Casuse family's move to Gallup when Larry was a teenager and where he witnessed the in-your-face misery of the bordertown. The KIVA Club, a University of New Mexico Native American student group that Casuse had led before his death, issued a statement. Larry, they wrote, "was tired of seeing everyday drunkards lying in the streets, lying in jails, of Indians trying to survive in a conquered oriented society." He'd come to Gallup that day to cleanse the city of that evil, they guessed, and hoped to "make his death a symbol" for something better.[4] Some pointed to his work feeding people at the many protests and actions he helped organize. He'd listen to the people talk to him as they ate the fry bread and mutton stew he served. How can you do work like that, some said, and not come to hate the enemies who governed them? Others agreed with Donald that Larry sacrificed his life to help Native people and did it because of a deeply felt need to connect to a world he'd been robbed of as a child. Born in Santa Rita, New Mexico, far south of the Navajo Nation, raised among the English-speaking and Spanish-speaking children of copper miners, Larry didn't grow up on the Navajo reservation, didn't learn the language, didn't participate in the ceremonies, didn't hear the stories, wasn't part of the traditions. Some, however, found no solace in explanations and no answers in his death. Whatever Larry's reasons may have been, they died with him on that sidewalk in Gallup on March 1, 1973. "To this day," his friend Phil Loretto said, years later, "I can't figure out why he did that."[5]

An Enemy Such as This attempts to answer Donald's question by telling the story of the Casuse family, a family born in the blood of colonialism, torn apart by the wars and occupations that marked the birth of a world hostile to their own. To follow the generations of Casuses introduced in this book is to enter their world, a world made and remade by war and occupation. The story of Larry Casuse and his family is a story of a long, unbroken line of generations that links the shootout with police in the sporting goods store in 1973 that killed Larry to the Johnson Massacre of 1837 that killed Juan José Compá, another Native leader killed by vigilantes or by police. The Johnson Massacre (examined in the book's third chapter) established US control of the world's most profitable copper mine, where a century later Larry would be born, where his father, Louis, would work as a miner, and where the most radical labor union in the US would organize mine workers. The story of the Casuse family links the rough streets of Gallup, where Larry would live and die, to the war-torn streets of occupied Salzburg, Austria, in the 1930s and 1940s, where Larry's mom, Lillian, was born into a crumbling empire and raised in another, and where Louis would patrol as an occupation soldier during the postwar occupation of Austria. Theirs is a story that links the reservation trading posts on the Navajo Nation, an industry that sentenced generations of Navajos into debt servitude, to the company stores of the Kennecott mine in Santa Rita, where Larry was raised.

The arc of the Casuse family follows the arc of US colonial war and occupation. The important moments of their lives overlay like a map on the world-historical events of the nineteenth and twentieth centuries. Larry's great, great grandfather, Jesus Arviso, the subject of the fourth chapter, is famous and revered among Navajos. He was kidnapped from his Mexican family as a child, traded from the Apache to the Navajo as a boy, and raised among the Navajo, to whom he became a legendary leader. Larry's maternal grandfather, Richard Hutzler fought in two world wars. The Royal Bavarian Army of the German Empire drafted him into the military on the same day it declared war on France in 1914. He fought as a lowly private in the wars that ended empires in Europe and was discharged from the army the day after Kaiser Wilhelm II abdicated and the German Empire collapsed, and the day before the doomed Weimar Republic was declared. Larry's mother, Lillian, celebrated her third birthday watching Nazis march through the streets of Salzburg, Austria, her hometown. She celebrated her eighth birthday hiding from Allied bombs that nearly destroyed Salzburg. She was almost ten when the Soviets invaded from the north and the Americans from the west, ending the war and beginning the postwar occupation of Austria. Lillian's personal story is part of the apocalyptical story of war and occupation in midcentury Europe. War and occupation are apocalyptic for all, but more so for girls and women. Allied troops raped tens of thousands of women during the occupation. After the war, thousands more migrated to the US from war-torn Europe as war brides, including Lillian.

Larry's father, Louis, fought in the two bloodiest European battles that American troops fought in World War II, was captured by the Wehrmacht in the Battle of the Bulge, and was held in a Nazi POW camp until his liberation. Louis rejoined the army after the war. He met Lillian in Salzburg, where he patrolled the prisoner-of-war and displaced-persons camps during the US occupation of Austria. After he was discharged, Louis returned to New Mexico and worked in the same mine made possible by the genocidal Mexican war against Apaches of a hundred years earlier. He was one of only two Navajo mine workers ever to join the radical union made famous in the film *Salt of the Earth*, which chronicled the strike by the International Union of Mine, Mill, and Smelter Workers against Empire Zinc. No history of that union or that strike tells his story.

So, forget Plymouth Rock and all the other stories of American exceptionalism that celebrate colonization. Look instead at Santa Rita, New Mexico, where settler colonialism was born in the blood of Apaches murdered by American mercenaries, where it was raised by settlers in copper mines that existed only because of the bloody murder of Apaches, and where it came of age in grim and violent bordertowns such as Gallup, New Mexico, those horrible machines of Native misery, suffering, and resistance.

To understand Larry Casuse is to understand this history, so we start in Santa Rita, New Mexico, where violence against the Apaches established the conditions for windfall profits for American mining companies. And then there's Larry's father, Louis, who led a life that explodes the stereotype of Navajos as passive or helpless victims of colonial conquest. He escaped boarding school. Survived tuberculosis. Fought a world war. Patrolled a European city as an occupier. Brought a war bride home with him. Joined the most radical labor union in the US in the 1950s. And then there's Gallup, a city calibrated to convert the suffering and misery of Navajo people into great wealth and security for settlers. This is still true today. And this is where the Casuses would eventually move, and where Larry would come of age.

◄·······►

Settler colonialism is a mode of sustained violence, as the story of the Casuse family makes clear. The violence of colonial conquest requires a vast war-making infrastructure and a complex network of institutions for justifying, rationalizing, and extending colonial violence into an occupation. Among the most potent, persistent, and least acknowledged of these is law itself. The violence of colonialism is a violence inaugurated by law. How has law, which depicts itself as rational, established and sustained the conditions for colonial violence despite its professed commitment to rationality and justice? Law relies on origin stories to make and enforce its claims. Perhaps the most important, and consequential, of these is the one found in the 1823 Johnson v. M'Intosh opinion written by the chief justice of the

US Supreme Court (and prolific land speculator) John Marshall. Marshall took an obscure property dispute and spun it into a sweeping, world-making legal doctrine. Native people might live on the land, he declared, but we conquerors own it. The decision defined what is called the discovery doctrine, and there would be no United States as we know it without it. "From time immemorial," he wrote in his Johnson v. M'Intosh opinion, the Native nations of North America held "no separate property in soil." What land and territory they claimed, he wrote, they held "in common." The "whole theory of their titles to lands in America, rests upon the hypothesis, that the Indians had no right of soil as sovereign, independent states." It is "discovery" he wrote, that "is the foundation of title." The whole "history of America, from its discovery to the present day, proves, we think, the universal recognition of these principles."

The principles of the doctrine of discovery are the principles of colonial conquest: The discovery doctrine defines property as a product of Indigenous genocide. It is this, and not some objective notion of justice, that constitutes the "whole history of America." Ruthless, colonial violence, which law calls "discovery," brought property to life in order to bring Indigenous worlds to an end. As Casuse would write weeks before his death, colonialism brought wave after wave of settlers who "raped our women, killed our brothers—the animals, murdered our elders, leveled out the vast forests, polluted our rivers, filled our air with chemicals, called us savage, pagans, Indians."[6]

Casuse called colonists and settlers a "cunning and ruthless" enemy that disguised its violence in the language of law, a machine that manufactures legal doctrine. Lawyers and judges have many definitions for legal doctrine. The phrase "legal doctrine" refers to the principles that judges draw from a specific set of facts in a particular case in order to establish and apply a set of legal standards. In goes the specific, the personal, the political, and out comes the universal, the objective, the legal. Or better yet, in goes colonial violence, out comes private property. In goes Indigenous genocide, out comes justice for settler society. In goes Native dispossession, out comes what settlers call America.

Johnson v. M'Intosh, along with two related cases collectively referred to as the Marshall trilogy, condemned Native nations to the status of domestic, dependent nations. Where the Marshall trilogy promised progress, Larry Casuse found suffering. "They split us apart ruthlessly and tried to assimilate us into believing we were the white man's children. They told us theirs was the best way." Law, it turns out, tells us very little about the "whole history of America." For that history, we need the story of the Casuse family.

Blood Contracts

Rita of Cascia, patron saint of impossible dreams and murdered women. Eighteen years married to a violent, abusive man. Instead of leaving him, she remained forever faithful. Hers was a life spent in suffering and prayer for the salvation of an abusive husband. Her salvation came only with his death, whereupon she became a nun of the Augustinian order. Mother and mystic, she was revered during her life and after her death in 1457 for the miraculous power of her prayers and the Christ-like stigmata on her forehead. In what is today southern New Mexico, more than six thousand miles and nearly two hundred years from Rita and where she made her home in Renaissance Italy, lies the mineral-rich Sierra del Cobre, in the heart of Gran Apachería, a vast Apache homeland that stretches from what is today southwestern Texas all the way to California and south into Mexico. The Spanish, then Mexicans, and finally Americans, occupied the region beginning in the eighteenth century, where they mined copper at a spot they called Santa Rita del Cobre. It quickly became Mexico's most important mineral deposit and largest producer of copper. By the mid-twentieth century, it was the largest and most profitable open-pit copper mine in the world, named after the peasant girl Rita, patron saint of abused wives and lost causes.

If you visit the mine, even today, you'll see an enormous rock monolith perched on a promontory above the open pit. The Kneeling Nun, as it is known, is a volcanic tuff of ignimbrite rock, shaped by wind and water in the image of a woman, a nun, wearing a habit, facing the mine, and, like Rita, forever knelt in prayer. It is no accident the Spanish soldiers and mining speculators who would dig deep into those copper veins named the place after Rita of Cascia. The entire enterprise was based on great violence and suffering. And forgiving them for all of it was the Kneeling Nun, forever praying for her tormentors' salvation. If those prayers were miraculous, as Rita's are said to have been, they were not meant for the Apaches who fought the Spanish, the Mexicans, and finally the Americans. From her perch above the mine, the Kneeling Nun watched an Apache homeland become a Spanish copper-mine village populated during the Mexican period by American mercenaries waging a bloody war against Mimbreño and Gileño Apaches. She watched as soldiers and mercenaries plundered Apache rancherías. She watched as they killed men and women, kidnapped Apache children, and took bloody scalps. She watched the wagon trains of slave-mined ore and ingots travel from Cobre to Chihuahua City.

Mexico waged a war against the Apaches that it could not win and could not afford. By the mid-nineteenth century, the Mexican government desperately turned to American mercenaries to fight the Apaches. The Mexican treasury established a fund to pay mercenaries to hunt and collect scalps. Mexican officials enticed soldiers-for-hire, most of whom were Americans, into Chihuahua by the promises of a bounty for every child they could kidnap and every scalp they could collect. *Contratos de sangre*, Mexican officials called them, Blood Contracts. These were first proposed and initially funded by the American and French owners of the mine in Santa Rita, who sought to harness the power of market-based exchange to reap efficiencies in colonial violence. Scalps for copper—colonialism's commercial analog to the Christian practice of the mortification of the flesh—purification through violence. The invisible hand of the market gathering up the hair above the scalp lock. The invisible foot of the market stepping on the neck of an Apache child. The other hand of the market holding a bowie knife and cutting deeply into the skin along the forehead, making the cut around the skull and under one ear. Then, stepping harder on the neck, the quick yank of hair then the scalp coming loose from the cranium with a quick, vacuum-like sound.

The Kneeling Nun added all this to her prayers as she looked down at the accumulating scalps flying like flags above presidios and churches from Santa Rita del Cobre to Chihuahua City.

◄•••••►

The story of Santa Rita del Cobre is also the story of Juan José Compá. Much of what we know about the origins of the Santa Rita del Cobre mine comes from the archives of the Spanish and later Mexican presidio in Janos, ninety miles south of Santa Rita. The name Compá appears over and over in the archives, in letters he wrote and in those he received. He was the only known Apache child ever educated at a presidial school. The second oldest child of the Apache chief El Compá, whom historians describe as an important Apache leader and Spanish ally. El Compá first made "peace" with Spain in 1786 at Bacoachi, Sonora. It was a peace like all others in that it wasn't arrived at peacefully, and it didn't produce peace. It required certain concessions on the part of El Compá, which included disarming and remaining settled at a Spanish presidio. When El Compá failed to adhere to these conditions, Spain kidnapped his wife in 1787. With the threat of exile looming, El Compá finally and permanently settled at Janos in 1790, where he remained until his death in 1794. While at Janos he served as a scout for Spanish authorities, who frequently enlisted El Compá into military campaigns against other Apaches. Spanish census records show that he lived at Janos with a woman named Maria, who the Spanish identify as his wife, and three other women, possibly sisters of Maria. Census records list four children. When El Compá died, the Spanish enlisted his oldest son, Juan Diego, as his replacement. His younger son, Juan José, was only eight or nine when his father died. A third child apparently died before El Compá did. The Spanish didn't bother listing the name of his youngest child, a daughter.

Juan José Compá attended the presidio school at Janos, an Apache boy among the sons of military officers.[1] He learned Spanish and gained a familiarity with Spanish soldiers, and later, Mexican officials. It would be to Juan José, and to a lesser degree his older brother, Juan Diego, that Mexican military officials would turn in the late 1820s and early 1830s for help in securing Santa Rita del Cobre against Apache raids.

There is no physical description of Compá anywhere in the archives. Not what he looked like, or how he talked, how good he was on a horse, how he handled a knife, or how well he shot a rifle. His letters reveal that he was more than merely bilingual—he was fully literate. In perfect Spanish, and with handwriting far better than the educated Mexican officers from Janos with whom he maintained a lifelong epistolary relationship, Compá demonstrated a keen understanding of the risks of Mexico's complicated colonial campaign against the Apaches.

Mexico relied on information from a network of what it considered "pacified" Apache leaders against "the evils and damages of the traitorous Apaches, conspiring against all living things."[2] They had many such arrangements with Apache leaders, but they considered El Compá, and later his son Juan José, their most important Apache ally. Juan José was constantly cited by military leaders as providing crucial information on Apache troop movements and intentions. But he was cautious in what he said, and often warned his Mexican contacts when campaigns in his view had gone too far. So influential and trusted was he that his letters would circulate among various presidios and often influence Mexican military strategy.[3] In an April 1833 letter to a wealthy hacienda owner, he correctly anticipated that Mexican military raids on Apache rancherías would have disastrous results. "I have heard news," he wrote Mariano Varela, "that in the north they have attacked the peaceful Apaches. . . . They killed Apaches in their homes, and others were also killed on the road to Chihuahua. . . . I am warning your government."[4] In that same letter he admitted that he was a flawed messenger for all sides. His long relationship with Mexican military officers had created suspicions among Apaches near Santa Rita del Cobre.[5]

Despite their doubts about him, Mexican negotiators relied on Juan José. There was no other Apache leader like him, fully fluent in Spanish and able to move so easily between worlds. "We value the good deal he plans to provide us," they explained.[6] But some among the Mexicans came to distrust him completely and blamed him for every failure in their efforts to "pacify" other Apaches. This placed Compá in an impossible position. Mexican soldiers in Chihuahua rarely negotiated in good faith. When Compá refused to go along with the subterfuge, he became a military target. "I don't know why they would search for me," wrote Compá once after refusing to participate in a plan to ambush an Apache ranchería, "for I have committed no crime."[7] Despite these doubts, he was too important to Mexican military leaders at Janos to abandon. By 1835, they declared him the "capitancillo of the pacified Apaches" and paid him a small monthly stipend.[8] His influence was greatest when it came to Mexico's efforts to defend its copper mine in Santa Rita del Cobre.

◀ ▪▪▪▪▪ ▶

The Spanish origins of Santa Rita del Cobre begin in 1799 when a group of Gileño Apaches, which English-speaking settlers would later call Coppermine Apaches, led a Spanish presidial colonel named José Manuel Carrasco to a valley in the heart of the Copper Range of the Mimbres Mountains. Colonel Carrasco had recently retired from a career as a *carabinero*, or frontier cop, whose job it was to patrol and "hunt down Apaches" in northeastern Sonora.[9] Carrasco operated during a chaotic time in northern Chihuahua and Sonora. Official Spanish policy of 1786 directed Spanish carabineros to seek out Apaches and convince them to settle on the *establecimientos de paz*, or Apache reservations, that surrounded Spanish presidios. But Mimbreño, Mescalero, and Gileño Apaches were wary of such offers. To settle was to submit to a peace administered by officers and carabineros prone to violating peace agreements. In late spring of 1787, eight hundred Mimbreños rose up at the San Buenaventura presidio and attacked Spanish soldiers while, at the same time, Mescalero Apaches escalated attacks throughout northern New Spain.[10] In response, Spanish troops killed or captured more than five hundred Apaches. Those captured were exiled from their homelands south to Mexico City under armed guard in forced marches, a policy of permanent deportation that the Spanish called *remesa*, or remittance. For Apaches throughout the northern frontier, 1788 brought an increase in both the intensity of Spanish warfare and an expansion in its policy of exile for Apache prisoners of war. This was Carrasco's trade: supervising the deportation of Apache prisoners of war from Janos and Chihuahua City to points further south.[11]

Carrasco's El Cobre origin story mentions none of this. It reads like a children's book. In 1799, in semiretirement, an old man once expert at exiling Gileños from their homeland, not only finds himself welcomed into the Copper Range by an Apache chief but is invited to take up mining at El Cobre. It is absurd, but it's a fiction that hews closely to the conventions of the colonial property claim, the genre in which Carrasco wrote. The conventions of Spanish colonial property making required a story of property's origins, one that included a single claim and a first discovery, free from preexisting or adverse claims. In Carrasco's petition, which under Spanish law would literally become a deed to property, he carefully avoided mention of any others—particularly missing is the long-standing and ongoing Apache presence in the area—in order to ensure that his claim would be approved. Colonial property claims—all property claims in fact—required an origin story, and truth had little to do with it.[12] Stop at the chamber of commerce offices in Silver City, New Mexico, and ask for the brochure on the Santa Rita mine. It retells this story in one sentence: "Carrasco was shown a copper deposit by a friendly Apache Indian."[13]

There are other ways to tell the story. Carrasco's petition was significant not only for the mineral potential at Santa Rita, but also for the enormous risk that Spanish colonization of the Copper Range posed. El Cobre lay days of travel north of the nearest military garrison at the Janos presidio. Santa Rita del Cobre thus marked a point well beyond Spanish influence, in a territory controlled entirely by Apaches. It was no place to be Spanish in 1799. To approve Carrasco's request would require extending Spain's already stretched military presence into the heart of the Apache homeland.[14]

Spain eventually permitted Carrasco's claim and expanded colonization efforts into the Copper Range, and it did this because the need for copper outweighed the likelihood of failure. The mineral potential at Santa Rita, even today, is hard to overestimate. The heavily forested Copper Range shelters huge deposits of lead, zinc, and iron, but it is copper that gives it its name. The Copper Range is a product of geological forces, millions of years in the making. For millennia, oxygenated water percolated down from the forested surface through igneous and sedimentary rock, leaching copper-bearing minerals along the way. The resulting copper-rich solution eventually found its way to the water table where it slowly mineralized into thick layers of enriched copper. Erosion and uplift brought these layers of copper, or veins, to the surface. Gileño Apaches described finding abundant copper just below the surface, and even scattered about the forest floor. At the site of Carrasco's claim, the copper mineralization mixed with gold to create a unique color that gave the rocks an appearance of "blue veins running through white marble."[15]

When he staked his claim to El Cobre in 1801, Carrasco explained to the Deputación de Minería in Chihuahua the familiar discovery myth that comes with all colonial property claims. "Divine providence," not fifty years of war and occupation, made his claim possible. But constant Gileño attacks on the mine thwarted his plans. Carrasco never named the Apache chief who led him to the site of the mine. It could not have been El Compá, however, who died five years earlier. It may have been Juan Diego, to whom the Spanish turned as El Compá's replacement. Not only did Juan Diego initially replace his father as "General of all Apaches," but he knew the mine as well. In 1805 Juan Diego and his nineteen-year-old younger brother Juan José petitioned for their own license to mine at Santa Rita, noting the "many signs of gold in placers and veins" along the San Francisco River west of what would become the village of Santa Rita del Cobre. The request makes no mention of Carrasco's claim, but given their influence among Spanish authorities, there's little doubt they were aware of it.[16] The Janos archive includes no evidence of any response to the petition by the Compás. Only Carrasco and his successor, Francisco Manuel Elguea, a wealthy and connected Chihuahua politico who purchased Carrasco's claim in 1803, received official recognition.[17] When Elguea began mining at Santa Rita he relied on Spanish soldiers to provide security, used prison labor to mine copper, and hired private security forces, augmented by Spanish soldiers, to escort the mule trains of copper ingots and ore along the copper road south from Santa Rita to Chihuahua City.

Elguea introduced underground mining at Santa Rita, which meant misery for everyone but him. Miners chased after copper veins by digging narrow trenches deep into the earth with enormous pickaxes. Muckers then descended into the narrow shafts on rough-hewn juniper ladders, shimmying through deep tunnels barely wide enough to fit them. With leather bags strapped to their backs, they dragged copper ore up through shafts prone to collapse and frequent rockfalls.[18] When the first shipments of copper from Santa Rita reached the royal mint in Mexico City, the copper's purity quickly established Santa Rita's ore as "the cleanest, most malleable, and best suited for coinage."[19] Between 1805 and 1809, Elguea shipped nearly a million pounds of refined copper to Mexico City, usually in the form of enormous ingots, mostly used by Spain for the manufacture of military weaponry.

When Elguea died in 1809, an heir continued operations at the mine, but low copper prices and increased Apache raids reduced the copper yield at Santa Rita. It wouldn't be until 1827, when the American Robert

Early Santa Rita del Cobre copper miner posing beside juniper ladders and the type of mining equipment common prior to the mechanization of the mine. Courtesy of Special Collections/Center for Southwest Research (UNM Libraries), 995-051-0046

McKnight and his French partner, Steven Curcier, leased the mine, that Santa Rita would return to large-scale production. Under McKnight and Curcier the mine produced annual profits estimated in the millions.[20] McKnight and Curcier assumed authority of daily operations at Santa Rita after first establishing silver and copper mines throughout Chihuahua and Nuevo Mexico. Like Elguea before them, they relied on prison labor and private security to operate their mines. Most men working security for the mine, which briefly included Kit Carson, moonlighted as trappers and hunters, and many would eventually turn to scalp hunting in the 1830s and 1840s. McKnight was based in Santa Rita, from where he managed the daily operations of the mine. Santa Rita relied on military security, and for this reason McKnight was in frequent contact with Mexican military officials at Janos. Shipments of copper no longer traveled all the way to Mexico City but instead to the state mint in Chihuahua City. Curcier rarely spent time in Santa Rita, instead living in Chihuahua City from where he organized the twice monthly supply trains north to Santa Rita that brought provisions, equipment, and weapons.

The son-in-law of one of Santa Rita's many mercenaries called the mine "the most fearfully dangerous enterprise that any man could think of engaging in."[21] The archives of the Janos presidio describe the beginning of McKnight and Curcier's tenure in Santa Rita as corresponding to the start of an extended war with the Apaches that would last for decades. There is an enormous amount of historical scholarship on this period largely based on those archives. These histories tell a story of a mine struggling to stay afloat amid a sea of Apache hostility and violence. It is easy to conclude that the beginning of copper mining at Santa Rita del Cobre coincided, coincidentally, with the rise of Apache resistance during this period. But it would be a mistake. Mimbreño and Gileño Apache raids on military garrisons and mining camps did increase in the late 1820s, but only after McKnight and Curcier expanded operations at Santa Rita in 1827. It was no coincidence that the start of intractable conflict between Mexico and the Chiricahua Apaches corresponded directly to the beginning of mining in Santa Rita. Santa Rita del Cobre, in other words, was not part of the story of Apache-Mexican conflict, it was its author. There is no better way to understand Mexico's genocidal policies of Apache extermination, particularly the scalp-bounty program that would come to define it, than through the prism of copper mining in Santa Rita.

The years McKnight and Curcier operated the mine at Santa Rita del Cobre were marked by two related trends: dramatically increased copper production and an even more dramatic increase in Mexican military activity in the Copper Range. Elguea had proved that the mine harbored unparalleled copper deposits, but unlocking the commercial potential of the mine was a logistical and security problem that Elguea and his heirs never solved. The problem was finding a way to reliably deliver regular shipments of ore, or refined copper in the form of ingots, through the heart of the Apache homeland along the copper trail that connected Santa Rita to Chihuahua City. The only way mining in Santa Rita would be possible would be through the reliable and long-term commitment from the government of Chihuahua to fund, no matter the cost, ongoing security at the mine. And not just at the mine, but the entire region. Colonial conquest, it turns out, required an expansion of Mexican settlements in Apache lands, and this required an expanded military force in the region. McKnight's and Curcier's partnership was designed precisely around the related problems of logistics and security. McKnight recruited mercenaries to provide security both at the mine and along the copper trail. Curcier, as a Frenchman, qualified for Mexican citizenship, and he used his citizenship to become not only a wealthy businessman in Chihuahua City but an elected member of the legislature, where he used his influence to expand the Mexican military presence near Santa Rita and throughout the copper trail.

◄••••••►

Mexico adopted many of the war-making policies first practiced by the Spanish. Among the most enduring of these was what some historians who wrote of this period mistakenly described as peace making and what Mexican soldiers at the time called "pacification." Chihuahua used violence or the threat of violence to force Apache leaders into peace negotiations where military negotiators would demand total fealty to colonial authority. They offered conditional protection and occasional rations to those Apache groups that submitted. To those who refused, they waged war. These "peace" treaties, once agreed to, included compulsory service on the part of Apache leaders to presidial units as scouts or interpreters in military campaigns against other Apache groups. Spanish, and later Mexican military officials, sought out influential Apache leaders, or men who they thought were influential leaders, and offered them rations—food, supplies, shelter, and protection. These "pacified" leaders would vouch to other Apache groups that the Mexicans wanted peace. When Apaches submitted to peace negotiations, Mexican soldiers often took "hostages from Apaches who came to them on peaceful missions" and then used those hostages to establish other "peace" agreements with other groups.[22] The choice was not war or peace, but war or an expanded colonial authority over Apache territory and every facet of Apache life.

When McKnight and Curcier began mining at Santa Rita, both Juan Diego and Juan José lived at Janos. Juan Diego left in 1831. Juan José maintained a ranchería at Janos but increasingly spent his time at a ranchería near Santa Rita del Cobre. By this time, the Spanish had begun calling Juan José, like his father before him, the General of all Apaches. It is not surprising that Mexico focused its interest on Juan José Compá. He was the only fully bilingual Apache leader, and to Mexican military officials this made him invaluable as a translator and intermediary.[23]

Juan José maintained a nearly lifelong epistolary relationship with a Janos hacienda owner who historians assume was his godfather, Mariano Varela. Varela was influential with Janos military authorities and frequently delivered Juan José's letters to the commander at Janos. As a result, both brothers were given preferential treatment at Janos, often receiving rations of clothes, food, and weapons. In his carefully written letters, Juan José would pledge his allegiance and then ask for gunpowder and ammunition.[24] But Mexican officials began to doubt his fidelity to Mexico and his influence among Apaches.[25] Though he was responsible for brokering peace agreements, and routinely gave Mexican authorities the names of Apaches who violated various peace agreements, his loyalty to Mexico and his influence with other Apaches had its limits.[26] It is possible he was genuinely loyal to Janos, and most historians of the period assume as much, and there is plenty of evidence to suggest it. He was at the center of efforts to broker peace agreements among other Apache groups. But it is also impossible to ignore the fact that much of what Compá did, and many of the claims he made in his letters, proved consistently unreliable. Some historians have suggested that his patrons assumed a regional influence that Compá never had. The Spanish and Mexican practice of naming Apache leaders reflected a profound misunderstanding of Apache social structure and organization. Juan José Compá was the "General of all Apaches"—in other words, to everyone but the Apaches. But it could also be true that Compá took advantage of this situation and manipulated the Mexicans, trading false loyalty for guns, ammunition, and information. And there is compelling, if circumstantial, evidence to suggest it. Apache attacks in the Sierra Cobre took one of two forms: raids on Santa Rita or on mule trains along the copper trail. The raids along the trail targeted supply trains, which included official correspondence traveling between Santa Rita and garrisons and presidios to the south. It would only have made sense to intercept Mexican military correspondence if someone could translate the letters, and Compá was the only Apache leader who could have done so.[27] It was also true that Compá cultivated a relationship with Robert McKnight, along with the trapper and notorious mercenary James Kirker, who worked security for McKnight at Santa Rita del Cobre. Mexican law prohibited foreign trappers from operating in Mexico without a license. A common way that American trappers got around the law was by moonlighting as security at Santa Rita in order to use the mine as a base of operations. They hid their otter and beaver pelts from Mexican officials in Santa Rita mine shafts until they could ship them north to Santa Fe or Taos. Kirker traded guns and ammunition to Compá, and in return Compá traded information to Kirker about Mexican troop movements.[28]

◄▪▪▪▪▪▪►

By the early 1830s, Santa Rita had grown to more than six hundred people, nearly half of them soldiers posted by Chihuahua's military chief, José Calvo, but the cost of security quickly exceeded Calvo's budget. In January of 1832, Compá sent two Apache messengers to Janos, who explained that while Apaches wanted "peace and tranquility" they were equally ready to "take up arms" against Mexican aggression.[29] As the Apache raids on Santa Rita continued, Calvo pursued pacification strategies and invited Apache leaders to Santa Rita to negotiate a peace treaty. In August of 1832, a delegation of twenty-nine Apache leaders, including Juan José Compá, met Mexican authorities in Santa Rita. There they agreed to the Treaty of Santa Rita del Cobre.[30] It could not have been more one sided. Each Apache group agreed to cease attacks on Santa Rita, return cattle and horses claimed by the Spanish, and refrain from any travel south into Chihuahua. Mexico offered nothing in return. No rations were provided or promised, and no limits were placed on Mexican military activity north of Janos. The peace treaty collapsed as quickly as it was agreed to and Mexican military operations continued, as did Apache attacks. In a letter to the Janos presidio, Compá warned that Mexican attacks would backfire and provoke a return to hostilities.[31] In April of 1833, Compá complained again of Mexican attacks on Apaches that were being launched under the pretext of peace making and in the presence of military leaders.[32] As he predicted, coordinated Apache attacks focused on Santa Rita, and in response McKnight fully militarized the mine, building a *torreón* and new barracks to hold more soldiers. But attacks continued and mine laborers abandoned Santa Rita. Terrified soldiers deserted their posts. The victorious Apaches celebrated with "days of dance and festivities."[33]

Santa Rita remained under siege through 1835. In the spring of 1836, Calvo received reports that Gileño Apaches were now moving toward Santa Rita del Cobre.[34] By the summer a coalition of Chiricahua Apaches, which included Juan José Compá, surrounded Santa Rita and enforced a total blockade that cut off Santa Rita from its supply lines in Mexico. The blockade effectively ended copper mining in Santa Rita.[35] As if the siege of Santa Rita was not enough, a coalition of more than one thousand Utes and Navajos moved to attack the presidio in Bavispe, Mexico.[36]

Calvo sought out Compá's help in restarting peace negotiations to end the ongoing and coordinated Apache attacks.[37] Throughout 1836, Mexican military leaders relied on intelligence regarding Apache troop movements from Compá himself, who provided near daily reports on various Apache "capitancillos."[38] Mexican officials at Cobre, including McKnight, had tried to end the siege on Santa Rita by offering Compá permanent residence at the mine, which in letters he claimed to desire, but Compá never took them up on the offer, asking only for rifles and ammunition.[39] In late June of 1836, he served as an intermediary between the Apache leader Pisago Cabezón and Mexican officials at Santa Rita. Mexican soldiers had captured an Apache leader named Chato and jailed him at Santa Rita. Compá spent much of June in negotiations for the release of Chato amid a buildup of Apache troops surrounding the mine.[40] But Compá had grown increasingly suspicious of Mexican desires for peace.[41]

Compá's suspicions of Mexican intentions were proven right when Calvo responded to the buildup by ordering soldiers and militias, "on pain of death," to intensify attacks on Apaches everywhere, which would continue "until the complete extermination of the barbarous nation."[42] Throughout 1837 and 1838, the war with the Apaches escalated with report after report describing Apache attacks from Janos in Chihuahua to the north in Santa Rita del Cobre against Mexican villages and ranches, "reduced to horrifying ruin."[43] The intensification of the conflict threatened not only the continued copper mining operations at the reinforced Santa Rita del Cobre but also the very presence of presidios and garrisons throughout northern Chihuahua.[44]

◄▪▪▪▪▪►

The Apache blockade on Santa Rita that had begun in 1832, and which in one form or another continued until the US invasion in 1846, provoked a sea change in the way Mexico organized frontier security. In October 1834, Curcier—by then an elected member of the Chihuahua municipal council—donated 50,000 pesos to a new war fund.[45] With the decline in regular military personnel and supply, Curcier proposed augmenting an increasingly ineffective and underfunded Mexican military with a cadre of soldiers of fortune. His proposal would come to be called the *contratos de sangre*, or blood contracts. Chihuahua should create a war fund, he proposed, which he seeded with his donation of 50,000 pesos in order to place cash bounties "on Apache captives and scalps." The scalp bounty would offer an incentive for "paid killers and hit squads, frequently North Americans and other foreigners, to exterminate Apaches."[46] While

Spanish and Mexican soldiers engaged in scalping prior to this period, the Contratos de Sangre transformed the gruesome practice into an official policy of Mexican war making.

The Mexicans were not the first to use scalping in warfare against Indigenous people. The Puritans enacted head bounties on the Pequod in 1637. By 1694, Canada included a line item in its official budget to pay for its scalp bounties. The Dutch preferred bounties on Indian hands. The Spanish used vicious dogs to hunt and kill—to literally tear apart—Indigenous peoples, but preferred methods that allowed for the collecting of human body parts. The Spanish strung ears together on necklaces and hung enormous garlands of these ears from church balconies in places like Santa Fe. They cut off hands, feet, and fingers and turned them into trophies. They stretched and tanned scalps and flew them as flags above Spanish presidios. But with the Contratos de Sangre, the American owners at Santa Rita del Cobre who proposed the Mexican bounty, and the Mexican government that enacted it, created something entirely different: the merging of colonial violence with market forces. The mercenaries killed Apache women and removed their genitals for use as hatbands. They tanned the skin and used the "leather" to make saddles, pouches, belts, and razor strops. The men sometimes kept the scalps and gave them to their wives as gifts. "Scalps hung on the church of Santa Fe as a sacrificial offering for the saints, on the gates of the Mexican Presidios and on Sutter's Fort in California."[47] Scalping became so common among American trappers in the Apache homeland that the verb "to scalp" came to replace the verb "to kill." The human scalp as a commodity.

There has been little reckoning with this horror in the stories that US historians have told about scalping. Nearly all who have written specifically about scalping and torture claim that it was, first and foremost, a pre-Columbian Indigenous practice. These were remnants of "a vague tradition" that survived colonization."[48] Europeans were said to be shocked by this frightening and unfamiliar violence. This "new experience" horrified European settlers in North America.[49] So disturbing was the practice that one historian speculated that the cultures of the Indigenous peoples of North America must lack social taboos against torture. How else to explain this gruesome practice? They must find enjoyment in the physical suffering of others.[50] Indeed nearly every report by European missionaries or colonial officers includes at least one account of the scalping of a settler, whether against colonial agents or other Native people. "The list of Europeans who found scalping among the eastern Indians in the earliest stages of contact," according to two historians of scalping, "could be extended almost indefinitely."[51] The sheer number of claims in colonial report after colonial report offer what seems like overwhelming evidence of scalping as a common practice among Indigenous people, and one that was completely unfamiliar to European settlers. Most early academic histories of scalping drew liberally from these sources in order to advance the idea that before they took up scalping themselves, the first colonists—from the French in present-day Canada and the Spanish in what is today Florida, the US Southwest, and present-day Mexico, to the English settlers in the Massachusetts colony—bravely, and barely, survived this frightening brutality and savagery. None of this is true.

The historical literature that relies on this colonial claim about Indigenous scalping can be organized into two categories. One category would be the many studies that make the claim that scalping was a pre-Columbian practice. All of these relied on colonial and missionary reports. These accounts, which dominate the English-language scholarship on scalping during the first half of the twentieth century, described scalping as a vicious tactic of pre-Columbian warfare, unrelated to European colonialism. Since scalping was a practice that apparently existed prior to the arrival of Europeans, historians claimed that it was used first used by Indigenous peoples against colonial settlers. The eventual use of scalping as a tactic of warfare against Indigenous people by Europeans, they argue, should be understood as reactive and defensive in nature and therefore not as evidence of any sadistic policy of genocidal extermination by colonists.

The other category is work that examines the act of scalping itself. The practice of scalping, particularly the version promoted in Mexican Blood Contracts, came usually after a surprise attack on a camp or Apache ranchería. In general, Mexico only paid bounties for those scalps "harvested" by what is called a "total compound scalping."[52] As the victims of a raid lay dead or dying, a scalp hunter searched for a good candidate—preferably one that he had killed or injured himself, since every man in the raiding party was a mercenary paid only by the scalps they collected, and it was considered bad form to scalp another man's kill. A good candidate was someone with long hair and a large scalp, preferably an adult male. Scalp hunters were not all that selective, and they frequently killed Apache children, but Mexico paid for the scalps of women and children at a cheaper rate, and the scalp hunters were there to make money.

With one hand, the scalp hunter gathered up the hair of his victim at the crown of the head, or scalp lock. With a knee on the victim's back, or a foot on the neck, he held his victim in place. With the other hand, he unsheathed his knife and placed it against the forehead. Moving quickly, he dragged the knife along the forehead, making the first cut. The knife sliced through skin to forehead bone. He then slowly drew the knife around the head, continuing the cut. At this point he would pivot and adjust his stance and his hold so that he could continue the cut around to the other side of the skull, where he had begun. If the victim was alive when this started, they were now in shock, with eyes full of blood. With the sharp edge of the knife the scalp hunter carefully dug into the cut around the head in order to raise the skin of the scalp. He then resheathed his knife and stood behind the victim in order to dig his fingers into the raised cut on the forehead. With a strong grip on the scalp, he slowly peeled the skin from the skull, front to back.

Scalp hunters took their bounty to an official repository in Chihuahua or El Paso where a government official inspected the scalps and paid the bounty. Some of these agents were sticklers and demanded that a scalp include proof that the bounty hunter hadn't cut multiple scalps from one skull. The standard way to deliver a scalp required that it include the right ear. If the bounty hunter anticipated this requirement, he would drag his knife under the right ear when cutting a scalp. Often, however, there was no time because this was all happening in the middle of a bloody killing field, and there were always more scalps to collect and more money to be made; or else the victim was alive and struggling and the scalp hunter couldn't take their time. So, in those moments they would skip this last step, hoping to find an understanding official in Chihuahua. He would simply take hold of the hair of the scalp lock with both hands and pull until the skull released the scalp.

It is best to be dead when being scalped. The bleeding that follows is nearly impossible to stop. If by some miracle the bleeding does stop, infection sets in quickly and death comes painfully by sepsis or meningitis. On rare occasions when the bleeding stops and infection is somehow fought off, necrosis comes next, and worst of all. The scalp, torn from the head, leaves the cranium "deprived of its blood supply, [to become] dry and black." It slowly rots away.[53] Fissures and foramens develop on the skull, through which oozes "the substance of the brain."[54] It is a gruesome way to die but entirely preferable to a "scalping by sabrage." When scalp hunters were particularly rushed by time, or cared little about the condition of the scalp, they would use an entirely different method. A scalp hunter would gather up the scalp lock in one hand and pull as hard as possible. This would lift the skin of the scalp away from the skull. With the other hand, the scalp hunter slashed quickly with a knife or long saber as close as possible to the top of the crown of the head.[55] This took the scalp and with it a portion of the periosteum, or the tissue that attaches the scalp to the skull. The victim might survive, only to die in the days that followed when their cranium disintegrated like wet cardboard.

Chihuahua's scalp bounties constituted a public "subsidy," according to Ralph Smith, a historian who spent a career writing about scalping, "for the production of dead Indians."[56] The bounties enticed mercenaries like James Kirker to Santa Rita, from where he staged enormous "scalp hunts" when he wasn't escorting copper ingots from Santa Rita to Chihuahua City. For Kirker, coming upon an Apache rancheria was like "discovering a mine."[57] Scalps became more valuable than beaver pelts.[58] And US trappers and mercenaries cornered the market. Kirker, in particular, killed and scalped so many Apaches that the Chihuahua treasury strained to find the funds to pay him. His "success" enticed other Apache killers into Chihuahua, Sonora, and Coahuila. "Each white frontier soldier, trapper, mountain-man and miner who reached these parts from the east by land was a scalp hunter."[59]

The scalp was death's "certificate of authenticity" and proved that a contract had been fulfilled. Mercenaries traded these *piezas*—Mexico's preferred euphemism for the scalp—for state treasury warrants at state-run trading houses and then traded the warrants for pesos at the state treasury. Kirker led "hunting expeditions" from Santa Rita del Cobre into the

Portrait of the murderer James Kirker, who worked for the American owner of the Santa Rita mine in the mid-1800s. He became among the most notorious scalp hunters during the early years of mining in Santa Rita. Courtesy of the Missouri Historical Society, St. Louis.

Apache homeland and returned to Chihuahua City with scalps by the hundreds, where he and his hired assassins "piled their trophies on tables where municipal officers inspected the scalps and paid out treasury warrants."[60] Or he traveled to El Paso, which served as a regional marketplace for scalps. There, state functionaries "inspected, verified and hung out scalps for public view, and issued warrants for them redeemable at the state treasury."[61]

Much of the early history of Indian scalping by US historians advanced the claim that the gruesome version of scalping practiced against Native people paled in comparison to the version practiced by Indigenous nations. Beginning in the 1970s, however, Native scholars, in particular, revisited these histories of scalp bounties and found the claims by non-Native historians of scalping's supposed Native origins rooted not in the historical record but in the familiar colonial tropes of Indians as savage enemies. The Standing Rock Sioux scholar and author Vine Deloria argued that scalping as a tactic of trophy taking and torture was never an Indigenous practice but rather an official European policy of colonial violence. "Scalping, introduced prior to the French and Indian War by the English, confirmed the suspicion that Indians were wild animals to be hunted and skinned. Bounties were set and an Indian scalp became more valuable than beaver, otter, marten and other animal pelts."[62]

The historian James Axtell and Smithsonian curator William Sturtevant took umbrage at Deloria's claims. In their 1980 essay, "The Unkindest Cut, or Who Invented Scalping," they exhorted historians to defend history against what they considered "Indian activism and white guilt."[63] They doubled down on the idea, based on a close read of the colonial archive, that scalping had Indian origins.[64] If Europeans were guilty of anything, it was only for "perpetuating a sanguinary Indian tradition."[65]

Nearly every non-Native scholar of scalping begins with the work of the German author and anthropologist Georg Friederici, who called the scalp "the characteristic trophy of the New World." Axtell and Sturtevant, in particular, pointed to Friederici's "thorough study of the distribution and history of scalping in North and South America," which, they claimed, "proved beyond a doubt that scalping was a pre-Columbian Indian practice."[66] Friederici published *Skalpieren und ähnliche Kriegsgebrauche in Amerika* (Scalping and similar warfare in America) in Germany in 1906. The Smithsonian published a short English-language summary ("Scalping in America") a year later. Axtell and Sturtevant based their claims on the short English-language summary, which didn't include Friederici's full examination of scalping found in his more complete German-language study. Friederici's longer study is fascinating for his interest in exactly the thing Axtell and Sturtevant ignore—the relationship between Indigenous scalping and the version that European settlers, particularly American mercenaries at Santa Rita del Cobre, used against Native peoples.

What we know about "Indian scalping" comes to us solely through the "accounts contained in Spanish, French, English, and American records of exploration, colonization, trading and missionary activity," which constitute "the sole sourses of information" that we have on Indian scalping.[67] Friederici was deeply skeptical of these colonial accounts. Most relied on secondhand information impossible for any historian to verify. Many of the reports, particularly the ones by colonial agents, provided detailed accounts of Indian aggression and violence while scrupulously avoiding any description of colonial violence. As one historian pointed out, "the 'Civilized' invaders unquestionably did practise [torture] on the Indians for the customary European motives of abstracting information or supplies and as a punishment for refractory behavior." These were not accounts of Indian scalping by disinterested bureaucrats. They were the stories that colonial agents told of Indigenous people, people they found important "only insofar as they still had land that one could take from them."[68] In other words, most had a vested interest in offering exaggerated stories of Native "savagery" to serve as "propaganda for colonization."[69]

Colonial reports of Indian scalping and torture played a key rhetorical role in the theft of Native land. Their so-called savagery legitimized the taking and occupation of their land and, even more importantly, excused the extensive colonial use of scalping against Native people. As one historian of scalping suggested, "we might well expect an overdrawn picture of Indian cruelties to serve as an excuse to wipe out these 'savages' who resisted the depredations of the whites, and in general this may be true."[70]

Friederici, however, made a distinction between the limited, often ceremonial, version of scalping practiced by some Indigenous peoples in North America and the scorched earth, genocidal scalping unleashed by *all* European colonial powers on Native nations. According to Friederici, scalping, when and where it was practiced by Indigenous peoples, was a ceremonial part of funerary practices. It was only rarely "carried out on the body of the enemy." Much of the archaeological evidence of pre-Columbian scalping confirms this view. It is rare to find archaeological evidence of scalping and rarer still to find it associated with warfare or violent conflict.[71] There is evidence for scalping in pre-Columbian warfare, but as Friederici notes, it does not appear related to torture or trophy taking and was not widespread. Scalping as terror and trophy taking was a European innovation. Pre-Columbian scalping, when associated with warfare, was "an act of the nation: a declaration of war or a statement of the state of war."[72] Also, it was not common among all Native nations. There are no records of Apache and Navajo people, for example, ever engaging in scalping, whether as a ceremonial part of burial or in warfare. Never, that is, until Spain, Mexico, and finally the US began using it against them and other Native peoples. This was Deloria's argument. Scalping, as Friederici argued, "grew into its familiar style and expanded significantly because of the Whites who came to North America."[73] Scalping was a colonial tactic, one practiced and perfected at Santa Rita del Cobre.

◄▪▪▪▪▪▪►

Historians date the start of the Mexico-Apache wars to 1831 or 1832, which corresponded to the years McKnight and Curcier ramped up production of copper at Santa Rita.[74] Some historians have downplayed the importance of the mine to wider conflict with Apaches, but there was no Spanish presence in the Copper Range prior to the establishment of Santa Rita del Cobre in the early 1800s. And the move by Mexico into the Copper Range came only after the copper produced at Santa Rita del Cobre became Mexico's most important source of copper. Mexico had few other reliable sources of copper for the mint in Chihuahua City and for the production of armaments. The military strategy prior to the use of scalp bounties was based on a ration-based pacification strategy. But Chihuahua refused to provide rations during the peace negotiations at Santa Rita in 1832, and as a result the entire pacification strategy collapsed, which led Chihuahua to turn instead to scalp bounties.

Sonora had run a de facto scalp-bounty program from at least 1835.[75] As early as 1825 there were reports of American mercenaries operating in both Chihuahua and Sonora. Janos received reports of Apache attacks on villages in 1825, which they suspected were actually attacks by "men of bad faith" disguised as Apaches who used the chaos of the territory to engage in their own raiding activities.[76] In short, there had been a long presence of American arms traders and mercenaries in Chihuahua and Sonora for years and the official scalp bounty program merely formalized an existing practice.

The arrival of the scalp bounties, and the mercenaries that followed, eroded the importance of men like Juan José Compá. Mexico discovered that it was cheaper to pay Americans to kill Apaches than to maintain Mexican armies to pacify them. In April of 1837 an American named John

Johnson set out for the Copper Range from Moctezuma, Mexico, leading a group of seventeen heavily armed American mercenaries. They were accompanied by five Mexican laborers, who hauled the weapons and supplies not carried by mules. In a letter that Johnson later wrote to the Commandant General of Chihuahua, he explained that he had received permission from Sonora to pursue an Apache raiding party heading toward Santa Rita del Cobre. The scalp hunters followed cattle tracks along a familiar trading route into the Las Animas Sierra. They arrived in Narbona in mid-April where Johnson acquired "a small canon or swivel gun."[77] He and his party found Apaches camped along a stream. Johnson was vague about what happened next. The Apache leaders in the party appeared "prepared to attack," he wrote, which seems likely since Johnson and his men were hunting them. His men were on edge, Johnson explained, from certain "acts of mistrust and betrayal" shown by the Apaches. Johnson does not explain why the Apaches should have shown any trust toward an armed party of scalp hunters, or what confidence they might have betrayed. Likely this is a reference to the fact that Johnson and his party were disguised as traders, but that the Apaches were suspicious of his intent nonetheless. Johnson claims he launched an attack that lasted more than two hours. When it was over, he and his men had injured twenty Apaches and killed another thirty Apache men and women, including five children. Among those killed were Juan José Compá, his brother Juan Diego, and an Apache chief named Marcelo. Johnson took their scalps and brought them to Janos where he presented them to the presidio's commander.[78]

The assassination of Juan José Compá became known as the Johnson Massacre. Josiah Gregg writes about it in his travelogue *Commerce of the Prairies*, based on his time spent along the Santa Fe Trail, largely in New Mexico and Mexico, in the 1830s. Gregg reports that Johnson's party was motivated by the 1835 bounty that Sonora had placed on Apaches. He described it as a coordinated ambush. Johnson tricked Compá and used a "little field piece" to kill more than a dozen, and then cut down by rifle fire those who had escaped the initial attack. He lists the dead at more than twenty men and women.

Philip St. George Cook, a commander of a Mormon battalion, retold the story in his 1846 memoir. Cook calls it a "treacherous massacre" by a party of mercenaries hired out by Johnson to plunder the Apache. In Cook's account, Johnson's party pretended to be traders looking to make a sale and slaughtered a dozen men and women with a hidden swivel gun as the Apaches looked over the goods for sale. Johnson's men chased down the survivors of the initial attack and executed them at gunpoint.

An 1854 account written by John Bartlett, who learned of the massacre from miners at Santa Rita del Cobre in the mid-1800s, described it as "a fiendish act" and Johnson's role as a "disgrace to his nation." Bartlett also attributed the attack to the Sonoran bounty of one hundred dollars per scalp that drew plundering parties into Apachería. This is similar to an 1886 account by J. P. Dunn, who cited the Sonoran bounty but also suggested that Johnson was "induced to this by pay from the owners of the Santa Rita copper mines."[79]

If McKnight and Curcier hired Johnson to assassinate Juan José Compá, there is no evidence of it in the archives. This has led historians to conclude that the assassination was unrelated to the mine, despite the fact that McKnight and Curcier only abandoned the mine during the "total Apache siege of the Santa Rita settlement" that followed the Johnson Massacre.[80] This would have been the second siege of Santa Rita. The first followed the collapse of peace negotiations in 1832, which led to a temporary abandonment of the mine. When mining restarted in the mid-1830s, low copper prices and declining yields contributed to a slowdown, or possibly even a temporary shutdown, but the mine was operating at the time of the Johnson Massacre. And it would be the mine that would become a focal point of Apache attacks following the murder of Compá. Apache leaders Mangas Coloradas and Pisago Cabezón launched the second siege of Santa Rita and renewed a blockade on the copper trail only after the assassination of Compá.[81] The response of the Apaches to the assassination of Compá, in other words, gave every indication that it had everything to do with Santa Rita del Cobre.

◄▪▪▪▪▪►

The Apache siege on Santa Rita following the Johnson Massacre spread throughout northern Chihuahua. To the Mexican military leaders who fought the war, the Apaches were skillful warriors. They "use the rifle, lance and arrow, which is like a pistol which is always prepared; they are excellent at using all of these arms, and are also very good horsemen, good hunters and excellent campers." Apache groups were in constant movement, launched skilled, clever attacks, even when outnumbered. To Mexican settlers in Chihuahua, it was like living in a state of "prolonged death." [82]

In response to the escalation on warfare that followed the killing of Compá, Chihuahua expanded its bounty program. In July of 1837, Chihuahua announced the *Proyecto de Guerra*, which established a voluntary fund with a goal to raise 100,000 pesos in order to attract more killers to Chihuahua.[83] Once again, it was Curcier who proposed it. The difference in 1837 was that, for the first time, Chihuahua established an official state-regulated price on Apache scalps: one hundred pesos for an adult male, fifty pesos for an adult female, and twenty-five pesos for the capture of a child twelve years old or younger. Curcier and McKnight, the owners of the mine, recruited Kirker, their employee at the mine, to take up scalp hunting in Chihuahua and New Mexico.[84]

Some historians have described the Contratos de Sangre as a bounty or price placed on the head of Apaches; and, although that's true enough, it's not entirely accurate. The bounty established a labor contract, or piece-wage, or price *per scalp*, which was intended to replace the salary, or time-wage, paid to military soldiers, which to that point had been the way that Chihuahua had funded the war against the Apaches. Despite an 1838 plan to tax wealthy residents for security, Chihuahua could barely afford to maintain a standing military. By stablishing a per-scalp bounty, Chihuahua transformed not only how Chihuahua paid for its war against Apaches but also how the war itself was waged. Instead of paying a man to become a solider and covering all the costs of maintaining an army, they paid a man who demonstrated he'd killed an Apache. The piece wage promised to reduce Chihuahua's financial burden for waging war while creating an incentive intended to attract mercenaries into Chihuahua, who would wage the war on its behalf. The political economy of scalping produced intended and unintended effects. The primary stated goal was to wage a cheaper war. The scalp-bounty program reduced the burden on the state treasury of funding the war, as it transferred most of the costs of warfare—both fixed and recurring—to the mercenaries who did the killing. Through piece wages Chihuahua anticipated receiving certain efficiencies by shifting production—in this case, the "production of dead Apaches"—from timework (i.e., salaries to regular military) to piecework (i.e., prices paid for scalps). No longer would Chihuahua pay salaries, maintain and supply presidios and garrisons, or provide provisions and weapons for all campaigns against the Apache at its previous levels. The quality and quantity of work (i.e., the successful killing of Apaches) would now be governed by the piece wage and would no longer require costly years of military training and expensive layers of military command and supervision. In other words, in return for the salaries and time wages that Chihuahua paid its military, it received a military, whereas in return for the piece wages that Chihuahua paid soldiers of war, it received dead Apaches.

The scalp constituted, therefore, a kind of commodity, and through piece-work wages, Chihuahua intended to produce more of them. It is interesting to note that at the same time that Curcier sought efficiencies and production increases in colonial warfare through the use of piecework in Chihuahua, Karl Marx, writing about colonialism and capitalism half a world away, was considering precisely the same idea. As Marx would later write, piece wages were the "form of wages most in harmony with the capitalist mode of production." This is because piece wages, "served as a lever for the lengthening of the working-day, and the lowering of wages." The idea that piece wages lower overall wages appears counterintuitive. After all, piece wages promise to raise individual compensation. Kill more, make more. But the difference between time wages and piece wages are only partly about the incentives (and thus efficiencies) they promote. As Marx would write of piece wages, "it is naturally the personal interest of the labourer to strain his labour-power as intensely as possible; this enables the capitalist to raise more easily the normal degree of intensity of labour."[85] The incentive buried in the logic of the piece wage was thus not only an incentive to kill Apaches but also an incentive to *intensify* the labor that goes into the killing of Apaches. Piece wages establish the conditions among those who work for a piece wage to both *choose* to work longer and *choose* to work harder, which theoretically results in the production of more scalps—that is, the production of more dead Apaches. And moreover, the piece wage shifts authority over the supervision of that labor to the laborers themselves. "The exploitation of the labourer by capital is here effected," wrote Marx, "through the exploitation of the labourer by the labourer."[86] Since wages are now based on "pieces" produced, the worker who produces more "pieces" receives a higher wage. If the Mexican military or civilian militias couldn't win the war against the Apaches, mercenaries working piece wages would. It's not for nothing that Mexicans referred to mercenaries as "entrepreneurs," and the Spanish word for scalps was *pieza*, or "piece."

It was through piece wages that Chihuahua sought to harmonize a colonial mode of warfare with a capitalist mode of production. Where a soldier saw an enemy, a scalp hunter saw a payday. The scalp bounty transformed a colonial relation of domination into an economic relation. But there were certain difficulties and unintended consequences that Curcier failed to consider, or more likely ignored altogether. For one, the scalp-bounty program was based on the idea that the brutal colonial war with Apaches could be won by transforming economic relations within colonial society, which assumes that the failure of Chihuahua to completely eradicate the Apaches was a question of labor productivity. The logic of the scalp-bounty program begins with the basic unit of those relations: the commodity. Scalping and trophy taking was not new in colonial warfare but establishing a price per scalp was. Chihuahua waged its genocidal war against the Apache using the logic of a capitalist mode of production, which is a mode of commodity production. The scalp-bounty program reduced the entire enterprise—colonial warfare—to one commodity, in this case the scalp. But consider the implications of transforming a scalp, a human head, into a commodity. A commodity is the bearer of value. Among the first things Marx wrote about commodities was that "a commodity is, in the first place, an object outside us." Unless you're Apache, of course. A scalp is only a bearer of value if you value the murder of Apaches.

According to Marx, a commodity is only a commodity if it is an object or product of labor with a dual character—that is, if it has both exchange value and use value. A commodity can be said to have use value if it has some social utility that makes it desirable. Use values do "not dangle in mid-air," which is to say that utility is defined by the physical properties of the commodity itself. Copper, for example, has use value in the production of armaments because of the particular properties of copper. Similarly, exchange value, like use value, does not magically inhere in the object itself. It is through exchange value that use values come to life. This is deeply ironic in the case of the scalp because the only way to bring to life the use value of the scalp is to put to death the Apache.

There is a profound way in which the scalp-as-commodity anticipated a capitalist mode of production that Marx could never have imagined. "Value," wrote Marx "does not have its description branded on its forehead." This is true unless one's forehead *is* the value form of the commodity. The capitalist mode of production, as Marx understood it, placed two great classes in conflict: a capitalist class, that owned the means of production, and a working class, that had only its labor to sell. But the scalp-bounty program merged a colonial mode of domination with a capitalist mode of production. This suggests that an analysis of the scalp bounty exceeds the limits of a strictly economic analysis. For all their antagonisms, the working class (i.e., mercenaries such as Kirker) and the capitalist class (i.e., mine owners such as Curcier) shared one very important thing in common: a desire for the production of dead Apaches. The scalp-bounty program produced, therefore, a set of related but distinct contradictions. The first of those follows from a strictly class analysis. The second only comes into view by understanding the production of scalps as exceeding the logic of a capitalist mode of production.

The first contradiction requires examining how the class antagonisms reflected in the circulation of the scalp-as-commodity might become apparent. The war with the Apaches was dangerous and prior to the scalp-bounty program Chihuahua managed this risk through the construction of a vast network of presidios and garrisons. Shifting these risks onto mercenaries, however, did not mean that soldiers of fortune assumed all the costs of managing them. Quite the opposite. Scalp hunters found ways to avoid risk entirely. This might have been an unintended consequence of piece wage compensation in Chihuahua, but Marx anticipated the outcome. While piece wages raise individual wages (assuming, of course, piece-wages have the intended effect of intensifying labor), they also tended to lower the overall average wage. The *Proyecto de Guerra* permitted scalp hunting of "indios de armas" (armed indians) only. The only permissible scalp to take, in other words, was one from an Apache at war. But there was no way to distinguish one scalp from another. And as a result, scalp hunters sought out the easiest possible targets. "The scalp hunters," according to William Griffen, "preyed on the more docile, easy-to-get Rancherías, leaving the hostile Rancherías even more hostile."[87] In addition, scalp hunters used a familiar Mexican tactic. According to the newspaper *El Faro de Chihuahua*, scalp hunters murdered Apaches they had tricked into engaging in peace negotiations. For instance, a group of scalp hunters attacked an entire party of Apaches they caught sleeping in Agua Nueva following official peace talks with Mexican officials.[88] Piece wages, in other words, lowered overall wages and thus the mercenaries who worked for piece wages engaged in tactics designed to manage their risks, and thus constantly lower their costs. Chihuahua had hoped that the scalp-bounty program would augment existing regular military, but it had the opposite effect. It intensified Apache attacks on the Mexican military in retaliation for the indiscriminate violence at the heart of scalp hunting. It was certainly indiscriminate if you were an Apache being hunted by a mercenary. But there was nothing indiscriminate about the pattern and practice of scalp hunting as mercenaries practiced it. There were reports of Apache attacks on Mexican villages, but investigations revealed them to be by American mercenaries, who dressed as Apaches, scalped Mexicans, and then sold the scalps as though they were from the Apaches.[89] The bosses wanted scalps and paid a piece wage for them, and so mercenaries found scalps everywhere.

"If commodities could speak," wrote Marx, "they would say this: our use-value may interest men, but it does not belong to us as objects."[90] What if, and this is the second contradiction, the commodity could speak? Not in the metaphorical way Marx meant, but literally, in flesh and blood. Consider what it meant that Chihuahua transformed through exchange the living head of an Apache into a commodity that congealed colonial use value. It was possible only because Apaches were already understood by settler colonial society as other-than-human. There is here a second contradiction, or better yet a second, profound irony, that escaped Curcier. The capitalist mode of production is defined by the production of commodities. The goal is the capture of surplus value through the production of more and more commodities, ever more efficiently. But this is not the logic of settler colonialism. There is only one goal of settler colonialism, and it is genocide. Settler colonial domination in Chihuahua sought the extermination of all Apaches. The scalp-bounty program reveals what happens when two divergent goals collide: The piece wages were intended as a way to create an incentive to kill as many Apaches as possible, which would culminate in the extermination of all Apaches. But this violates the logic of capital. The piece wages did not create an incentive to exterminate Apaches; rather, it created an incentive to produce as many scalps as possible, *indefinitely*. The merging of colonial conquest and capitalist production established an enduring irony. Colonial conquest never reaches the only goal it gives itself—the total extermination and complete replacement of an Indigenous society with a settler society. Settler colonial genocide, in other words, is a lousy business model. It is far more profitable, it turns out, to establish and maintain a suffering Native population forever exploited by a colonial society.

◄▪▪▪▪▪▪►

There was significant support for the scalp-bounty system in Chihuahua. The most influential newspaper, *El Faro de Chihuahua*, lobbied for and defended the scalp-bounty program because of what it called the intrinsic viciousness and violent nature of all Apaches. The fight was between "the lazy savage" and the "industrious and useful citizen" and therefore the end justified the means, according to *El Faro*, no matter how gruesome. After all, the newspaper reminded its readers, the entire state of Chihuahua was "overcome by a swarm of bandits who rob as if it were the only and the most delightful job, and that love assassinations merely because of the pleasure of the blood." The scalp-bounty program was, as a result, depicted as necessary against a foe portrayed as other-than-human, and anyone who would oppose the use of soldiers for hire, whether on moral or practical grounds, could only do so because they didn't "know the Indians [or] the type of war in which they are occupied."[91]

The critics called it a "bloody industry" and condemned the "fatal vertigo" that had seized Chihuahua officials in making it. Some assailed the program on both moral and practical terms. The result was not a resolution of war, but rather a situation in which the people in the region "have never suffered more cruelties."[92] To critics of the scalp-bounty program, it produced the opposite of what was promised. It didn't end the war, it escalated it. It didn't exterminate the Apache, it galvanized them. Though none provided an explanation for why that might be, the results were obvious: the scalp-bounty program may have been genocidal in intent, but it created the opposite, a shockingly brutal and highly profitable *permanent* war. Genocide not as a goal but as an industry. The longer the scalp-bounty program lasted, the more profitable it became; and the more profitable it became, the more it expanded.

Chihuahua officials, having not read Marx, thought maybe the problem was that the bounties weren't large enough. So, they raised the scalp bounty to two hundred pesos per scalp with the idea that this would attract more professional "foreign entrepreneurs and speculators," which it did, of course, but not because any of those mercenaries shared Chihuahua's colonial goals. They came because Chihuahua made an already enormously lucrative industry even more lucrative. Next, Chihuahua merged the scalp-bounty program with its regular military personnel in order to extend the benefits to all. But this just guaranteed that soldiers would now also have a vested interest in endless, permanent war. A former Mexican military commander, Juan Nepomuceno Armedariz, traveled throughout Chihuahua in the late 1840s hunting Apache scalps.[93] He wasn't alone. The scalp-bounty program attracted scores of regular soldiers who took up scalp hunting. A mixed unit comprised of regular Mexican soldiers and militia led by the commander of the Janos presidio, Baltazar Padilla, attacked an Apache ranchería near Laguna de las Palomas, south of Chihuahua City, killing twelve. They took scalps from the dead and seven more from captives taken during the raid.[94] Padilla had been an early critic of the bounty program and, in particular, the most prolific scalp hunter, James Kirker. But by the late 1840s, he had become an enthusiastic scalp hunter himself, commanding regular military as well as mercenary units comprised of American "guerilla bands," as he called them, on scalp raids.[95] The private sector transformed the public sector, and now everybody killed for profit.

The presidios, particularly at Janos, became staging points for scalp-bounty warfare. American and Mexican soldiers of fortune launched their raids from presidios, where they returned with their scalps, which then flew from garrison flag poles. As a result, the presidios, whose security the scalp-bounty program was designed to increase, came instead under constant attack. In mid-October of 1849, more than two hundred Apache fighters attacked the presidio at Janos and, over the course of a day-long siege, took thirty-five prisoners, including thirty-one of the American mercenaries garrisoning at Janos.[96]

There is one final irony to the scalp-bounty program, and it serves as an introduction to all that follows. Scalp hunting led to the total abandonment of Santa Rita del Cobre, the very place and the very thing—copper mining—that Curcier's scalp-bounty policy was designed to defend. The story that follows is not one limited to a place, Santa Rita del Cobre, or a thing, copper mining. Rather it is a story told through the lives of the Casuse family, witness to the merging of colonial domination with capital accumulation in Santa Rita, where capital emerged, was incubated by colonial authorities, and then sprung, finally and fully, into the world, "dripping from head to toe, from every pore, with blood and dirt."[97]

The Story of the Boy Who Was Traded for a Horse

After the Mexicans and their mercenaries from the north, there was the coming of the American army. The story of their arrival starts with a man named Red Hair, a full-blooded Mexican raised by the Navajo who was one of the great men of those early days. This was during the time of the great war with other tribes. Red Hair lived on the east side of Tohatchi Mountain, out where it is flat. He could shoot an arrow like a gun. He never missed and the arrow always found its mark. It could pass through a body like a bullet. Red Hair could outkill a whole army of other warriors

■▶ ◀■

Red Hair had a Little Black Pony. The pony was fast but gentle, and Red Hair could ride him without a bridle. Little Black Pony was wild, and when Red Hair wanted to ride, he would whistle and the pony would come. They were so fast together that neither were ever hurt by the arrows of other fighters.

■▶ ◀■

Red Hair was a good friend to the Apache people. He would ride the Little Black Pony south and stay for a month or more and bring with him braided rope, braided whips, braided bridles, saddle blankets, buckskin made into coats, shoes made out of buckskin. Some say Red Hair met with Cochise, others say Mangas Coloradas. When Red Hair returned, he returned with arrows, stout and well made.

47

■■▶ ◀■■

During a celebration marking one of his visits, Red Hair saw a little boy among the children. A boy different than the other Apache children. He had curly black hair. His face and body were white. The boy had been born in 1850 in a small village in Mexico, from where he had been stolen as a young child. He was returned but then he was stolen again. The last time he was taken, Apache warriors on horseback found him chasing a colt, took him from his family, and brought him to a ranchería along the Alamosa River in the valley between the Black Range and the San Mateo Mountains.

■■▶ ◀■■

It was now some years later. The boy watched as the Apache chief admired Red Hair's Little Black Pony. All saw how strong and fast the pony was. The chief asked Red Hair to trade him the pony. This was during the days when the Apache fought the white people and the Mexicans. Red Hair refused the trade. The Apache chief persisted. "I cannot sell," protested Red Hair. "What could I do without him?"

■■▶ ◀■■

It was then that Red Hair turned to the little white boy called Jesus Arviso. His hosts told Red Hair that they'd taken the boy years ago and had raised him up. Red Hair saw that the boy could ride a horse. He saw that he spoke like the Apaches but also like the Mexicans. The Apache chief asked again to trade for Little Black Pony. This time Red Hair said, "I will take the little Mexican boy." The Apache chief traded the little boy to Red Hair along with some fur made from the skin of a buffalo.

■■▶ ◀■■

This was when Jesus Arviso came to the Navajo with Red Hair. He lived in the family of Kla (Tla, Lefthand), a headman, who some say was the same man known as Black Shirt, a tall man of the Ashiihí Clan, the Salt People.

He learned how to shoot the arrow and how to run and how to herd sheep. He had a thick black mustache. He wore a black felt hat with a round brim. He became a trusted warrior.

■■▶ ◀■■

Jesus Arviso married a Navajo woman named Yohazbaa' of the Naneesht'ézhí Clan and daughter of Asdzáá Sání Ałs'íísí, "Small Old Lady," and Tsii'wooli, "Shaved Head," of the Ta'neeszahníí Clan. This was Arviso's first wife. He lived with her and their children on top of Tohatchi Mountain. He became known as Jesus Arviso Bí éé' łizhiní Adits'a'ii. One day he was out hunting deer on the west side of the mountain. While he was away the American army seized his wife and children along with some other Navajo people and took them away to Fort Defiance. This was during the time when bands of American army took Navajo people. Took them to Fort Defiance, or to Fort Wingate, or to an army depot in San Fidel, and eventually to Fort Sumner.

■■▶ ◀■■

Jesus Arviso was now alone, and he wandered for two years from Tohatchi Mountain to Black Mountain and up to San Francisco Peak. In the high mountains around the Grand Canyon he saw the people hiding from the Americans. He became the one who told the people what was happening, that the American army was looking for them, that they should stay hidden. Jesus Arviso was the only one who knew where everybody was.

■■▶ ◀■■

He began to think about how alone he was, about his family at Fort Sumner. He decided he would join them. Jesus Arviso knew that the American army had taken some Navajo people to the Apache country. He followed them on their march to San Rafael. He made a flag out of a blanket of white sheep-skin and waived it as he rode toward the American army. They took him and he came into the crowd talking Navajo and the Navajo people knew him by heart. To the American army he spoke as a Mexican, and there were some among them who also spoke like the Mexicans. The army took his horse and tied his hands. He spent long days walking and long nights tied up.

■■▶ ◀■■

He told the American army that the Navajo did not want war and he agreed to be a scout and interpreter. They sent him to find the Navajos who were still hiding. He came to his people in the Canyon of Taholi where they were hiding. He told them that it would be better for them to join the other people at Fort Sumner. He explained that a band of the American army will come to kill them unless they came to Fort Sumner. Many did as Jesus Arviso said and made the long walk to Fort Sumner.

■■▶ ◀■■

When they arrived at Fort Sumner they were given shovels. They dug holes in the ground like open graves and this was where the American army made them live. The Navajo prisoners at Fort Sumner ate rations that made them sick. Some refused and died of starvation. Most every day at Fort Sumner the Navajo people would gather and talk of their homeland. They learned the American army planned to send them to Oklahoma. The people asked Jesus Arviso to talk to the general. He explained to the general that it will be worse in Oklahoma, but General William Tecumseh Sherman told him Oklahoma will teach the Navajo the lesson of obedience. This is the reason the American army planned to send them to Oklahoma.

■■▶ ◀■■

The Navajo people at Fort Sumner refused to leave their homeland for Oklahoma. A letter arrived from Washington to the general and it said that the Navajo could only return to their homeland if they promised to send their children to boarding school. The general said that they would have to give up their children to be educated by the Americans. "We shall put up schools in the Navajo reservation," he told Jesus Arviso. "I want for every child that is born from today on to be sent to school. There they can learn a better way of living and behavior," he said. Arviso brought this to the Navajo people. This is what the general said, they shall send their children to school, boarding school. An agreement was made in May of 1868.

■■▶ ◀■■

They traveled home across the Manzano Mountains and past the Rio Grande. Each morning the strongest Navajo runners raced ahead while the rest would go slow. The fire was already going when all arrived. They made it back to their homeland and rebuilt their homes. The American army required they come once a week to receive rations and supplies.

■■▶ ◀■■

This was during the time that things being made in the East were being brought to the West. Machines and also ideas. Many Navajo people worked on the railroad. Built dams. Lived on rations they were made to eat.

■■▶ ◀■■

This was during the time of the American army's war against the Apache people. The American army sought Mangas Colorado and also Goyathlay, the one the army called Geronimo and who refused to surrender. Cochise, who is said to be the descendant of the great Juan José Compá, the one who made the mistake of befriending two white men, refused also to surrender. The American army hired Navajos to hunt and capture the Apaches. Some agreed to this because they remembered the long walk and the lesson of Jesus Arviso and they knew there was no other way that the Apache chiefs would live to old age.

■■▶ ◀■■

Jesus Arviso had two wives in his life, and they had many children. One child among them was called Lamon Jesus. He married Winona and they had only one son and named him Harry Jesus. Harry Jesus married a woman named Alheejiibaa who would die in 1924, but before she would die she would have a son in the summer of 1922 and they would name him Louis Casuse. Louis was born in Tohatchi into the People from the Middle of the Rock People Clan.

■▶ ◀■

Louis Casuse would fight a war in Europe, would toil in the mines at Santa Rita del Cobre, would marry an Austrian girl named Lillian Hutzler. Lillian Hutzler would escape war and bear seven children. The last of these children would be Joseph. Dashija and Ursula would come before Joseph. These three would be their youngest children. Nijoni and Erika would come earlier. Donald too, who would be born a year before Erika. Their first child, who came when Lillian was very young, would be born in a town that today floats in the sky, suspended between worlds. They would name him Larry Wayne Casuse.[1]

Blood for Soil

According to the Bureau of Indian Affairs, Louis Casuse was born somewhere "in the vicinity of Tohatchi," in the Chuska Mountains, a thin range of peaks that erupt from arid plains along what is today the New Mexico–Arizona border. Each document that mentions his birth—Bureau of Indian Affairs (BIA) birth certificate, army discharge papers, obituary—list a different date. Most family members, including Louis, place his date of birth in mid-August of 1922, during the second annual Gallup Inter-Tribal Ceremonial. When Louis was young, his father, Harry, found wage work building the railroad, and on various dam construction projects. Louis's mother died when he was young and he was sent, along with an older brother, to live with their grandmother in Standing Rock, near Chaco Canyon. When Louis was seven or eight his father remarried, and Louis returned. They lived in hogans at a summer camp in Mexican Springs, near Tohatchi. In the winter, they moved to a lower elevation camp east of Coyote Canyon.

His was a large family. Two siblings before his mother died, and then six half-sisters when his father remarried. Louis lived with his sisters, Louise, Ella Mae, Alice, Mary, Pauline, Virginia, and Julia. The children collected water from the creek, husked and ground corn, and herded sheep. Louis attended an elementary school in Tohatchi until eighth grade. At fifteen or sixteen he was sent to the boarding school at Fort Wingate, forty miles southwest of winter camp. The military previously used Fort Wingate to store weapons and military surplus. In 1925 the War Department transferred a portion of the old fort, which by that time had become the largest munitions dump in the world, to the Bureau of Indian Affairs. The old barracks became the classrooms and dormitories for a boarding school for Navajo and Zuni children.[1]

Louis stayed at Fort Wingate only long enough to contract tuberculosis. By the late nineteenth century, tuberculosis replaced smallpox as the "great destroyer" of Native nations.[2] Chronic and highly contagious, the disease attacks the lungs. The coughing and sneezing of an infected person releases and suspends bacteria like an aerosol in the air. It was an epidemic on the Navajo Nation, where tuberculosis infection rates were greater than anywhere else in the United States.[3] Some medical professionals at the time assumed the high rate of tuberculosis infection on Native reservations reflected some deep pathology among Native peoples, some profound inability to assimilate to the modern world. Louis's experience, however, offers a different explanation. Crowded, poorly maintained boarding schools, such as Fort Wingate, constituted a lethal vector for disease. The unsanitary and overcrowded conditions, and the lack of medical services, established the perfect conditions for a variety of infectious diseases. Louis ran away from Fort Wingate and returned to Mexican Springs to recuperate.

He didn't stay long. When US war planning accelerated following the Battle of France in June 1940, the War Department selected the Fort Wingate Ordnance Depot as a key munitions storage facility for a coming war.[4] Construction on the ten-million-dollar project began in February 1941. More than two thousand workers labored on the project and nearly all were Navajo or Zuni, and they included a nineteen-year-old Louis Casuse, who worked as a carpenter's helper and lived, as nearly all did, in a nearby camp below sandstone cliffs at Indian Springs. "It was a common sight," according to a War Department press release, "to see them trotting back to their dwellings after completing eight hours of strenuous toil."[5]

The work at the depot had not yet finished when Louis registered for the war draft in June. He enlisted into the army in August. While a small number of Diné men served in the Marine Corps as code talkers, most like Louis served in army infantry units. The Navajo Code Talkers have become mythical figures, revered and celebrated both on and off the reservation. Louis would say of them only, "They just talked their way through the war. I carried a gun and fought on the front lines."[6]

The Diné and other Native peoples had not been subject to the draft during World War I because they weren't citizens of the United States. The 1924 Snyder Act extended citizenship status to Native Americans, but a number of states, including New Mexico, disqualified Native peoples from voting.[7] Despite this, all states expected Native peoples to submit to the draft. John Collier, the Commissioner of the Bureau of Indian Affairs, proposed special "all-Indian divisions" to be administered by the BIA, not the War Department. The army remained segregated by race when Louis joined, but this racial segregation did not formally extend to Native soldiers. Collier, however, argued that "large numbers of Indians did not speak English" and would struggle to adapt in English-language-only military units.[8] This was a concern shared by the Gallup draft board, which ruled in December of 1940 that non-English-speaking Diné men would not be subject to the draft. The head of the Navajo Tribal Council, J. C. Morgan, objected to the ruling and also to Collier's "all-Indian unit" proposal. Morgan, who has been described as the "Navajo apostle of assimilation," demanded that the Diné be subject to the military draft and serve in regular units.[9] "It's discriminatory," he declared. "Navajo are extremely patriotic and want to serve."[10] The Governor of New Mexico, John Miles, also objected to Collier's proposal. The exclusion of Native peoples from the draft in New Mexico would mean that non-Native people would be drafted in greater numbers. The draft board relented and required that all Native men register for the draft. It promised remedial English classes for those inducted. According to some accounts, Native people served in the US armed forces during World War II at a rate greater than any other group.[11] The highest rate came from New Mexico and Arizona, where three thousand Diné men and women, 6 percent of the population, entered the armed services.[12]

Draft registration for Native men began in New Mexico in October of 1941. Nearly five thousand Navajo men registered. Throughout the US, between November 1940 and October 1942, more than six thousand Native men were drafted into the military.[13] In his 1944 report to Congress, Collier wrote that the war "brought about the greatest exodus of Indians from reservations that has ever taken place. Out of a total of approximately 65,000 able-bodied men from eighteen to fifty years of age, 30 percent have joined the armed forces."[14] By war's end, the War Department determined that "24,313 male and 357 female US Army and US Air Force personnel, who indicated their race as American Indian upon enlistment or induction from 1 July 1940 through 31 December 1945" served during World War II.[15] Louis was too young to register and too young to be drafted, but he registered anyway and then was either drafted or enlisted into the army in August of 1941 in Santa Fe, New Mexico.[16]

The War Department refused to create "all-Indian units," but it did create "all-Indian training platoons . . . that existed solely to ease the transition from the reservation into military life."[17] Louis spoke English but it's possible he spent time in training platoons with other Native men in the all-Indian units created in Gallup and Phoenix. Navajo Code Talkers were sent to Camp Elliott in San Diego, California. Other army inductees, likely those who passed the literacy test, were sent to Fort Bliss in El Paso, Texas.

The Navajo Tribal Council complained in 1942 of "stories of discrimination and mistreatment" toward Navajo men and women in the military.[18] Native soldiers rarely received promotions.[19] Louis won three Bronze Stars for his combat service in Europe but mustered out of the army as a private, the lowest possible rank, despite receiving an honorable discharge during four years of service, which included months in combat. Some were "treated as undesirables and passed around from camp to camp, they often endured hunger" while in training. Dan Benally, a Diné man from Crownpoint, New Mexico, was drafted and trained with the army but told he would be assigned to the air force. Before going to Europe, he trained at camps all over the US, passing from one to the next: Texas, Louisiana, Arizona, California, and Pennsylvania. He described traveling to camps with other Native soldiers by train under armed guard. He recalled first arriving for training at Fort Bliss in Texas. "Some Pueblos that had long hair. They were mad when the officers cut their long hair off. Next, military clothes were issued to us to wear. Some of us had long hair and some Navajos had queues. Our queues were cut off and sent back to our wives, parents and relatives . . . We were forced to sleep anywhere, sometimes hungry, at that training center."[20] They also drew "some of the worst wartime assignments."[21] The white soldiers they served with called them "Chief," and many of their officers considered them "natural" scouts and fierce "warriors" and drew on the

warrior myth as a rationale for placing them in the most "precarious assignments" in battle.[22] The secretary of the interior, Harold Ickes, celebrated
what he called Native peoples' total lack of fear and their "uncanny ability"
to reconnoiter difficult terrain as scouts.[23] Louis Casuse and Dan Benally
spent years in "training" before joining regular units. Both were made rifle-
men, the most dangerous job in the wartime army, and both were assigned
to infantry units that fought in the western front's bloodiest battles.

Louis sailed for Europe on the Queen Mary on November 3, 1944,
along with nearly twelve thousand other soldiers bound for war. The
Queen Mary was among the largest and fastest troop ships in operation,
with a capacity of sixteen thousand men. It could move an entire division
in one voyage. The sheer number of soldiers meant the ship was cramped
and lacked enough bunks. Soldiers slept in rotations, ate kidney stew and
Brussel sprouts in shifts, and bided their time.[24] Louis arrived in Gourock,
Scotland, on November 9, 1944.[25]

From Gourock, Louis traveled by troop train south to London and
eventually crossed the English Channel. He made his way through France
and finally into Belgium, where he joined K Company of the 3rd Battalion
of the 18th Infantry Regiment, part of the famed 1st Infantry Division—
The Big Red One. The 3rd Battalion had recently moved from Aachen,
Germany, to the Münster forest, near Stolberg, where it bivouacked until
November 17. By the time Louis arrived as a replacement soldier, the unit
had fought in North Africa, landed on D-Day at Omaha Beach, and raced
across France and Belgium through rain and mud until, finally, attacking
the city of Aachen, along the German-Belgian border.

◄■■■■■►

Before the ground fight for Aachen began in October 1944, Britain and
the United States launched a relentless bombing campaign. By this time
in the war, military scientists had realized that "a city was easier to burn
down than to blow up."[26] The character of the bombing campaigns of late
1944, which focused on the North Rhineland, Germany's industrial engine,
shifted from a previous focus on high explosives to one that included liquid
incendiary devices. British and American planes dropped tens of millions

of bombs on the Ruhr and Rhine River valley towns and cities such as Aachen. They bombed the shipyards, the coal mines, and the coke plants. They bombed the forests and the residential areas of cities. They cratered the whole of western Germany in an unprecedented firestorm of destruction "outstripped only by nuclear weapons."[27]

They dropped huge explosive weapons on nearly every Rhineland city, and also smaller liquid incendiaries. The high explosive bombs blew buildings open. The incendiaries burned them down. Incendiary bombs were really multiple bombs encased together. The casings were designed to open in midair and release and scatter smaller "bomblets." The liquid incendiary attacks usually began with a "phosphorous rain" of flares dropped in clusters by an armada of lower elevation bombers. The flares glowed red or green upon impact and marked targets for higher-elevation bombers that thundered in after the flares had been dropped. The people who looked up from Rhineland cities in the moment before their destruction rarely saw the planes that attacked them. By the time the bombs hit their targets the planes were miles away. Instead of the sound of planes, they heard the sound of bombs, an eerie sound like a waterfall suddenly roaring open in the sky and pouring down on them. These were carefully engineered terror weapons. Before the war and during its first years, British scientists "investigated the properties of German furnishings, since the first things to catch fire were the contents of the houses. Junk in attics, food in pantries, clothing, cushions," and they designed their incendiary devices with these homes in mind.[28] They made no distinction between military and civilian targets. Liquid-incendiary bombs fell on hospitals and burned patients alive.[29]

The bombing campaign served as a prelude to the slaughter that would come for the soldiers fighting east of Aachen. The town of Duisburg, a key industrial hub of the German war machine not far from Aachen, all but disappeared in a firestorm that engulfed every building in the city in the course of just a few moments during mid-October 1944. "In twenty minutes, 1,063 British planes dropped 3,574 tons of high-explosive bombs and 820 tons of incendiaries."[30] The attack destroyed much of Duisburg and instantly incinerated, or slowly asphyxiated, three thousand people.

Louis arrived in Aachen after the attack. He walked through the rubble and saw the charred bodies trapped in collapsed buildings. He reported to

Lieutenant William Russell, the commander of K Company since D-Day. By the fall of 1944, the German Army was in retreat under the barrage of bombing and artillery attacks, and army planners assumed that the heavy fighting was over and the war might end by Christmas.

Louis joined the war in Aachen, but the fight he joined would not be one fought in cities and towns; instead, it would be a battle waged in the Hürtgenwald, the pine and fir forest southeast of Aachen. Had they not come to Europe to kill people, they may have seen beauty in those woods. The low, rolling hills of the Rhenish massif sheltered thick forests. Peasant farms and hamlets spread out along the valleys of the Ruhr and Rhine Rivers. Raised bogs crisscrossed woods and mountains and gave way south of Aachen to the wide moorlands and heathlands of the Hohes Venn, where the grasslands burned in summer and everything dissolved into fog and mist under heavy snow in winter.

Louis found his unit bivouacked in the cold and mud along the Belgian border with Germany. "The men constructed living quarters of logs for shelter and protection as foxholes could not be dug because of the water-soaked earth."[31] The replacements arrived in trucks and carried carbines and gas masks. They arrived in time to watch the enormous German V-1 rockets roaring past them in the sky "headed for the rear."[32] If Louis arrived before November 17, he was with the battalion when it mustered out of Münster and moved south into the Hürtgenwald.

◀■■■■■▶

The Hürtgenwald begins along the Belgian border with Luxembourg, in the mountainous Ardennes region, which stretches more than twenty miles south into Germany's Eifel Mountains. The Allies fought the Germans in the Battle of Hürtgen Forest in a patchwork of farms and forests, or rather tree plantations mostly comprised of nonnative pine and fir trees densely planted in rows. The southern stretch of the Ardennes includes a number of distinct smaller forests—the Wenau, Hürtgen, Rotgen, and Monschau woods among them. Combined, they create the nearly eighty-square mile, triangle-shaped Hürtgenwald. Those who lived in the "Huertgen" or "Hurtgen" Forest, as the Allies called it, occupied a working landscape of dense woods and isolated peasant farm holdings interspersed with small villages, forest hamlets, and larger commercial and even heavy industrial towns at the edges. Every October and November, before the snows arrive, the Hürtgenwald transforms itself into a rainforest. Narrow forest trails cut through steep and heavily forested terrain marked by swollen rivers and sodden soils hidden by a dense, water-logged canopy. Deep ravines and gorges bottom out into bogs and ponds that thwart easy travel. The wide-spreading, heavy boughs of the Douglas firs—some more than one hundred feet tall—drop nearly to the ground and interlock with those of other trees, blocking natural light from reaching the forest floor. The fall rains in 1944 turned the Hürtgenwald's loamy soils into an oily, concrete-like mixture that stuck to everything.

The battle for the Hürtgenwald had dragged on for months by mid-November. Army planners had been convinced that weakened German forces were in retreat after the fall of Aachen and on the verge of surrender. The army sought to deal German forces a deathblow in the woods and planned an attack that would send a broad front of men and machines into and through the forest, beyond the Ruhr River and past the Rhine toward Cologne. The Allies could have swept past the Hürtgenwald, ignoring it entirely, but military planners had no idea how many Wehrmacht soldiers occupied the woods, and they feared an attack along their forest flank. But the Germans largely had abandoned the Westwall, as the line of fortifications along their western border was known, following the Fall of France and had only recently and "hastily reoccupied the line, at first mainly with second-rate troops: teenagers, old men, and battalions formed of men suffering from the same ailment, such as stomach ulcers."[33]

The 1st Division's battle plans called for the six thousand men of the 16th and 18th Infantry Regiments to fight their way southeast from Aachen, through the small villages of Hamich, Heistern, and Langerwehe, and attack the Westwall directly.[34] By this time the army already had sent thousands and thousands of men into the forest, and all had been cut down and thrown out by weather and artillery and mortars. It was a battle strategy of attrition whose victory depended on an unlimited supply of men. How else to win a battle with a casualty rate that exceeded 100 percent for some units.

To the soldiers bivouacked near Aachen, the Hürtgenwald looked like "a vast undulating blackish-green ocean" of horror into which the Nazis had planted minefields along nearly every trail, strung barbed wire between the more than three thousand concrete and steel pillbox bunkers, and built and installed thousands and thousands of antitank, pyramid-shaped concrete blocks known as "dragon's teeth."[35] This unbroken network of military reinforcements bisected the Hürtgenwald and stretched all along Germany's western border from Holland south to Switzerland. How to pierce the Westwall—or Siegfried Line of fortifications, as the Allies called it—preoccupied army planners through the summer and fall of 1944.

War destroys everything, except for the Hürtgenwald, which grew more lethal when the shooting started. The men who fought in the woods worried more about the trees than the Westwall, for the Hürtgenwald was a forest carefully designed with "plenty of malice afterthought" to kill and maim a man as quickly and efficiently as possible.[36] And not just because of the reinforcements of the Westwall. A mature fir tree, it turns out, is the perfect military weapon. Its boughs obscured German observation posts and minefields. The woods were so dense with closely planted fir trees that American soldiers often did little more than return fire into the trees. But the firs provided more than a defensive advantage for the Germans. The forest served as a tree plantation devoted to the production of timber, firewood for smelting, charcoal and tannin for the leather industry, but also as a resource for war making. The "German forces exploited softwood anatomy to weaponize conifers" by firing mortars and artillery directly into the dense fir canopy above the foxholes and forward observation posts of Allied troops.[37] When targeted by artillery or mortars, fir trees, which lack the cellular fibers and structure found in hardwoods, "separate easily into shards upon impact." The whole forest, it seemed, would explode on impact and rain down fire and "airborne daggers" of wood and metal shrapnel on US troops.[38] There was nowhere to hide in the Hürtgenwald, where "the forest sucked at the lifeblood of a man's body and spirit."[39]

This was not a place to learn how to fight. Everything was lethal. The skies greeted the Allied assault by opening up in September with rains that never ended. When the clouds would briefly part, German mortars, artillery, cruise missiles, and 88 antitank guns took their place. Death came from above and also from below because the Germans laced the forest with minefields. "One mine was buried every eight steps."[40] And the mud seemed alive. It climbed up men's boots, found its way into trucks, tents, and foxholes. It gummed up everything and stopped tanks in their tracks.

A 16th Infantry Regiment truck plows through a muddy Hürtgen Forest road in the fall of 1944 after constant rains made travel nearly impossible. Courtesy of 1st Infantry Division archives, public domain.

By late November, when the ground froze solid, the men needed dynamite and pickaxes to dig foxholes. They could never dig their foxholes deep enough, and the fir boughs were never strong enough to protect them from the constant German mortar and artillery attacks. The Germans knew the woods well, and every pillbox with mortars or artillery—and there were thousands of them—seemed to have the coordinates to every bivouac, every crossroads, every clearing, and every farmhouse. If a soldier's footfall cracked a twig, mortars came as if attached to the man by string. And the horrible trees blocked every advance, obscured every German bunker, exploded into a million lethal shards under every German barrage. If anvils had started falling from the sky no one would have been surprised.

The "Germans were everywhere" in the woods, or at least it seemed like they were.[41] And Louis's unit never had enough ammunition or fuel.

The 1st Division had raced so far ahead of its supply lines in its race through France and Belgium that the men had no cold weather gear and rarely enough to eat.[42]

The geographer, writer, and artist J. B. Jackson fought in the Hürtgenwald as an intelligence officer in the 9th Infantry during September and October of 1944. He interrogated German POWs, interpreted aerial reconnaissance photography, compiled battle reports, and wrote intelligence briefings on German military movements in a "desolate countryside" reduced by artillery and bombs to "rain soaked ruins." In an essay titled "Landscape as Seen by the Military," he wrote about the aerial, mortar, and artillery carpet bombings of the Hürtgenwald that "obliterate roads and fields and forests and house types and settlement patterns as if they had never existed."[43] Jackson's job required that he represent the battle in the forest through photos, maps, and written reports and interpret these into military terms. What tactical advantage can be gleaned from the study of the forest ecology and political and military geography of the Hürtgenwald? Are the bridges blown? Are the dams a threat? Who controls the high ground? Where are the minefields and the passable roads? This work required a close, careful read of the places—natural and human built—that Jackson found around him. "I began to see that regimented landscape in front of us," Jackson would write, "as a kind of formal eighteenth-century garden, and the eighteenth-century formal garden as the regimented militarized state in miniature."[44] The Nazis, Jackson realized, had converted the Hürtgenwald into a weapon "as relentless as the enemy himself."[45]

Jackson, the future scholar of cultural landscape studies, tried to make sense of this new kind of military landscape and the carnage it produced. Nearly all studies and analyses of the Battle of Hürtgen Forest highlight the Westwall and German military strength and tactics. Critics of the decision to attack through the woods often emphasize the miscalculation on the part of the Allies in entering the forest to begin with. Jackson, however, considered the problem of the forest itself. He realized quickly the danger of thinking of the forest as "a kind of setting or empty stage upon which certain alarming and unpredictable decisions and actions took place." The Hürtgenwald only appeared "natural." The carnage it inflicted was by design, and this "design was manifest in every detail."[46]

Elements of the 9th Infantry Division, particularly the 60th Infantry Regiment, Jackson's outfit, suffered heavy losses while fighting in the Hürtgenwald in September and October. They were among the first units into the forest and "suffered almost 100 percent turnover in combat person-nel."[47] Whole infantry companies—hundreds of men strong—entered the woods only to emerge days later with just a handful of men alive. Whole units ran out of the forest screaming. The sheer terror the place provoked in the men, and the shocking rate—and way—they died, suggested to Jackson an unnerving explanation to the unique brutality of the battle. They weren't fighting *in* the forest, they were fighting *against* the forest. The men "hated its cold and dampness. They hated its lurking death."[48] When the Hürtgenwald "trembled from an artillery barrage and burst into flames" following a German attack, it produced a hellfire so lethal that the forest seemed to suddenly transform itself into a terrifying killing machine. It was his first lesson in what he would later come to call *the vernacular land-scape*, "where the slow, natural processes of growth and maturity and decay are deliberately set aside and history is substituted."[49] A forest as a living and botanical expression of Nazi aggression, one as lethal as a German V-2 rocket and as terrifying as an 88 antitank gun. This is a "war," Jackson wrote, that "organizes space." A fight in a forest of beheaded tress that the men in Louis's unit called a "death factory."

◀▪▪▪▪▪▶

The first Allied artillery attack in early September did little to soften German lines behind the Westwall. The constant fog and cloud cover limited air support. Germans held all the high ground in the woods with "about 200 artillery pieces that could fire on any part of" the Allied Army in the forest.[50] When German artillery and antitank fire arrived, it came with a rising shriek that sent men running for cover. The mortars came in silently, without warning. Sniper and machine-gun fire came from every direction. Some units fought in the forest for weeks without relief. They left their dead in the woods because the ambulances couldn't reach them. Nearly every infantry regiment sent into the woods experienced unheard-of fatality rates. Truckloads of replacement soldiers arrived, only for the men to be killed before even making it to their assigned units.[51] The army sent replacements to replace replacements.[52] In one unit, the fatality rate for rifle company commanders was over 300 percent.[53] Entire companies disappeared in the woods. In its official history of the fight, the 1st Infantry Division described the fighting in the Hürtgenwald "as deadly, as miserable, as unrewarding, and as relentless a battle as the 1st Division ever engaged in. The woods were treacherous; the mud was slick and slimy. The roads were practically nonexistent and the weather became worse and worse."[54]

There were nearly three thousand enlisted men in the 18th Infantry when Louis arrived.[55] Few of them would survive the forest. The casualty rate in Louis's unit eventually exceeded the rate at which they could be replaced. Entire platoons were gunned down as if by firing squad. It was understood that the men were being sent to their deaths. Eventually so desperate for replacements, division sent the regimental band into battle.[56] They sent the veterinarians into the fight.[57]

Louis's first days with his unit were spent trying to stay warm in small lean-tos made of logs "because foxholes could not be dug in the water-soaked bivouac."[58] The cold had settled in, and tank gears froze during the night. It snowed. Few infantry soldiers had winter boots or cold weather gear. The cold and unremitting combat never let up and despondent men froze to death in foxholes.[59]

Dan Benally, who arrived in Europe four months ahead of Louis, fought in the same woods. "In November the weather was really cold. We dug holes to stay in. The holes contained water, and the water would easily freeze. Sometimes we stayed in a hole for a week, in the frozen water from our waists down . . . Some of the white men in the freeze holes had frozen to death."[60]

The initial battle plan placed Louis's company in reserve while the 16th Infantry Regiment lead the assault.[61] When the offensive started on November 17, they attacked a small village. The previous day, four thousand planes of the US 8th Air Force "dropped more than ten thousand tons of bombs on German positions in the Huertgen Forest."[62] According to some reports, the bombing campaign killed tens of thousands of people.[63] The next day, against "loses quite heavy," the 16th and 18th Infantry attacked the village of Hamich.[64] The previous day's aerial and artillery attack had largely destroyed the village, but German panzers still patrolled the town.

The Wehrmacht controlled the high ground, too. The soldiers spent that first day dodging "German heavy artillery and automatic weapons fire" as they fought to take "Bloody" Hamich, as the soldiers called it.[65] Intelligence reports warned of five German panzers in the village and an entire company of German infantry hiding in the reinforced cellars of ruined homes.[66] German infantry tank and artillery fire, both from the high ground and from the village, repelled the 16th, which "requested maximum amount of artillery support to make up for lack of heavy weapons."[67] Hundreds of shells rained down on German positions from more than a dozen different artillery units.

The rain finally let up the next morning, and the 16th Infantry attacked again, this time capturing nearly forty German soldiers and taking the southern edge of town.[68] The Wehrmacht, as it always did, counterattacked. Fifteen tanks and an entire company of soldiers, supported by German planes, overran 16th Infantry positions. This would be the pattern. The 16th or 18th would take a village or a sector of the forest one day, lose men and ground to a German counterattack the next, and bring in reinforcements or replacements to launch another attack on the third. The division was now bogged down in a "bloody foot-by-foot tree-by-tree struggle . . . each house, each hill, each hole in the ground was fought for, and gains were reckoned in yards—not the miles of the race through France and Belgium."[69]

The men would move in the rain and fog through mud and forest into a village, fire rifles and mortars at German bunkers and reinforcements, scramble into a defensive position, desperately dig foxholes, call in artillery, dig deeper into muddy or frozen ground, cut down trees to use as cover for their holes, string barbed wire, send out patrols, post forward observers, and prepare for a German counterattack at night. Their wet socks covered swollen feet slowly decomposing inside their boots.

One company from Louis's battalion joined the attack of Hamich on November 18. With the 16th hiding in the basements of blown-out buildings, multiple field artillery battalions fired directly into town, and at every road into Hamich, and destroyed three German tanks.[70] The German counterattack came from the north, "swinging around to the east part of town."[71] The Wehrmacht roared in with tanks, hundreds of infantry soldiers, and so many self-propelled guns that "the only way the Germans could be beaten

Infantry soldiers fought through nearly impenetrable forests in the Hürtgen Forest in the fall of 1944. Courtesy of 1st Infantry Division archives, public domain.

off was by the 1st Division Infantry calling down artillery fire on their own positions in the town."[72] German snipers and mortars killed five men in L Company of Louis's battalion during the fight. Louis avoided the carnage. Most of his battalion peeled off from Hamich and marched through thick forest toward Wenau, a hamlet surrounded by woods a mile to the southwest.[73] They trudged "through the heavily wooded area south of Wenau and German artillery inflicted many casualties."[74] As they went, they managed to drag 5-ton, 155mm guns through the mud and minefields, which they used to flatten Wenau with a barrage of 100-pound rounds.[75]

With Louis and K Company dodging snipers and minefields, the rest of the battalion took cover alongside the 16th Infantry in Hamich, hiding in half-destroyed buildings, firing bazookas at German armor, and taking cover as US artillery blasted German positions in the town.[76] It would take two days of fighting and cost more than one hundred US soldiers their lives, and another five hundred injured, to take both the village and the high ground. Hamich was even bloodier for the Germans. "It is estimated that at least a battalion of infantry a day was destroyed in the fighting around Hamich."[77]

Louis's unit was still in the woods that night, "receiving quite a bit of direct fire and air bursts."[78] It was his first real introduction to the Hürtgenwald. Some men who fought there were convinced "they could smell the dead inside" the woods when they entered the forest.[79] Louis's unit spent most of the next week fighting in woods near Wenau and a larger village called Heistern. German artillery and mortar always followed them.[80] German mortars pinned them down along a tree line two hundred yards south of Heistern. One of the officers in Louis's company was injured and evacuated in the fighting.[81] Over two terrifying days, his entire company came under constant automatic weapons fire and mortar and artillery attacks.[82] Trees exploded above their heads without warning. They had no time to dig foxholes, so they dove under fir boughs when shrapnel and wood rained down.[83] "In the Hürtgen Forest every shell was a tree burst."[84] Even if they'd had time to dig into the frozen ground, it wouldn't have helped. "Foxholes, without cover, were no protection whatsoever" from the air bursts.[85] The tall firs "dropped like javelins on troops below."[86] The 32nd Field Artillery Battalion fired more than six hundred rounds of artillery into Heistern beginning just before midnight on November 20.[87]

The sheer number of wounded men during the months-long Hürtgenwald campaign swamped medic stations behind the front lines. The injured who made it out of the woods "would just sit there and shake. Others would be in a daze and have to be helped around. When given a place to sit, they would stay there, staring with vacant faces."[88] Medics stacked amputated arms and legs like cordwood.[89] The casualty rates were so high, and the US advance so slow, that some company commanders began refusing orders to attack. Entire platoons were wiped out. Whole battalions of infantry soldiers—hundreds of men—simply "ran away" from the fighting, screaming, shell shocked and "walking away as if in a dream."[90] Some of the injured men were evacuated to replacement depots where they "were treated like prisoners and kept inside barbed wire enclosures. They were even beaten if they gave the depot people a hard time."[91] If they didn't go AWOL, they were shipped back to different units as replacement soldiers. So many men were killed in the fighting—tens of thousands—that the dead were often left in the forest.

First Hamich, then Wenau, now Heistern. Louis's company attacked from the left while another company attacked directly into the village. "German artillery fire was on a heavier scale" than they'd seen to that point.[92] They set up defensive positions in Heistern's few buildings that weren't on fire and spent the night in "fanatical house-to-house fighting."[93] Louis's company commander, Captain Russell, established a headquarters in a partially destroyed building. The next day, November 21, started cold and windy. An entire German battalion counterattacked before dawn. For more than two hours, US artillery saturated the village.[94] Some German soldiers took "refuge in buildings" occupied by Louis's battalion.[95] House-to-house combat turned into room-by-room fighting. They fired at each other through living room walls, fought with bayonets in dining rooms. By midday, Louis's unit took the crossroads at the north end of town, while other units continued to fight German forces in the streets and houses of Heistern.[96] At dusk, K Company, with tanks in support, finally seized the village.

German artillery and infantry fire killed nearly seventy-five men from 3rd Battalion in Heistern, including Captain Russell, who died by a sniper's bullet to the head.[97] Multiple companies in the battalion suffered catastrophic casualties amid "some of the most intense artillery and mortar fire" in two years of fighting.[98] Heistern nearly wiped out all of K Company, which needed nearly fifty replacement soldiers to reform platoons.[99] A new company commander, Captain Paulsen, took command of K Company. Louis, in the woods less than a week, was now among the most senior men in his company.

It rained on November 22, and for the first time since Louis joined the fight there were no German counterattacks against their position.[100] His battalion went into regimental reserve and spent Thanksgiving in Heistern's rubble, hiding from the rain that flooded the river valleys.[101] Each morning, for days, they dragged themselves out of muddy, waterlogged foxholes or damp, ruined buildings to send patrols out of Heistern. On November 27, under a heavy smoke screen laid down by mortar fire, they attacked the industrial city of Langerwehe from the south. This was the final push. Langerwehe had been the crucial target since Aachen. The plan required they take Hamich, Wenau, and Heistern and then fight toward the Ruhr River villages of Langerwehe and Düren. The Ruhr ran south-to-north to the west of both Langerwehe and Düren, where a railhead linked to a German supply depot further east.[102] The Germans fortified Langerwehe as "a defensive strong point" against the Allied assault, but mostly teenage fighters, some as young as sixteen, defended the town.[103]

As Louis's unit launched the attack, US artillery, and British and US planes, bombed both cities into "smoldering ruins."[104] But the German reinforcements held the town as Louis's unit swept in from the south. By afternoon, they occupied the high ground in Jungersdorf, a stone's throw from Langerwehe, from where two other units launched attacks directly into Langerwehe over open terrain.[105] Between Louis and Langerwehe lay chaos. "Front lines became jammed close together."[106] There was no discernable front. Artillery came from every direction, and "the fight seemed to have no end."[107]

K Company cleared buildings in Langerwehe, which was like playing hide-and-seek to the death. They occupied the southern half of the city, while two other companies pushed further north into town. "The fighting was very bitter, from house to house all the way," with tanks and tank destroyers supporting the advance.[108] The Germans finally retreated across the Ruhr on November 28, abandoning Langerwehe. By November 30, the 1st Infantry Division established a line west of the Ruhr River. It took months of fighting and thousands of dead to push the German Army ten miles east of Aachen. In the two weeks that Louis fought in the Hürtgenwald, the 1st Infantry Division lost nearly 3,500 men, more than it lost on D-Day.[109]

The 2,800 men of the 18th Infantry Regiment, mostly replacements by this time, rotated out of combat and fell back to what they thought would be a month's leave. They spent the first few days of December in Langerwehe before relieving another unit in Luchem, a mile north. Luchem was under sporadic mortar and artillery attack when they arrived. Louis's unit was relieved on December 7 and spent a night back in Hamich before rotating out off the front lines to Gemmenich, Belgium.[110] From December 8 to December 15, they were assigned to "training, regrouping, care and cleaning of equipment, recreation."[111] Everyone got new uniforms. "All men were paid; trips to Paris and Verviers were initiated; men were given the opportunity for hot showers. Company parties were held and movies, USO shows and ARC Clubmobiles were also available."[112] The men billeted in the homes of grateful Belgians.

They slept in beds and ate hot food. It was in Gemmenich, on December 11, that Louis may have received two of his three Bronze Stars.

Division placed the battalion on a six-hour alert on December 16, when the Germans launched a surprise attack. Hundreds of thousands of Wehrmacht soldiers and paratroopers, 1,500 tanks, and thousands of heavy artillery pieces and antitank guns thundered into Belgium like an avalanche. The Germans were after Allied supply dumps and the crucial shipping port of Antwerp.[113] The 18th Regiment raced back to the front lines the next day and dug into defensive positions on the eastern side of Eupen, Belgium, in dense fog and waist-deep snow near the northern shoulder of the bulge in the Allied lines.[114]

Hundreds of German paratroopers dropped behind Allied lines.[115] Each day came another report of more German paratroopers. Multiple German panzer divisions roared into the heavily wooded Ardennes, re-taking positions south of Hamich, Heistern, and Langerwehe. These were not the teenagers and the elderly who fought in the Hürtgenwald, but battle-tested troops taken from the eastern front for this counteroffensive. Some had spent years in the brutal fighting against the Soviets. For the plan to succeed, the Germans would have to race through Allied lines in a fighting sprint. It was an impossible strategy that depended on surprise, ruthlessness, and rainy weather. They murdered entire platoons of captured US soldiers in order to avoid slowing down with POWs. The Allies ad-opted a mostly defensive posture, and some criticized the British General Montgomery for this approach, but Montgomery had seen the grinding horror of the Hürtgenwald.

◄■■■■■►

Louis's unit took turns patrolling in waist-deep snow.[116] They wore white ponchos and looked like ghosts in a haunted forest. K Company reinforced L Company on December 18 to keep the paratroopers out of Eupen.[117] They spent an evening in a firefight with a German patrol and chased German soldiers into the woods with percussion grenades.[118] They spent the next day sweeping a sector near Malmedy, firing wildly at German attackers.[119] German paratroopers and supplies dropped from the sky throughout the day, and K Company took twelve prisoners and rescued twenty-three Americans in the woods near Eupen.[120] There were reports of entire companies of German soldiers speaking English, wearing American uniforms, and driving American jeeps, sowing confusion.[121] Small patrols of German soldiers probed their lines and K Company "fired on them and they threw three percussion grenades and took off into the woods."[122]

They moved south of Eupen on December 20, traveling in a convoy of trucks and tanks to Ovifat, Belgium. A cruise missile or buzz bomb—the same weapon the Germans used in the terror bombing of London (vengeance weapons, the Germans called them)—exploded near their position, wounding one man.[123] It was as if the unique and shocking viciousness of the eastern front arrived suddenly in Belgium. An entire battalion of German troops and tanks broke through the line between Louis's unit and another company. The men dove into foxholes fortified with timber. A dozen German panzers were suddenly on top of them, "firing point-blank at the infantrymen's [fox]holes and running over their holes with the tank treads."[124]

The survivors of Ovifat moved to Nidrum on December 23 and bivouacked in the mud, where they spent day after day in late December patrolling, laying minefields, and stringing concertina and barbed wire between positions. The cold and snow drove the men underground, where they huddled under roofs of reinforced timber, in holes heated and poisoned by makeshift wood-burning stoves.[125] Mist and low clouds on December 23 made air cover difficult. Four US bombers dropped explosives directly on 3rd Battalion troops, killing six men.[126] The Germans moved heavy armor into Faymonville, Belgium, on Christmas Day.[127] Louis's unit relieved another in Bütgenbach, Belgium.

If K Company had a radio, Louis may have heard Hitler's defiant New Year's Eve speech. At midnight, while the men tried to stay warm in foxholes covered by snow drifts, Hitler broadcast a New Year's proclamation in which he mocked the "coterie of drawing-room politicians and drawing-room generals" who have assumed for over a year a coming German surrender. There will never be "a German capitulation," he boasted, only "a German victory!" Louis's division commanders were listening, and shortly after midnight, "Division Artillery and attached units fired concentrations on all known and suspected assembly areas and installations." The bombardment would last all night and into the next day. The Germans responded with rockets that hit Louis's company in the early hours of New Year's Day.[128]

The long cold night gave way to dense morning fog. The men wore snowshoes out on patrol and used dynamite to dig foxholes. There were never enough combat engineers because there were always too many mud-bound trucks blocking the road, always too much snow that needed bulldozing. Reinforced platoons from Louis's battalion moved south of Bütgenbach "cleaning out" German positions as they went, inflicting heavy casualties on a large German infantry unit.[129] Low-flying German planes buzzed their positions throughout the day.[130]

Louis's unit spent the first few days of 1945 aggressively patrolling the Bütgenbach ridge through deep snow. They defended their line by "stringing additional tactical wire and by laying more mine fields across their front."[131] Four army divisions launched a coordinated diversionary attack on January 3, "supported by artillery, in such strength as to drive in enemy outposts" but "conducted as to lead the enemy to believe an attack in force was under way or in prospect."[132] It did nothing. German forces responded aggressively, and most of Louis's unit withdrew under heavy snows and even heavier German mortar fire to shallow foxholes south of Bütgenbach.[133] All along the line the Germans attacked. To the south, near Bastogne, Belgium, the 6th Armored Division retreated in the face of a German tank assault. "Reports from men drifting back from the front were alarming. Entire units, claimed many wild-eyed refugees, had been cut off and were being wiped out."[134]

Louis's company sent a patrol out on January 3 in sleet and snow. German mortar attacks scattered it. A wounded man separated from the others found his way back, only to die at the aid station. Two or three other men died in the mortar attacks in the woods.[135] Mortars and tank fire continued through the night and increased in the morning with machine-gun fire from their right flank.[136] Louis's unit was less than one thousand yards from German positions and radioed in for more concertina wire and trip flares to string between platoons. They didn't want to waste their dynamite, so they dug foxholes in frozen ground with pickaxes.[137]

The snow continued on January 8 and K Company must have felt increasingly claustrophobic in the woods. To their left, they heard German burp guns, ahead of them mortars, and all around them the sound of Germans chopping and felling timber for God knows what.[138] The next day, either from the weight of the snow or the bitter cold, land mines spontaneously exploded.[139] Near midnight, they heard engines starting up and revving.[140] The entire forest seemed to catch fire two thousand yards in front of them on January 10, amid shouting and explosions just beyond the tree line. They launched star shells into the night sky to illuminate the forest but saw nothing.[141] Combat engineers cleared snow with enormous bulldozers and spread sand on roads, but the snow kept falling and burying the sand.[142]

Every day now was the same. Drifting snow, frigid cold, nighttime ambush patrols through the woods that lasted for hours, mortar attacks, exploding trees, causalities. An assault on January 14 sent an armored division north to take Saint Vith from the Germans. The 16th Infantry took the villages of Faymonville and Schoppen. Louis's battalion cleared the railroad tracks and took the high ground near their current positions.[143] They hiked into dense forest and down into a steep valley, across a half-frozen river, and then up into the German high ground. Mortars followed them as they went.[144]

They used their hand grenades to dig shallow foxholes.[145] The next day, January 15, started warmer but grew colder when snow and fog arrived. Division sent 150 replacement soldiers to reinforce the battalion.[146] In the morning, Louis's unit "raised itself from snow bound foxholes and launched an attack" in support of the 16th Infantry.[147] Louis's battalion "attacked over open terrain covered with deep snow to reach a wood line where the Germans were dug in with excellent vision and fields of fire."[148] So many men fighting on January 15 and 16 "would get wounded and go throughout [the] aid station and return to their units and then get wounded again."[149] Louis's unit "drew considerable small arms and mortar from the draw and the woods to the east of" German positions.[150] German mortar attacks pinned down I Company. L Company "was caught by daylight in the open."[151] Two platoons were nearly wiped out by automatic weapons as artillery and mortars "rained down" on the men.[152] Under cover of smoke that provided no cover, L Company retreated back to Bütgenbach amid "murderous machine gun fire" and "frightful casualties."[153] Louis's company attacked into the woods to the south, where they set up an observation post on the high ground overlooking Schoppen, but "could do little more than dig in for the night."[154]

Bütgenbach must be German for misery. Wehrmacht soldiers occupied a line of bunkers along the Bütgenbach Heck, a remote, high elevation ridge. Louis's water and food rations froze. "The foul weather and deep snow made the supply and evacuation problem very difficult. There were only trails and they were piled high with drifted snow."[155] Platoon commanders spent the dawn hours trying to reassemble shattered rifle companies gutted by the previous day's battle. Scores of men from Louis's battalion had been killed and "the bodies were still lying where they had fallen."[156] Louis didn't talk much about the war later in life, but he talked about the patrols on the Bütgenbach Heck. "They would send a few of us out on patrol at night, and I would be the only one who would return alive," he told Ursula once. "It's a miracle you survived," Ursula would reply. "I was a good shot," he would answer, and that was all he'd say.[157]

The sun rose to a clear and cold day on January 16. No one had slept for three days.[158] What was left of Louis's company "moved forward into the woods against heavy enemy opposition and heavy concentrations of artillery fire."[159] They linked up with a company from the 16th Infantry Regiment and moved south toward German positions.[160] Within an hour, they found themselves in woods "full of enemy and they received [a] heavy barrage" of machine-gun fire, mortars, and artillery that lasted for hours.[161]

By evening, Louis's unit was pinned down. Division sent an infantry battalion to reinforce their position. Their commanders ordered them to fight through the "enemy's rear and attack from there," but there was no one left to do the fighting. Louis's battalion had suffered hundreds of casualties over the previous few days.[162] Nearly two hundred men were wounded, and eighty-five men were killed or missing in action.[163]

It would be here, where so many men died and would die, in the remote and snowbound Bütgenbach Heck, that the Wehrmacht would capture Louis Casuse.[164]

◄▪▪▪▪▪►

There are no military records of Louis Casuse's capture by Germans on the Bütgenbach Heck or of the seventy-nine days he spent in a German POW camp, or even in what camp the Nazis held him. Most of his service records burned in a 1973 fire in the National Archives in St. Louis. He appears on no roster and on none of the thousands of pages of operations reports, official histories, or regimental or company reports and rosters. He was a ghost in a haunted forest, like most of the men who survived the Hürtgenwald.

The Wehrmacht force marched their POWs out of frozen and smoking ruins. Entire villages destroyed, tens of thousands of bombs, months of constant artillery and mortar shelling, and the grinding toll of tanks through the woods had converted the Hürtgenwald into a vast wasteland. Over the course of the more than four-month battle, the army sent seven infantry divisions—the 1st, 4th, 8th, 9th (twice), 28th, and 83rd—an armored division, and dozens of other units into the Hürtgenwald—altogether around 120,000 men.[165] More than 25,000 men were killed or captured and nearly 10,000 wounded in the fighting.[166]

Louis may have spent time in the same POW camp as Dan Benally, who was captured by Germans the same day that Louis's unit entered the Hürtgenwald. Benally spent much longer than Louis as a POW. "I was lost for seven months," he said years later. "I guess they notified all of my relatives that had been writing to me. The letters that were sent to me were all piled up in Fort Leavenworth. That was where dead letters went. All of my belongings and property they did away with I guess. The awards that I had won were forgotten. The white men's were not forgotten."

After his capture, the Germans marched Benally through mud and snow for days. Louis described a similar forced march. His German captors force marched him and other POWs through a blizzard. On the few occasions he told the story, he described the cold as otherworldly. The man marching alongside him suffered severe frostbite to his face and hands. A fourth-degree frostbite is strangely similar to a scalping. The skin, deprived of its blood supply, turns black. Louis, marching beside the man, watched as rotting flesh fell from his face.[167]

Benally met one other Navajo man in a POW camp. They talked briefly once while eating bloody meat. "I don't know, it could have been human flesh," he would say later.[168]

Louis was stooped at the shoulders when he returned from the war, and he explained that this was because a Nazi guard slammed a rifle butt into his back while he was praying on his knees once.[169] Another kicked him in the face and broke his nose.[170] We know that Louis spent seventy-nine days as a German POW, which places his liberation on the same date as the 47th Tank Battalion's liberation of Stalag 13-C on April 6, 1945, where the Nazis held more than a thousand American GIs captured in the Battle of the Bulge.[171] If true, the forced march he described to his children would have lasted for a week or more.

When he was finally liberated, he was an inch shorter and twenty-five pounds lighter than when he arrived in Europe.[172] Benally lost eighty pounds. "The meat on parts of our bodies was nearly gone, and the part that was left was transparent-like."[173] Benally didn't think his relatives would recognize him when he got home. "They probably thought a man that burned to death in the war had returned."[174]

◄■■■■■►

In the years after the war, the Hürtgenwald would occasionally erupt in flames from "remnant phosphorus grenades."[175] Some bodies have never been recovered and the "search for missing soldiers continues until the present day."[176] The fighting in the Hürtgenwald transformed the structure of the forest and even the biology of the trees in it. There are new species now growing in the Hürtgenwald. The fir and pine trees, splintered by war, gave way to saplings that absorbed the metal from the battlefield—the helmets, grenades, rifles, and more—directly into the root structure and xylem of the trees that replaced them.[177] So much shrapnel and ordnance, so many minefields, and the debris and ruins of so many firefights and artillery bombardments littered the battlefield, that the detritus of war became an engine of ecological succession.

After his liberation from a German POW camp, Louis sailed home in mid-April from La Havre, France, on the USS *General W. P. Richardson*, along with a thousand other liberated POWs.[178] Benally made it home the next month. When asked about the war and his time as a POW, Benally described seeing starved men thrown into mass graves. He cut a man's head

off in fierce fighting during the war and said only that "he hated to do it."
Louis said little, often just, "What's the use?" What could he have said to
explain it all? That he fought alongside wounded men who lost themselves
in blizzards and froze to death in snow.[179] That he fought alongside or
against men who killed and took scalps, took ears, took teeth from men
they'd found dead or slaughtered. Wore them like jewelry; showed them
around like souvenirs from the Death Factory.[180] These were not his stories,
so he never told them.

Child War Bride

Louis Casuse arrived in New York on April 26, 1945, along with a thousand other liberated POWs. From New York, the army shipped him to Camp Fannin in Texas, where he received an honorable discharge in October 1945. He briefly returned to Coyote Canyon, but by mid-December he joined an exodus of men traveling south from the Navajo Nation to Santa Rita to work in the copper mine. By then Kennecott Copper owned the Santa Rita mine, among the largest and most profitable copper mines in the world. The war draft starved Kennecott of labor, so it found replacement workers among the Navajo miners of one of its subsidiaries, the Gallup American Coal Company, or GAMERCO, as it was known. Kennecott recruited more than a thousand Diné men beginning in 1940, and Louis joined the tail end of this labor migration, taking a job as a trackman building narrow-gauge rails for the coal-powered trains that hauled copper ore out of the mine. The work was dangerous, and the pay was lower for Navajo workers than other miners. Most Navajo men who worked the mine stayed only long enough to cash one paycheck. Louis lasted eight months.

In August 1946 he reenlisted in an army that no longer needed infantrymen, so they shipped him off to Europe as a military policeman bound for the postwar military occupation of Austria. He sailed from New York in May of the following year and arrived in Italy in June 1947, eventually making his way to Austria that summer, where he joined the 16th Infantry Regiment, and later the 350th Infantry Regiment, in Salzburg, Austria.[1] He was twenty-seven years old.

◄▪▪▪▪▪▪►

Kennecott Copper Company's vast Chino Mine in Santa Rita, New Mexico, around the time Louis returned to Santa Rita following World War II. At the time, the Chino mine was among the largest copper mines in the world. Courtesy of Chino Mine Collection, Silver City Museum, Silver City, New Mexico.

Lillian Hutzler was ten years old in the summer of 1945 when US military occupation forces first marched into Salzburg. It would be the second occupation that she would live through. Born in July 1935, she was the second oldest of five children and lived not far from the city center in a small apartment. The first occupation began just before her third birthday, when the German 8th Army rolled into Austria, taking Salzburg on the morning of March 12, 1938. These were not yet the battle-hardened Wehrmacht soldiers that the Allies would later fight across North Africa and Europe. Their panzers ran out of gas on the way into Salzburg. They hauled artillery behind rickety horse-drawn carts. No matter. The Austrian Army surrendered before most of the Germans even crossed the border.[2]

Western Europe greeted the invasion with trepidation, fearful that it put the continent on a path for war. For many Austrians, however, the moment marked the final unraveling of the punitive Treaty of Versailles, which had ended World War I and established Austria as an independent country. But Austria's forced independence by the Treaty of Versailles did not "represent the wishes of its inhabitants, most of whom felt it could not survive without being linked to Germany."[3] The Nazi Party agreed and made Austrian annexation a priority of the Third Reich. Most Austrians greeted the Anschluss, as the German annexation of Austria is known, with delight. The German Army received an enthusiastic welcome in 1938 by "throngs of people in the streets" of Vienna and Salzburg.[4] The groundwork for the invasion and occupation had been laid years before the Anschluss. The Nazi Party—officially, National Socialist German Workers' Party or NSDAP—had long "infiltrated into every branch of public and business life" in Austria.[5] The NSDAP found its strongest support in Salzburg where, prior to being declared illegal in 1932, it received more than 20 percent of the vote in the provincial election. And just days before the panzers stumbled into Salzburg, Austrian Nazis seized power in all Austrian provinces.[6] The city of Mozart would be a city of Nazis during most of Lillian's childhood.

The overwhelming, but largely underground, support for the Nazi Party by business owners, elected officials, police, and schoolteachers prior to the Anschluss burst into the open after it. Lawyers, judges, engineers, doctors, and police were all "strongly Nazi" and cheered the NSDAP in the streets.[7] A Nazi cell had long operated within the Salzburg gendarmerie, whose police chief was a Nazi group leader.[8] Professors and schoolteachers, in particular, were among the most hardcore Nazi supporters. "Schools and universities proved specially fertile ground for Nazi penetration. Many teachers and students were among the most ardent Austrian Nazis, with numerous secret organizations of their own, run undercover often by the schools themselves."[9] The Boy Scouts pivoted after the Anschluss and rebranded itself as Hitler Youth. Lillian's grade schoolteacher, her doctor, if she had one, were all likely devoted to the Nazi Party. Nazi propaganda in pamphlets, books, journals, and newspapers "poured into Austria" after the Anschluss, distributed by a network of Nazi booksellers in Salzburg.[10]

Anschluss translates into English as *connection* or *following*, and this describes perfectly the annexation of Austria by Germany—more homecoming than invasion. The Austrian Army, full of "loyal fighters" for Germany, refused to defend Austria against the Wehrmacht. After the Anschluss, the Nazis folded the existing Austrian Army into the Wehrmacht and quickly drafted a million more Austrian men into Ostmärkische divisions, such as the Wehrkreis XVIII, an army corps created in August 1939 and composed entirely of Austrian men drafted after the Anschluss. Austrian soldiers would eventually make up nearly 10 percent of the Wehrmacht.[11] Lillian's father, Richard Hutzler, may have already been a soldier in the Austrian Army when the Wehrmacht arrived. If not, he was drafted and would eventually fight alongside German soldiers in North Africa.

By mid-March, after the Wehrmacht solidified its control of Austria, Hitler arrived. Hundreds of thousands of Austrians thronged Vienna's Heldenplatz (Heroes' Square) to cheer Hitler at a "liberation rally" where he declared "the entry of my homeland into the German Reich."[12] Behind him came Heinrich Himmler and his Gestapo, which "descended on the *Ostmark* and threw the political opposition into concentration camps."[13] This cleared the way for Austrian soldiers and Nazi bureaucrats in Austria, who enthusiastically found themselves "over-represented in the terror system that committed mass murder on the Jews of Europe."[14] Austrian Army divisions, in particular, proved to be among the most ruthless units of the Wehrmacht. The German 6th Army, almost entirely Austrian, participated in the murder of more than thirty thousand Jews in the massacre at Babi Yar in 1941.[15]

The Nazis established Salzburg as a regional administrative headquarters and immediately set about enforcing its Nuremberg racial laws, unleashing an "Aryanization" frenzy from Vienna to Salzburg. All those deemed "racially unworthy, criminal and anti-social Gypsies" were arrested. The Gestapo detained thousands of Austrian Jews and Roma and deported them to Dachau and Buchenwald, among other concentration camps. Half of all those sent to Dachau in 1938, more than ten thousand people, were Austrian Jews, Roma, or communists.[16] Germany appropriated Austrian companies, particularly Jewish-owned businesses, seized the gold reserves, commandeered the railways, and reoriented Austrian industrial works for German military production.[17] The Austrians who cheered the Nazis when they arrived spent the months after the Anschluss looting Jewish businesses. They seized homes, violently evicting tens of thousands into the streets in just a matter of days. Nazi bureaucrats did this on a larger scale, "resettling" thousands of "enemies"—Jews, Roma, communists—in camps or ghettos throughout Germany and Austria.[18] Austrians would serve among the upper echelon of the most notorious camps—Łódź, Belsec, Treblinka, and Sobibor, among others.[19] Hundreds of Roma were incarcerated at Maxglan-Salzburg, a slave labor prison camp just a stone's throw from Lillian's childhood home. Lillian may have seen the Sinti mothers trying to kill their children to save them from the Nazis. She may have seen them marched from the camp during the day and rented out as forced labor for local businesses.[20] From Maxglan, Nazi war planners deported prisoners to German extermination camps throughout eastern Europe.[21] By the end of 1942, the Nazis cleared Maxglan out and deported the approximately three hundred inmates held there to Łódź, where they were murdered in the gas vans of Chelmno.[22]

Lillian marked her birthdays by occupations, concentration camps, and bombing campaigns. The Allied bombing of Austria began just after her eighth. Germany had converted Austria into a factory for killing machines during the war and as a buffer against Allied attacks at the end of it. It built the majority of its Luftwaffe planes and tank armor in eastern Austria. "Allied bombers dropped some 50,000 tons of bombs" on Austrian targets, killing tens of thousands of people, destroying nearly 100,000 homes and buildings, and half of all rail lines.[23] Tens of thousands of bombs fell on the enormous warplane factories south of Vienna, all of which used slave labor.[24] Thousands died in the attacks. While western Austria escaped the worst of the Allied bombing, dozens of raids on Salzburg, in a bombing campaign that lasted more than eighteen months, destroyed thousands of buildings and homes in the city—every other building fell to the bombs— and killed hundreds of civilians.[25]

The bombing campaign and wartime rationing took a toll on Austria, particularly Salzburg. When those who fled finally returned, they found the city in ruins. The bombing campaign had destroyed more than seven thousand buildings in Salzburg alone.[26] The infant mortality rate quintupled; industrial production declined by nearly half and the death rate nearly doubled from prewar levels.[27] Other than her father, who fought with the Wehrmacht, Lillian and her family never left Salzburg and somehow survived the Allied bombing and the Nazi-imposed food shortages.

◄■■■■■►

When the war ended, it came without the parades. The Soviet 3rd Ukrainian Front, as if sprung from cages, thundered into Austria as the eastern front collapsed in early 1945. After destroying two panzer divisions in Hungary in

March of 1945, just months before Lillian's tenth birthday, the Soviet Army launched a final counteroffensive against the Wehrmacht and attacked into Austria, laying waste to everything in its path. Few English-language accounts of the April 1945 Vienna Offensive capture the viciousness of the siege. After razing Wiener Neustadt, a city at the industrial heart of the Nazi war machine, the Soviets turned toward Vienna and attacked with a ferocity nearly unmatched up to that point in the war. Some estimates of the fighting in and around Vienna count the dead at 250,000. They looted homes, businesses, and factories, sparing only those already destroyed or looted by the retreating German Army. They seized the harvest, killed breeding animals, stripped the factories of machinery, and shipped as much as possible back to the Soviet Union.[28] They took park benches. They cut leather from chairs.[29] The Soviet Army took Vienna on April 13, 1945, the day after Louis finally escaped Europe on the USS *Richardson*.[30] Vienna was mostly destruction and debris. A fifth of all buildings lay in ruins.[31] The Soviets suspended law and replaced it with the rule of bare force. Under Soviet occupation, there would be arrests but no charges, convictions but no trials.[32]

This marked the beginning of the Soviet occupation of Vienna, and it began in a drunken fever of sexual violence that came in waves. Some historians estimate that Soviet troops, "encouraged to regard German women as plunder," raped two million of them.[33] "Various sources report that between 70,000 and 100,000 women of all age groups were raped in Vienna" by Soviet troops.[34] In the month of July 1945 alone, Soviet troops assaulted more than one thousand women in Lower Austria and killed more than one hundred civilians.[35]

Other accounts of Soviet sexual violence explain the brutality and large-scale, organized rape of women and girls by Soviet troops as a reprisal for the patterns of German sexual violence during the war. German commanders and soldiers on the eastern front never considered rape a moral or legal offense. If sexual violence was a concern at all, it was a concern over "race mixing." For the Reich and the soldiers of the Wehrmacht, for example, this meant a strict prohibition on all sexual contact with what it considered non-Aryans, especially Jewish people.[36] The Wehrmacht carefully "managed" military sexual violence by maintaining "traveling brothels" of women they captured or "recruited" and forcibly sterilized or subjected to compulsory abortions.[37] Despite the prohibition on "race mixing," German military leaders forced tens of thousands of Jewish girls and women into these military rape camps.[38]

The idea that the Soviets might have retaliated against the Nazis for their campaign of sexual violence with their own campaign of sexual terror ignores the fact that every country and every military unit in the war engaged in sexual violence in Asia, Europe, and North Africa. In addition to Soviet atrocities, French, UK, and US soldiers raped hundreds of thousands of women, both during the war and during the years of occupation that followed. These were organized, military campaigns of sexual terror that served military and occupation goals, not "a by-product of conflicts [but] a pre-planned and deliberate military strategy."[39] Sexual violence was a central mode of US military war making throughout the war, as well as a central tactic of military occupation in the war's aftermath.[40] And even the "solutions" to the problem of sexual violence included more sexual violence. Some military commanders responded to the "group rapes of women and children on a global scale" by military units by turning "a blind eye on their troops' sexual engagements with prostitutes."[41] American soldiers used the word "liberate" to describe rape.[42]

The Americans in Austria arrived shortly after the Soviets, fighting their way to the Bavarian city of Teisendorf on May 3, 1945, where they paused briefly before the siege of Salzburg. Gestapo leaders fled in advance of the assault and the few Wehrmacht officers remaining quickly surrendered.[43] When the war came to a final end in June, the Allies carved up Austria. The British, French, Americans, and Soviets divided the country into four occupation zones. The United States Forces in Austria (USFA) occupied Land Salzburg, which included the city of Salzburg and the region surrounding Lillian's hometown. They established an occupation headquarters near the center of Salzburg, where Louis would eventually be posted.

International law generally accepts military occupation as a distinct, temporary mode of governance that follows, and claims to resolve, the violence and destruction of military conflict. A just occupation, according to law, is what comes after a just war. Just occupation provides the legal rationale for war in the first place and retroactively establishes a claim to legitimate versus illegitimate occupation in war's aftermath—rebuilding versus looting; ending political persecution versus imposing it; implementing peace versus waging war. A war, in other words, can only be justified by the character of what follows. But this is only in theory. In practice, occupation, such as the US occupation of Austria, seeks no resolution to war's conflict. Occupation extends war. Occupation always treats the destruction of war—the human misery, the annihilation of the nonhuman world, the razing of infrastructure, the wrecking of industrial and agricultural capacity, the bulldozing of social and political institutions—as a condition necessary to violently impose a new order. War's violence destroys the old order, the violence of occupation imposes a new one.

All four powers—the United States, the United Kingdom, the Soviet Union, and France—claimed two primary goals in the occupation of Austria: First would be the destruction of Nazi ideology and propaganda, and the banishment from public life of all Nazi Party members and leaders. Second would be the resolution of the European refugee crisis in Austria. On the ground, however, all four occupying powers had something else in mind. They looted the Austrian treasury, seized homes and farms for occupation personnel, unleashed a wave of sexual violence on women and girls, and established a black market for fuel, food, and all other essential goods.

The US transformed Salzburg into a massive open-air concentration camp, dotted by smaller concentration camps that held displaced persons, war criminals, and refugees. No records remain of Louis's initial post in Salzburg, but he most likely posted first at Camp Truscott on the outskirts of the city, which sits in the shadow of the Salzkammergut Mountains, where limestone alpine peaks give way to the Salzach River valley and the rolling plains north of it. The Nazis originally built the camp that later became Truscott in the late 1930s, and US occupation forces repurposed it after the war to hold war prisoners and to serve as the regimental headquarters for the 16th Infantry, and later the 350th Infantry. Louis served as a military policeman in Salzburg, where he guarded prisoners of war and displaced persons in various camps spread throughout the city. He walked security patrols outside the USFA headquarters in the center of Salzburg, and he rode the trains that brought the supplies into Salzburg and shipped refugees and displaced persons out of it.

◄■■■■■►

Nazi hunting structured the first phase of the Austrian occupation, a period in which USFA intelligence agents investigated every public official and private business owner in US-occupied Vienna, the city of Salzburg, and all the villages and countryside that surrounded it. In Salzburg, the US Counter Intelligence Corps, the precursor to the Central Intelligence Agency, investigated suspected Nazis and then turned incriminating information over to the occupation or to Austrian police, which arrested them. By the time Louis arrived, the US had already dissolved and abolished all political parties and organizations affiliated with the NSDAP. Occupation authorities removed five thousand Nazi members, sympathizers, or collaborators from public office and arrested 2,861 people for "political reasons."[44] The second phase, between July 1945 and April 1946, led to the removal of eight thousand people from public office and the arrest of 9,738 others. The third, revenge phase, which overlapped the second, began in December 1945. In this phase, USFA shifted its authority over denazification to the reconstituted Austrian government, which imposed a Nazi registry on all citizens.[45] The law required all to register their Nazi past, a requirement that imposed a kind of legally binding oath on every Austrian. Failing to disclose even the mildest connection or affiliation with the NSDAP could result in serious sanctions. This approach appeared promising at first. By November 1946, fourteen thousand people had been removed from public office and more than fifteen thousand people had been arrested. Countrywide the numbers were enormous. Of 300,000 civil servants, occupation authorities removed 71,000 Nazis or Nazi sympathizers from office, and 36,000 from leading positions in business and industry. All told, more than 250,000 Nazis were either arrested, banished from public life, or fled.

By late 1948, despite the thousands of Nazis in jail or removed from office, some occupation authorities declared the denazification program a failure. "Under denazification many registered Nazis were in fact removed from positions of influence. Many, however, remain (for numerous reasons) and the denazification law is such that their removal is impossible."[46] Among the "numerous reasons," one stood out. The job of hunting and removing Nazis and Nazi sympathizers was so enormous that the USFA relied on the Austrian criminal justice system to do it. While, officially, all members or sympathizers of the Nazi Party beyond "nominal participants" were subject to arrest or banishment, The US relied on a reconstituted Austrian bureaucracy dominated by former Nazis, despite denazification.[47] In order to "prevent the reconstitution" of the Nazi Party in Austria in any form, the USFA turned to the same Austrian cops, judges, and lawyers who had cheered the Anschluss eight years earlier. If you were a Nazi judge in Austria in 1945 and 1946, even one with "strong derogatory information" that identified you as a Nazi, you likely escaped punishment and remained a judge.[48] Cops remained on the job as long as it was determined (often by other Nazis) that the evidence against them fell into the "less incriminated" category, a category eventually applied to thirty thousand people in Land Salzburg.[49] This was denazification-by-Nazi, and to some it seemed as if by design. "The fact that most Nazi businessmen have been left unscathed by Allied and Austrian denazification measures has begun to convince many persons that effective action will never be taken against them and that as soon as American and Allied occupational forces leave Austria, the influential Nazis will return to power."[50]

Lillian's father probably escaped serious punishment despite his military service for Germany in both world wars. Richard Hutzler was born in January 1896 in Pirmasens, a small West Palatinate town near the French border in what is today southwest Germany. He worked as a cutter in a shoe factory and was raised by a father who worked as a bookkeeper. The milestones that marked his personal history corresponded to world-making events, as if the key moments in his own life served as a kind of barometer for world historical transformations. On the day the German Empire declared war on France, August 3, 1914, the Imperial German Army drafted Richard Hutzler into the army and assigned him to the 22nd Infantry Regiment of the Royal Bavarian Army. He spent the next four years remaking Europe in battles fought all over the continent—Serbia, France, Russia, Romania, and Belgium. He was awarded the Iron Cross 2nd Class for service in battle, and he was wounded first in January 1915 and then two more times—possibly three, earning him the silver Wound Badge. The Imperial Army discharged him from service on November 10, 1918, the day after the empire collapsed and Kaiser Wilhelm II abdicated the throne, which was the day before the establishment of the Weimar Republic. For the next year he served the Weimar Republic as part of a series of border protection forces, including in Wilhelmshaven, Germany's imperial shipyard and deepwater port city in the northwest, home of the German Navy during World War I and site of a rebellion by sailors and workers that hastened the empire's end.[51]

Richard emigrated to the newly established Austrian Republic after the war, sometime before 1925. When Germany annexed Austria a decade later, the now middle-aged Richard once again found himself in the German Army, fighting with the Wehrmacht in North Africa. Factory workers turned army privates rarely catch the attention of US Nazi hunters. The US didn't consider service in the Wehrmacht as evidence of Nazi collaboration, even among generals, as long as there was no evidence of a connection to the Nazi Party. If Richard Hutzler only served as a soldier in the Wehrmacht, and never joined NSDAP or related Nazi groups, he may have been categorized as a "follower" or a "lesser offender," two categories of collaboration that came with minor sanctions, such as travel restrictions or the curtailment of political rights.[52] If he were found to be an "offender," however, his penalty could have included imprisonment, hard labor, and

A young Lillian Hutzler and her father Richard pose for a war time photo in Salzburg sometime in the mid-1940s prior to Lillian's emigration to the United States. Courtesy of Ursula Casuse-Carrillo.

possibly the threat of execution. Denazification efforts focused on party loyalists, not Austrian soldiers forced to fight for Germany.

In addition to denazification, the other stated goal of the occupation was to manage the refugee crisis. In the first years following the war's end, the Austrian population more than doubled as tens of thousands of displaced persons and refugees streamed into Austria. Austrians, who were paid the lowest wages in Europe, suffered as much as the refugees and spent hungry years with no food other than what the occupation rationed them.[53] Some food rations came from domestic food production, but by the end of the war Austrian agriculture produced, on average, fewer than nine hundred calories per person. The Germans had commandeered most of Austria's agricultural capacity during the war, and Allied bombing and postwar looting by occupation forces destroyed much of the rest. While the US considered Austria a conquered country, the Soviets and French considered Austria no different than Germany and provided no rations.[54] The French and Soviets actually exported food back to France and the Soviet Union.[55] The Soviets even slaughtered Austrian breeding animals for military consumption. As a result, most food rations were imported into Austria by international aid organizations, such as the United Nations Relief and Rehabilitation Administration (UNRRA). Despite this aid, Austrians suffered a "hunger catastrophe" in 1945, with children in Salzburg "on the point of starvation."[56]

US occupation authorities in Land Salzburg subsidized meager domestic production through a ration system designed, on paper, to account for the limited local production and the unpredictability of food imports and aid. Every seventeen days, US military authorities revised its official ration, publishing circulars detailing which foods would be available and at what amounts, and it distributed new ration books based on these new daily calorie amounts—often revised down from the previous ration period. The military occupation authority controlled the production and distribution of *every* consumer product and public service in Austria. Food, water, clothing, shoes, coal, firewood, and more were all rationed, with specific amounts controlled by occupation authorities. Food and fuel rations were set by job type. "Normal consumers"—those out of work, or in less strenuous jobs—received the smallest ration: 2,100 calories per day in the fall of 1948. "Heavy workers," who labored in factories, received 2,500 calories.

And the "heaviest workers," who worked in construction or manufacturing jobs that required the most strenuous labor, received 3,100 calories, the largest ration. Children received the smallest ration of all, along with an unreliable 500-calorie supplement at school.[57]

But every Austrian learned quickly that what the ration coupon promised and what the occupation delivered were two different things. Ration coupons were distributed by food type and would describe a certain kilo of meat or cheese, a certain number of eggs, or a liter of milk. More often than not, however, the occupation authorities substituted meat and dairy with pulses, oats, and grits.[58] Meat, fuel, oil, and butter were rarely available. "[Austrians] feel bitter," military authorities admitted, "when flour, fat, and meat shortages are substituted by other items of the same caloric value, but not of the same cooking value."[59] Occupation planners blamed Austrian farmers for this problem, claiming that many farmers withheld their food deliveries in 1947 in order to find higher prices on the black market. Merchants, too, hoarded goods instead of distributing them as rations.[60] But even with substitutes, the minimum daily calories that the occupation promised, always barely above starvation levels, rarely materialized. Between the twenty-second and thirty-sixth ration periods—a stretch of nearly eight months—occupation authorities distributed ten million *fewer* calories in Salzburg than the official ration books promised.[61] Occupation meant "a slow starvation diet for Austrians."[62]

And somehow things got worse. By the summer of 1947, an extended drought led to the collapse of the potato harvest, which arrived alongside an epidemic of cholera and typhoid fever. And then the UNRRA, which provided around a thousand calories per person on average, decided to end its food ration program in Austria all at once.[63]

The result was desperation, but mostly a desperation borne by refugees held in camps and the working poor trapped in dangerous jobs with low wages. Wealthy refugees from Vienna and rich tourists from western Europe enjoyed a different experience. They flocked to Salzburg, where they found no shortage of food or luxury goods. "The Salzburg city is still short of bread, while at the same time long lines of cars are waiting in front of restaurants of the black marketeers and delicious dinners are serviced in luxury restaurants at exorbitant prices."[64] A bread shortage in Zell am

See was traced to merchants hoarding food for the nine thousand tourists expected for a music festival.[65] "Farmers sell butter to anyone for 100 Schillings, but report nothing to deliver to officials."[66] Restaurants catering to tourists bought it all up. The chamber of commerce recruited wealthy investors to Salzburg and the US occupation authority set aside "a daily ration of 5,600 calories"—more than twice what children received—for businessmen looking for investment opportunities.[67]

Meanwhile, because of the unreliable electricity grid, thousands of poor people slowly poisoned themselves in cramped apartments cooking with wood or coal.[68] These were the lucky ones. Thousands more had no place to live. The destruction of the war, the flood of refugees from Vienna, and the housing requisition by the occupation threw thousands of people out of their homes. Some squatted in the flooded basements of destroyed buildings, with ten to fifteen people per room.[69] School-age children lived on little more than 1,200 calories per day, supplemented by a bowl of soup and a roll if they went to school. They suffered from rickets, anemia, and tuberculosis. Desperate Austrians rioted, particularly in Vienna, over the lack of food.

Lillian had it barely better than most. Her family somehow avoided requisition and were able to keep their apartment. She and her brothers and sisters spent their days scrounging for anything they could get their hands on—food or consumer goods—to bring home or sell on the black market. They never starved. She would often join other children in the woods near her home, where they would wait for the slow-moving supply trains of the occupation forces. When one emerged in the distance, the children would race out of the woods and run toward the train yelling at the soldiers to throw food to them. Lillian ran faster than most and gathered more than the rest, and often gave some of the food she collected to empty-handed younger children. The rest she kept for her family, or to trade on the black market.

◄ ■ ■ ■ ■ ■ ►

It was from a supply or transport train that Louis first saw Lillian. He couldn't have missed the desperation in the children's eyes as they ran toward him, hollering in German or improvised English. He may have recognized the look and the feeling. He would say years later that the only reason he joined the army was because he was starving back in New Mexico.[70]

Lillian, like all the other children, did what she could, given the circumstances. According to the historian Petra Goedde, the children of postwar Germany and Austria often "eked out a meager existence through petty theft and break-ins." Lillian described smuggling trinkets and food in underground tunnels built below the city, where she found other children of the black market smuggling and trading items. Thousands of children, particularly those whose parents had been arrested, killed, or had gone missing in the chaos after the war, lived on the streets, begging, stealing, and trading on the black market. Occupation and Austrian police routinely arrested teenagers "for vagrancy. There is no other place for them but jails which ruin them for their whole life. We are the ones who drive children and even young kids into crime. Nothing could be too much to alleviate this misery." The problem was acute everywhere in Austria, "but in Salzburg this situation is faced helplessly and with empty hands."[71] Some teenage girls, either out of desperation or coercion, "resorted to prostitution in order to make a living."[72] And everyone turned to the black market. A 1947 Rockefeller Foundation report estimated around twenty thousand young people traded on the black market to survive.[73]

Occupation authorities considered black marketeering a threat to occupation authority, but in practice the occupation created and sustained the black market.[74] On the surface, military authorities opposed it, obsessively monitoring black-market prices and placing guards wherever they thought black-market trading happened. Soldiers patrolled hotels, railheads, political offices, gas dumps, bakeries, military commissaries, coalyards, occupation authority offices and installations, restaurants, and more. They posted guards on trains to Munich, and they guarded the trains that shipped ex-enemy POWs or refugee repatriations into Germany or Poland. But this just made black-market trading easier since US soldiers participated in the trade. The same occupation soldiers ordered by USFA to stop black marketeering were among its most enthusiastic traders. An investigation by Louis's own regiment concluded that soldiers fueled the black market. Soldiers saw a "rise in the calory level of food" that they received, but also saw that "a comparable rise was not evident among the civilians," which established the conditions that made the black market possible.[75]

Soldiers had access to goods constantly in demand on the black market. And since they were frequently reassigned, redeployed, and overworked at grueling and dangerous guard work, many decided they deserved the benefits of the black market despite the prohibition and the risks. Everything for the soldier was temporary and "inasmuch as a man will be leaving soon, he can get away with anything while he is here."[76] A 1948 occupation investigation found that "small items such as soap, cigarettes, etc., are still being stolen." Soldiers stole typewriters out of military intelligence service offices and beer kegs out of camp bars.[77] They sold cigarettes for nearly twenty schillings a pack, soap or candy bars for four or five schillings, and chocolate syrup for nearly one hundred schillings per can.[78] In an effort to restrict the flow of US dollars on the black market, the occupation paid soldiers in Military Payment Certificates, but soldiers traded those too. "The present rate of exchange for Military Payment Certificates on the black market is 30 to 35 Austrian schillings for one dollar MPC."[79]

"Cognac of poor quality is being peddled at eight (8) packs of cigarettes per bottle. Cigarettes are now selling at 200 Schillings a carton." Liquor, in particular, posed a specific threat as soldiers were "killed or made extremely ill as a result of this trade."[80] If a soldier crashed an occupation vehicle while driving drunk after consuming black-market alcohol, which was not unusual, he could avoid punishment by stealing occupation fuel and trading it to Austrian mechanics for repairs, thus avoiding having to report the accident.[81] Soldiers also often traded with local children. "All of us give them candy and gum we get in rations," one occupation soldier in Germany explained. "And whatever else we can pick up."[82] Children knew this. Run toward an occupation train, or beg an American soldier for candy, they were taught by older children; they'll almost always give you something you can trade on the black market.

Lillian was especially good at this. And she stood out among the children, her long, bright red hair trailing behind her when she ran toward a train. Louis spent weeks traveling on these trains, throwing food to children, including twelve-year-old Lillian, until one day he abandoned his post and jumped off the train to chase after her.[83] Imagine the terror Lillian must have felt. With Louis in pursuit, she ran the entire way home. She arrived home before Louis, and Lillian's older brother heard her screams. He came out of the house to find Louis in his military uniform chasing his sister. They scuffled and he broke Louis's nose with a punch.[84] None of this was unusual; not the interest by a US soldier in an Austrian girl, not the chase, or the girl's fear, and definitely not the violent confrontation that resulted.

Years later, Lillian would tell her children stories about the occupation. Short snippets from a faraway life. She smuggled black-market items through tunnels, she would tell them. She saw a Jewish woman swallow a ring to hide it from authorities. Nazi soldiers menaced her with German shepherds. But of all the things she had to fear, it was perhaps Louis's pursuit of her that frightened her the most. Even a young girl understood what it meant for a woman or a girl in Austria at that time to find herself the subject of a soldier's intense interest. The terror might have been the realization that she was a kind of military target, an object of interest caught between occupation soldiers on one side and Austrian men on the other, both of which organized themselves around the control of women's and girls' sexual and reproductive lives and futures.

◀■■■■■▶

For Austrians the black market was the only place to supplement the starvation rations from the occupation, find heating and cooking fuel, and even get medicine. Women traded GIs trinkets and souvenirs that they'd pilfered or scrounged—worthless reichsmark coins or Hitler Youth badges—for cigarettes, and then some would trade those cigarettes to farmers for food withheld from the ration system. They traded old wristwatches for butter or meat rations.

Soldiers, on the other hand, turned to the black market for alcohol and sex. Occupation soldiers traded food, cigarettes, and even clothing for sex from women or girls that occupation authorities referred to in monthly reports as "hostesses."[85] A May 1949 investigation by occupation authorities discovered a woman working out of the kitchen at Camp Truscott in Salzburg. Soldiers paid her as little as one dollar for sex.[86] Soldiers preyed on women and girls, and occupation authorities blamed women and girls for it. "Many girls from the Russian Zone are coming into the American Zone hoping to be picked up. This type of prostitute does not hang about the immediate vicinity of clubs, but lingers on a nearby corner, or by the nearest streetcar stop. This type of girl is dangerous, for many are gathering chocolate and cigarettes for civilian boyfriends."[87]

Black-market trading in Austria brought everyone eventually into contact with occupation soldiers, but this contact was more dangerous for women and girls as it placed them in a kind of double jeopardy. On one side were Austrian men, who attacked women and girls they considered fraternizers with occupation authorities.[88] They hunted them in "scissor clubs" and violently cut their hair. Unlike the victims of Mexican scalp hunters, the victims of the Austrian scissor clubs usually survived their attacks.[89]

On the other side were American GIs, who women risked their lives to trade with on the black market. These were coercive relationships, not consensual. They traded on the black market to survive, not by choice. Many soldiers took advantage of this and sought out sexual relationships with women in return for protection or food. Consider the risks women took to do this. Austrian men might viciously punish them for it, but women did it anyway because, for many, they had no other options. The black market was the only way to supplement meager rations for food or firewood, forestall possible deportation, avoid incarceration, or find a reprieve from forced labor. Some families pursued soldiers for their daughters, as in the case of Lillian, when they saw no future for them in Austria.

For Lillian it must have seemed as if an entire world war had been fought over her. And if she thought this, she would not have been entirely wrong. All the death and destruction of war, and all of the suffering of occupation, somehow led inexorably to her. It would be her life and her future that the war and the occupation would turn upside down. Lillian's parents allowed Louis to pursue Lillian even though she was only a child. What future could they have seen for her in Austria? An entire generation of young men had been killed, wounded, or imprisoned by occupation authorities. German and Austrian women, and the parents of some German and Austrian girls, pursued "personal relationships with individual GIs" in order to supplement rations or find protection.[90] And Louis must have known this would be the outcome despite the fistfight that marked his first meeting with her family. He convinced Lillian's parents to invite him to dinner, and he arrived with gifts of coffee, sugar, and butter. Upstairs, Lillian, the twelve-year-old, hid in the bathroom.

◄■■■■■►

The war bride, as Susan Zeiger notes, is nothing if not "a spoil of war."[91] Few accounts of war center the experience of women this way. To call a war bride "a spoil of war" is to insist that the impossible position in which war and occupation places women and girls is no accident. War and occupation so perfectly produce the conditions for it, it's hard to see it as anything other than the point of it all in the first place. Sexual violence has been so "central to military legal precedent" that it is impossible to understand the military, whether in combat or as an occupying force, without placing violence against women, and the control of women's sexual lives and futures, at the center of every effort to understand military tactics, strategies and goals.[92] According to military records, US soldiers raped more than fourteen thousand women and children between 1942 and 1945. *Time* magazine called the US an "army of rapists."[93] This pattern of sexual violence continued after the war, during a period one historian called "the rape phase of the occupation."[94] Every woman understood this, especially the ones who survived it all, only to become war brides.

War making, as the historian Ellen Wu argues "is central to US immigration history," and much of the effort around the question of fraternization focused on the question of war bride immigration.[95] Military occupation planners, as all military occupation planners do, paved the way for this at the very start of the occupation. They ended the formal ban on fraternization by the summer of 1945 and claimed this was only because the building of social bonds between soldiers and Austrians advanced the denazification goals of "domestic moral reconstruction."[96] The 1945 War Brides Act exempted the spouses of military servicemen from immigration quotas. Tens of thousands of German-speaking women emigrated to the US to marry US servicemen in the years after the war.[97] Thousands of women who American GIs intended to marry migrated to the US following the passage of the 1946 Alien Fiancées and Fiancées Act,[98] a law that permitted demobilized soldiers to receive marriage visas for German and Austrian women.[99] Louis had law on his side. Lillian and her family had only desperation on theirs.

It's possible that Lillian's parents willingly invited Louis into their home. If Richard had been declared a member of the Nazi Party or a sympathizer, he would have been unemployable in Austria and ineligible to emigrate out of it. Those with Nazi pasts often used "their wives or daughters to gain the sympathy of key representatives of the occupation powers."[100] For occupation soldiers, food, soap, and other goods "replaced flowers and jewelry as the most common instrument of courtship."[101] Lillian's parents likely saw a better future for her in America, despite her age. Various war bride acts and formal practices regarding the taking of war brides included girls as young as Lillian. While it was less common and came with greater scrutiny, the US Army approved marriage licenses to servicemen and young girls, and immigration authorities approved visas for unaccompanied minors.[102] "Underaged girls were regarded as fair sport."[103] Waiting periods were often imposed before US immigration authorities would approve immigration visa requests, and this likely applied to Lillian too.

Years later Lillian described the initial fear she had for Louis, but she was living in a destroyed country and Louis was from America. In postwar occupied Austria, those were the only logical reasons to get married. Lillian, who had traded with soldiers on the black market for survival, now found herself traded to one.

Red Scare

When his tour in Austria ended, Louis left Salzburg by train and traveled through occupied Germany to La Havre, France, where he boarded a ship to New York in late August 1949. When he arrived in New York he boarded another train and traveled cross-country to New Mexico, arriving in early September. Alice Bitsilly, one of his younger sisters, remembered his return. He came back to his hogan and his sheep, and he worked odd jobs in the Gallup area. His sisters would sneak into his hogan when he was away and rummage through his things looking for the picture of Lillian that he kept in an old tin can. "I'm going to marry her and bring her back here," Alice remembers him telling them, but none of them believed him.[1]

Louis left Lillian in Salzburg, Austria and returned to the United States immediately following their wedding. Here Lillian (left) and Louis (center) pose for a wedding day photo on the steps of a train car. Courtesy of Ursula Casuse-Carrillo.

He had spent more than two years in Austria, and another two more back in New Mexico before finally saving enough money to come back for Lillian. He returned to Salzburg in the summer of 1951, and they married on August 9. She was sixteen years old. The marriage certificate listed her occupation as a housemaid. They took no honeymoon. Louis stayed in Salzburg only long enough for the wedding. He left Lillian in Salzburg for a second time and retraced his steps back to New York, where he arrived eleven days after the wedding.[2] Lillian remained in Salzburg waiting for the visa she needed in order to emigrate, which she could only apply for after the wedding. In most cases the immigration approvals took months, but it would end up taking much longer for Lillian. Her young age may have caused a delay, but it's also possible Louis couldn't initially afford her travel to New Mexico.

When Louis arrived in New York in late August 1951, he was broke and alone. If he had money, he saved it for Lillian. When his ship docked in New York he disembarked and made his way directly to Manhattan, where he wandered through the city looking for the headquarters of the Kennecott Copper Corporation, one of the world's largest mining companies and the owners of the copper mine in Santa Rita, New Mexico. When he finally walked into their midtown offices, Kennecott rehired him on the spot and gave him an advance on his first paycheck so he could afford a train back to New Mexico.[3] His name appears on an early January 1952 track department roster for the mine, which suggests he may have traveled first to Mexican Springs before returning to Santa Rita in the winter of 1951.[4]

Lillian left Salzburg nine months later and traveled alone across Europe to Amsterdam, where she took an overnight flight to New York in early May. She was joining the tail end of an exodus of German-speaking war brides. By the early 1950s, more than fifteen thousand women and girls had emigrated to the US.[5] While Lillian traveled across Europe by train, Louis traveled across the US by truck and picked her up when her plane landed in New York. They drove back to New Mexico and Louis's sisters remember the day they arrived. As the green pickup truck arrived, the sisters ran up to it and pressed their faces against the passenger-side window hoping to get a first glimpse of Lillian. When Louis finally stopped the truck, the girls backed away, and Lillian stepped out, wearing high heels and a white blouse, her long, thick red hair dropping to her shoulders and beyond.[6] The wide-eyed girls, speechless, brought her into a hogan where they sat her in a chair and spread out on the ground, looking up at her. Louis's stepmother, Dahdebah Barney, served Lillian a meal and everyone watched her eat in silence.

The morning after she arrived, if not that first night, Louis explained that he had to return to work in Santa Rita in the morning. It was no place for her, he said. They'd have to live in a one-room shack with no plumbing or electricity in a segregated area called "Indian Village." She'd be better off staying in his hogan and looking after their sheep. He'd visit when he could, he told her. Though she spoke little English, she described a different plan, and it didn't include living in a hogan or a tent in Santa Rita. If he had to go to work at Kennecott, she'd go with him.

◄■■■■■►

Kennecott bought the mining claim to Santa Rita del Cobre from the Chino Copper Company in 1933. Chino mined copper at Santa Rita beginning in 1909, using methods little changed from the nineteenth century. Mine workers hauled ore out of vertical shafts on wooden ladders that reached more than three hundred feet below the surface. They cracked open rocks by setting fire to heaps of logs. These older methods limited copper production, so Chino increasingly mechanized the mine. Instead of miners in tunnels climbing up and down ladders, men operating ninety- and forty-ton steam shovels surface stripped ore that had been dynamited out of rock.[7] They hauled the ore out of the mine in narrow-gauge train cars rather than by teams of horses. Mechanization increased production, which increased the amount of rail needed, which made the operation at Santa Rita del Cobre look a lot more like a railroad construction site than a copper mine. Scores of trackmen worked in teams as section hands, or *traqueros*, since nearly all were Spanish-speaking laborers. Once built, the track conveyed fifty-car trains full of rock sent to a series of mechanical jaw and cone crushers that chewed up boulders to the consistency of powdered sugar. Apron feeders transferred the material to a precipitating plant, where sulfuric acid and giant agitators leached the copper from the ore. When the copper bubbled to the surface, mechanical arms skimmed off the concentrated copper. They dumped the waste liquid, or tailings, in Whitewater

Draw, contaminating the creek with toxic sludge. When the concentrate dried, they sent it to the smelter, where a 2,800-degree Fahrenheit blast furnace separated the copper matte from slag. They dumped the slag in ever-growing piles near the landfill, while mechanical ladles scooped up the molten copper and delivered it to a converter furnace, where the heat transformed the copper matte to a nearly pure copper. This required enormous amounts of water, gas, electricity, and miles and miles of narrow-gauge train tracks. Kennecott's power plant produced enough electricity to power a city of a hundred thousand people.[8] Chino and Kennecott dumped tons of waste rock each day, and they dumped so much polluted wastewater that downstream farmers found only toxic sludge when they tried to irrigate their farm fields.[9] Chino paid wages tied to the price of copper. When the price of copper dropped, so did the wages.

Chino smelted its copper in El Paso, but when Kennecott arrived, it built its own smelter in nearby Hurley in May of 1939.[10] Kennecott produced more copper in the US than any other mining company, even before it came to Santa Rita.[11] Along with Santa Rita del Cobre, it mined claims in Arizona, Nevada, and Utah. It also owned mines abroad, in Chile. Kennecott's domestic production accounted for nearly two-fifths of all copper produced in the United States. When combined with its overseas operations, it controlled a fifth of the world's copper supply.[12] Even before Kennecott arrived, the Santa Rita mine constituted the largest industrial operation ever undertaken in New Mexico and accounted for 12 percent of the company's total copper production.[13]

When Kennecott came to the scene, Santa Rita del Cobre had already been a company town for decades. The mining companies owned nearly everything. "Company housing, company store, company doctors and hospital. There were company swimming pools, club houses, and schools, one of each for Anglos, one of each for 'Spanish-American.'"[14] Even the police were company-owned. Chino hired deputies, including the brother of Billy the Kid's killer, to "keep the unions out."[15] When Kennecott bought Chino, it also acquired the Gallup American Coal Company (GAMERCO), which provided the coal Kennecott needed to run the steam shovels and trains. Through GAMERCO, Kennecott also hired Horace Moses, who had come to southern New Mexico in the late 1800s to prospect for gold and silver in Santa Rita. He hired on as the superintendent of the Santa Rita mine in 1897. When Chino bought Santa Rita, he moved north to Gallup to run GAMERCO. Kennecott brought him back to Santa Rita as its general manager in 1938.

To Moses, a safe worksite was a productive worksite, so if he wasn't compiling reports and writing memos about tonnage and wages, he was riding around the massive mine on horseback complaining to supervisors about clutter, messy worksites, or careless mine workers. Moses and his mine superintendent, Bill Goodrich, fired workers for carelessness but more often because they had talked to union organizers or complained about low wages. Goodrich came to Kennecott from Chile, where he worked as the general manager of Chuquicamata mine, the world's largest open-pit copper mine. He brought his Chilean housekeeper when he arrived. He reserved entire Pullman train compartments when he traveled, complete with plumbing, servants, and upholstered furniture.[16] The managers lived different lives than the miners.

The war draft slowly starved Kennecott of mine workers in the early 1940s, so Moses used his Gallup contacts from GAMERCO to recruit Navajos for the mine. "The labor shortage is becoming more serious," Moses explained in a July 1943 memo, "and consideration is now being given to shipping in a few Navajo Indians to work as trackmen at the mine."[17] The men Moses recruited worked strictly as laborers and trackmen, the most physically grueling and lowest paid job at the mine.[18] Despite the low pay, the job was crucial. Nearly everything moved by rail, and trackmen accounted for a fifth of the mine's workforce. Every new expansion needed a new rail line. Moses hired fifty-six new employees in July 1943 and thirty-eight were Navajo men hired as trackmen.

The Navajos recruited from the Gallup area spent their days swinging enormous double jacks and wrestling huge pry bars. They spent their nights in a segregated settlement far from Santa Rita that Moses called "Indian Village." As he explained, "The Mexicans can be housed at the Federal Housing Project at Hanover, and tents will be erected for the Navajo Indians."[19] He ordered fourteen tents erected adjacent to the precipitation plant, near the smelter, and a stone's throw from the landfill. The Navajo men who migrated to Santa Rita for work in the mine found living in Indian

Village like camping in a flood surrounded by a chemical fire. Smokestacks, slag piles, and toxic tailings encircled them.[20] Spanish-speaking miners had it better, but not by much. Kennecott limited them to Santa Rita's north side barrios that came with no paved streets, no water, and no sewers. These miners paid Kennecott rent for lots on which they built homes and back-yard privies with their own hands.[21] "The Anglos lived on the south side of the tracks," in comfortable company housing.

Kennecott Copper Company reserved the worst company housing for its Spanish-speaking miners. Courtesy of University of Colorado at Boulder, Rare and Distinctive Collections.

Kennecott limited the Spanish-speaking and Navajo mine and mill workers to the lowest paid jobs. As a result, the white miners paid a smaller portion of their wages back to Kennecott for housing and supplies at the company store. Between July and the end of the summer of 1943, Moses had recruited forty-two Navajo trackmen, but only eight remained on the job.[22] They were quitting as quickly as Moses could hire them. Moses blamed pull factors. "Steps are being taken to see if more of these Indians cannot be hired as they might remain in our employment longer now that the Indian ceremonials are over."[23] Only eight Navajo trackmen remained by the end of October, despite four additional hires the previous month.[24] Another twenty-one Navajo men arrived in November, which brought the total number of Navajo trackmen recruited by Moses to eighty-two, which would have composed the entire track department, and 10 percent of the entire workforce, if all had remained on the job. By the end of the year, however, only twenty-seven Navajo trackmen still swung double jacks in Santa Rita.[25] In memos Moses appeared genuinely perplexed at Kennecott's difficulty retaining Navajos in the track department, but it was no mystery. Kennecott paid the Navajo trackmen an average wage of $5.36 per day, the lowest in the mine. They contended not only with low wages and difficult working and living conditions but also with a hostile reaction from some rank-and-file members of the various union locals of the International Union of Mine, Mill and Smelter Workers, known as Mine-Mill, the union that represented workers for Kennecott and other mining companies throughout the region. Many among the union leadership actively recruited Navajo mine workers, but the union locals officially opposed Kennecott's Navajo recruitment program and spent years fighting with Kennecott over it. According to the personal papers of a Kennecott manager, the union "protested the accommodations. . . . The company, unhappily, yielded to non-Navaho pressure, evicted the tenants, and did away with the mini-village," ending the formal recruitment of Navajo mine workers from Gallup.[26]

Kennecott reserved its best company housing for management and Anglo miners in neighborhoods with paved, tree-lined streets, water and sewer service, and large lots. Courtesy Chino Mine Collection, Silver City Museum, Silver City, New Mexico.

Kennecott dismantled Indian Village and, in its place, built "Navajo Indian Settlement," a more permanent village with sheds, cooking facilities, corrals, and latrines for the men who remained. Moses started with twelve one-room, wooden structures without electricity or plumbing.[27] By this time, more than five hundred men had left Kennecott for the war. Even though Moses expected to lose another eighty men to the war in August 1944, he managed to retain only twenty-eight of the 175 Navajo trackmen that he'd hired since July of the previous year.[28] They walked off the job each month by the dozens—thirty-three in April; another twenty-eight in May. Moses suspended the hiring program and looked to other sources for labor. He hired thirty-five track women and twenty-four track boys (all sixteen or seventeen years old or less) in June and July of 1944.[29] By the end of August, a year after Moses had started recruiting Navajo trackmen, four times as many women than Navajos worked in the track department.[30] But some Navajo men continued to migrate south despite the end of the formal recruitment. "Though no great success has been had toward keeping the Indians on the job, still their presence has greatly helped during the scarcity of common labor."[31] Throughout the fall, a revolving door of Navajo men kept the number of Navajo trackmen working never much higher than a dozen.[32]

By the end of 1944, only thirty Navajo trackmen still worked for Kennecott out of a total of 223 hired. "At the present time," the mine superintendent Goodrich explained in his annual report, "it is not expected that any more Navajo Indians will be shipped from the Gallup district."[33] Some Navajo men continued to arrive, along with newly hired women into the track department, throughout 1945 and 1946, but in much smaller numbers. At the beginning of 1946, twenty-nine women still worked at Kennecott, but Goodrich "proposed to lay these women off during the first part of the coming year as fast as men are available."[34] By the end of 1946, only twenty-eight Navajos out of nearly 487 hired since July 1943 still worked in the mine. Moses and Goodrich slowly replaced nearly all of them with men returning from the war.[35]

Louis joined that migration to Santa Rita. Before he ever met Lillian, he worked as a laborer and trackman for Kennecott at the Santa Rita mine, which by then was a mile long, half as wide, and six hundred feet deep.[36] He first came to Santa Rita before he ever went to Austria, in mid-December of

1945.[37] He was among the very last wave of Navajo men to arrive, and one of only two Navajo trackmen to join the union. The Western Federation of Miners, which became Mine-Mill in 1916, organized mining camps throughout the US West and Southwest during the first half of the twentieth century, a job arguably as dangerous as mining. Throughout the 1920s, the Chino Mining Company fired employees it suspected of holding union sympathies and sent local police and hired goons after Mine-Mill organizers.[38] The organizing efforts during Chino's tenure collapsed when the price of copper bottomed out in the early 1930s and Chino closed the mine. When Kennecott purchased and reopened the mine, it rehired only those it considered "untainted by any experience or knowledge of unions."[39] The National Labor Relations Board (NLRB) declared Kennecott's union-busting tactics illegal, and the decision finally opened the door for Mine-Mill. A two-day wildcat strike in June 1938 marked the beginning of a four-year union campaign that included occasionally violent clashes between union organizers and supporters and the cops and hired goons of the mine.[40] Mine managers carried pistols and saw communist conspiracies everywhere.[41] In 1939, at the height of the union campaign, Kennecott refused to hire mine workers until they signed a "yellow dog" card pledging their opposition to union organizing.[42] It took four years before the NLRB finally certified the union at Santa Rita in 1942.[43]

Twelve different union locals represented workers at Kennecott: blacksmiths, boilermakers, carpenters, clerks and assayers, electricians, locomotive enginemen, machinists, operating engineers, painters, pipe fitters and plumbers, trainmen, and a unit for unclassified employees each had their own union local.[44] The union signed a contract with Kennecott in June 1943. It ended race-differentiated hiring and pay scales. The year before the contract, trackmen like Louis made no more than $5.88 per shift, the lowest at the mine. The first union contract included a 25 percent, across-the-board pay raise for trackmen in Santa Rita and another 25 percent raise in July 1948.[45] By the time Louis returned from Austria in late 1951, union-negotiated contracts had raised wages for trackmen to $10.48 a day, a rate twice what they made before collective bargaining.[46] The contract also, and most importantly for Louis, opened up "hundreds of job opportunities to Mexican-Americans" and Navajo trackmen that had previously been unavailable to all but Anglo workers.[47] When he returned in the early 1950s, he first worked as a trackman for a few months until finally transferring into the truck department as a driver in March 1953. His daily wage jumped to $14.86, nearly three times what he made when he first arrived in Santa Rita.[48]

◄■■■■■►

Mine-Mill was among the most radical and militant labor unions in the United States. Its locals in southern New Mexico were notorious for wildcat strikes and work stoppages that shut down production at mines and mills throughout the region. By the time Louis joined, Mine-Mill represented tens of thousands of mine workers organized into hundreds of local unions throughout the United States. Even during the height of the anti-communist witch hunts of the McCarthy era, many of its leaders and organizers were unapologetic communists and as a result were constantly targeted by red-baiting legislators and transnational mining companies. The 1947 Taft-Hartley Act required that union organizers and leaders sign anti-communist affidavits as a condition of legal union recognition. "The Taft-Hartley slave labor act" as Local 890 organizer Clint Jencks called it.[49] Nearly every union official from local affiliates of the American Federation of Labor and the Congress of Industrial Organizations signed the affidavits, but Mine-Mill leaders in Bayard and Santa Rita refused.[50] The local National Labor Relations Board, four members of which were Kennecott board members, decertified Mine-Mill in 1948 because of it.[51] Kennecott also retaliated, stonewalling the decertified Mine-Mill during 1948 contract negotiations. Two locals in nearby Hurley voted to strike in May in reprisal, but Kennecott still refused to negotiate. Communism constituted "a menace that presents a serious threat to our free way of life," claimed Kennecott in July 1948. The company's managers refused to negotiate a new contract with Mine-Mill until it pledged to "stamp out Communistic control."[52] Kennecott, emboldened by the NLRB ruling, fired union members in 1951 for distributing what it called "communist literature" and for what it considered the union's "pro-Communist positions."[53] It docked the pay of one truck driver one hundred dollars a month when he joined the union after decertification.[54] Even its own union federation opposed it. The Congress of Industrial Organizations expelled Mine-Mill in 1950.[55]

Mine-Mill union workers frequently walked off the job in wildcat strikes and organized work stoppages throughout the late 1940s and early 1950s, but most histories of Mine-Mill focus on only one action, Local 890's dramatic 1951 strike against Empire Zinc in nearby Hanover, New Mexico. The 1954 film *Salt of the Earth* chronicled the strike. Rather than professional actors, the movie famously included mine workers and family members of mine workers among the cast. Jencks and Local 890 President Juan Chacon played themselves in the film. The film's writer, director, and producer all had been among the Hollywood Ten, a group of artists blacklisted from filmmaking when they refused to answer questions before the US Congress on their relationship to, or membership in, the Communist Party. The film, which has come to occupy an exalted place among many union and social justice activists, placed Chicano mine workers and the militant role of women at the center of its story of union struggle. There's no shortage of books or articles about the film and Mine-Mill. Most focus on the role of women in the union or the film, the red-baiting of union organizers, and the plight of Mexican and Chicano mine workers in the 1940s and 1950s.[56] None of these take up the role or experience of Navajo mine workers in the union. If they are mentioned at all it is in passing or in a footnote.

The union's monthly and executive board meetings, held both in English and Spanish, regularly included lengthy discussions about "the need to eliminate racial discrimination" in Kennecott's hiring practices.[57] But if rank-and-file union members stood against racism and enjoyed the labor, racial, and gender solidarity depicted in the film, it wasn't a solidarity freely shared with Navajo trackmen. Among the hundreds of Navajo workers who came south in 1943 and 1944—men like Kee Chee Wally, Tom Yazzie, Fred Jim, Sam Begay, Tony Begay, John Shoe, Tim Benally, John Nez, John Yazzie, Sam Chee and Hayala Nez—only Hayala Nez joined the union.[58] Nez worked as a swamper, or general laborer, the same pay grade as the trackmen. He joined in October of 1945 but quit shortly after, even though he worked at Kennecott for years.[59] He would eventually return to the union and during the 1950s served on the union's negotiating committee.[60] But no other Navajo miners joined. The union wondered why Navajo men didn't join the union, but it might have been better to ask why any of them joined at all. The union's stand against racism and discrimination never included a stand against the treatment that Navajo men received in Santa Rita.

It's difficult to overstate the depth of violent, anti-Indian sentiment in New Mexico during the 1950s, a period in which Navajos died from tuberculosis at a rate nearly ten times that of white people; dysentery by thirteen times; invasive gastroenteritis by twenty-five times. Measles took the lives of Navajos at a rate nearly thirty times greater than white people. Where white people expected to live to nearly seventy, Navajos were lucky to live to twenty. Few unions took up their cause. Most developed red scare tactics of their own. Where the bosses busted unions using anti-communist tactics, the unions competed among each other to prove which was most anti-Indian. In the late 1950s, an Arizona AFL-CIO official told delegates at its annual convention that the "Indians of Arizona and New Mexico are posing a definite threat to labor."[61] Why would any of them join the union? The only two Navajo trackmen who did, and who stayed with it, were Nez and Louis Casuse. Casuse started at Kennecott in December 1945 and joined Local 63 in July 1946. Like Nez, he quit shortly after when he reenlisted in the army.[62] Also like Nez, he returned and reclaimed his job in 1951 and joined the consolidated Local 890. He and Nez would be the only Navajo mine workers to ever pay union dues and attend union meetings.

◄•••••►

The story of the Santa Rita mine is a story of Indian removal. The only reason the mine existed at all at the time of the Empire Zinc strike was because of Mexico's genocidal war of extermination against the Apaches in the mid-1800s. Kennecott's treatment of Navajo mine workers in the 1940s offered a twentieth-century version of the 1840s scalp contracts. Curcier and McKnight established the mine at Santa Rita del Cobre by funding Mexico's scalp-bounty system, and one hundred years later Kennecott made a fortune during the war by shipping a few "Indians from the Gallup district."[63] Curcier and McKnight waged the war; Kennecott managed the occupation.

It's easy to read the memos in the archives and assume Kennecott was desperate to stay afloat and this led it to seek out Navajo labor in order to save the mine. But the war years were not lean years for Kennecott. The company launched its Navajo recruitment program not out of desperation, but in order to cash in on the profits war promised. The demand for metals spiked during World War II and this stabilized the price and demand for copper, which meant Kennecott could expect record profits but only if it could replace the men lost to war. During the height of the Navajo labor recruitment, the track department removed more ore and rock from the mine than in the years before or after. In the decade prior to the United States entering World War II, annual copper production at the Santa Rita mine averaged less than fifty million pounds of copper. From 1940 to 1945, when Navajo trackmen and female track laborers comprised a majority of mine workers in the track department, production nearly tripled to more than 130 million pounds per year on average.[64] Before the war, the corporation's "earned surplus (undistributed profits) was $90,151,000." By war's end, "profits had increased to $164,552,000."[65] This earned surplus didn't include money Kennecott put in reserve or distributed to shareholders. Throughout the war, Kennecott recorded annual profits of nearly $50 million dollars a year, and by war's end its surplus increased by an astonishing 3,500 percent, from $500,000 in 1937 to $17,633,00 in 1946.[66] Meanwhile, Navajo trackmen lived in tents amid toxic sludge and slag piles and earned as little as $3.85 a day in 1943 for dangerous, backbreaking work.

The Navajo recruitment program wasn't a desperate effort to keep Kennecott afloat while its mine workers fought a war, it was a calculated strategy to maximize profits during the war's boom years. War meant profits for Kennecott, and the company cashed in by keeping its wage rates and expenses low. The union did little to oppose Kennecott's exploitation of Navajo workers. Juan Chacon called the trackmen, which included Navajo men, "some of the weakest men who are working for Kennecott," and he explained the union's apathy toward the plight of Navajo miners in the simplest terms: "We have been unable to get them to join our Chino Unity Council."[67] Chacon, as president of Local 890, raised the issue of Indian Village in nearly every union negotiation with Kennecott. In an August 1954 negotiation with Kennecott, the union noted that the "houses have had no repairs since 1945, no heating system, open sewerage ... no lights except kerosene lamps."[68] Kennecott refused to discuss the issue but promised to look into it. In November of 1954, the company told the union it had "a plan to do away with the Indian Village," with a Kennecott official writing that "I was going to give the Indians six months' notice and at that time we would move them out of those houses and tear the houses down. I am writing this letter simply as a confirmation of that oral statement. The Indian tenants in the Indian village are also being apprised of this move."[69] The displaced Navajo miners were not offered alternative housing in Santa Rita. Once soldiers began returning from war, and Kennecott's corporate coffers were full, all that remained for Navajo trackmen was an anti-Indianism as deep and wide as the mine.

◄ ▪▪▪▪▪ ►

Louis returned to work for Kennecott at the tail end of the Empire Zinc strike, while Lillian arrived the spring after it ended. Louis took Lillian to the Navajo settlement where men used the sheds as barns for their horses and lived in canvas tents instead.[70] She refused to get out of the truck and made Louis drive to Booth Hill, where Anglo miners paid Kennecott fifteen dollars a month to live in homes on paved streets with indoor plumbing. Kennecott distributed its Booth Hill homes, the barrio lots, and Navajo settlement sheds by racially segregated waitlists. It reserved Booth Hill "for accommodation of the white employees."[71] By the time Louis and Lillian arrived, Kennecott had been razing a few buildings a month for years, even in Booth Hill.[72] The copper below Santa Rita was more valuable than Santa Rita itself. Each explosion and every shovelful of ore expanded the mine and slowly and inexorably encroached on the town of Santa Rita. Everyone knew the town's days were numbered. It's possible Louis and Lillian skipped to the front of the Booth Hill housing queue because of this. Who wanted to move into a house and live under the constant threat of eviction? Each month, Kennecott destroyed a few buildings and evicted their tenants as the pit grew. If Louis explained this to Lillian, she ignored him. They drove through Booth Hill and Lillian made him stop the car in front of the first

Explosions like the one pictured here were a part of daily life for the residents of Santa Rita. The town can be seen in the background. Courtesy of New Mexico State University Library, Archives and Special Collections.

empty house she found, number 783.[73] They moved in that day and lived there for the next five years.[74]

Living in Santa Rita in the 1950s was like living on a sinking ship floating on a hostile copper sea. The sense of impending doom that pervaded Santa Rita during those years must have felt oddly familiar to Lillian. Nearly every day and on every shift, miners with rotary drills dug nine-inch diameter, sixty-foot-deep blast holes. Crews poured powdered dynamite into the trenches and ignited explosions that launched rocks everywhere. The blast produced a sonic boom that thundered into Santa Rita like an Allied bombing campaign. After the explosion, the miners brought two-story-tall electric shovels online to scoop up the rubble of waste rock and ore, drawing so much electricity that lights dimmed in Santa Rita homes and as far away as Silver City. Then trucks so big that mechanics needed cranes to change flat tires rumbled in and out of the mine all day.[75] The groan from the 25-ton diesel-powered Euclid trucks must have sounded like the roar of panzer tanks.

Louis no longer worked as a trackman. He drove a truck instead, a much less physically taxing job but equally as dangerous. The enormous trucks made one hundred or more trips in and out of the mine each shift

Lillian, holding Donald, poses with Louis, holding Larry's hand, in a 1955 photo in Santa Rita, New Mexico. Courtesy of Ursula Casuse-Carrillo.

and ferried as much as 2,500 cubic yards of ore each day along precarious dirt roads carved out of the steeply sloped sides of the mine.[76] Turning a fully loaded truck around required death-defying precision. Just receiving the ore from the shovels demanded a synchronized choreography that came with its own dangers. The shovels were larger than the trucks, and shovel operators were notoriously impatient. A missed connection, a truck out of place, or an irritated or careless shovel operator could flip a truck and send it tumbling down steep slopes. A truck driver named Natividad Perez suffocated to death in 1964 when a surge pile he backed his truck onto collapsed like quicksand and buried him alive.[77] It had been these lethal working conditions, as much or more than the low wages, that fueled union organizing efforts among the mine workers in the years before Mine-Mill. Before the union, runaway trains ran over trackmen, killing them or taking legs and arms. Mechanics lost eyes and fingers in shop accidents. Mill workers died of electrocution. Rockslides crushed men to death. Steam shovels flipped, killing their operators. Of all the jobs, however, the most dangerous were those on the blast crews, jobs that fell exclusively to Spanish-speaking mine workers. Powdermen worked with dynamite all day long and eked out a living risking their lives "on a daily basis."[78] They set explosions that

Louis peeks out of the cab of his 40-ton Euclid truck. The image appeared in an issue of *Chinorama*, Kennecott's glossy publicity magazine. Courtesy of Chino Mine Collection, Silver City Museum, Silver City, New Mexico.

launched boulders into the air that occasionally triggered lethal rockfalls on steep slopes. A 1954 explosion at a blast site killed five men, after which Kennecott abandoned hand-poured powdered dynamite and shifted instead to carbamite, a mixture of diesel fuel and dynamite, or a gelatinous mixture of ammonium nitrate and water, which they delivered by hoses attached to a powder truck.[79]

While Louis spent his workday in a truck hauling thousands of tons of ore out of the pit each shift, Lillian spent her days in their Booth Hill home tending their vegetable garden in the morning and writing letters home in the afternoon.[80] She'd walk to the company store to buy comic books to help her learn English. She dyed her hair dark brown and started wearing boots instead of heels. A year after first arriving in New Mexico, they returned to Mexican Springs for a visit and Lillian told everyone in her German-accented English that she was seven months pregnant.

Just days before her eighteenth birthday, on July 19, 1953, she gave birth to a boy, Larry Wayne Casuse, in the small Santa Rita hospital. Louis's sister Ella Mae moved in with them to help with the baby.[81] Donald arrived next in 1954 and then Erika a year later. Driving a truck for Kennecott was not a family-friendly occupation. Kennecott frequently changed shifts, lengthened shifts, eliminated swing shifts, created new shifts, ordered men to work, furloughed them, frequently changed workweek patterns, and arbitrarily altered sick leave amounts.[82] The other miners who lived in Booth Hill made a significantly higher wage than Louis and could afford the cost of living there. Louis, on the other hand, paid most of his wages back to Kennecott for rent, food, and supplies at the company store. He supplemented his low wages any way he could. When he traveled back to Mexican Springs for ceremonies, he often pawned scrap metal, copper wire, or tools, that he'd scrounged from the mine. As the kids got older and traveled with him back to Mexican Springs or Coyote Canyon, he'd remove the back seat of the car and the kids would sit on pilfered spools of wire or boxes of tools that Louis would pawn for gas money once they got to Gallup.[83]

◄▪▪▪▪▪►

The struggle to make ends meet and avoid dying on the job was not the version of mine work that Kennecott celebrated in *Chinorama*, its glossy, monthly magazine. Alongside "human interest" stories and miner profiles, it ran anti-union editorials that celebrated capitalist enterprise, Kennecott-style. In "Who's a Tycoon?," Kennecott bizarrely claimed that Santa Rita's birth rate projected a local "labor force of 88 million people" by 1975.[84] You might not like capitalism now, but you'll like it then, the editorial promised. In "Who Profits from Profits?," Kennecott tried to argue that profit wasn't "money withheld from laboring people who have sweated and slaved to earn it," even though by definition it was. Instead, Kennecott, confusing profit with revenue, claimed profits came "from the customer's dollar spent for the product the company produces." The company simply couldn't return profits back to workers, even if the workers deserved it, explained the editorial, because then Kennecott's "stock would be worthless." If that happened, "there would almost certainly be NO JOBS" in Santa Rita. The editorial concluded by admitting that the company makes "substantial profits," but it would be a mistake to hold this against Kennecott since "profits are the working man's best friend."[85] If so, Louis's best friend abandoned him. He could barely afford food for his family. Most editions of *Chinorama* included a list of the monetary winners of Kennecott's monthly suggestion

Louis Casuse (third from the left) poses with other Chino truck drivers in a 1960 photo of the Kennecott's Euclid Truck Department. Courtesy of Western New Mexico University, Silver City, New Mexico, J. Cloyd Miller Library Archives.

contest. Each month Kennecott gave awards to a handful of miners who made winning suggestions to "improve" the mine. In February of 1959, Louis pointed out that the location of the oil tank on the Euclid trucks forced drivers to spend all day sitting in cabs slowly filling with carbon monoxide.[86] He won twenty dollars.

As anti-union propaganda, *Chinorama* scrupulously avoided any mention of Kennecott's labor practices. It ran no lists of the men and women it fired or furloughed. There were no pictures of families evicted from their homes. The union kept those lists. "In 1935 and 1936 the company handed out sixty-one eviction notices to workers it had fired for union organizing and then forced them to remove or tear down their homes."[87] Every month at least one person who worked the mine came home from a shift and found an eviction notice nailed to their front door. If anyone wanted to place a wager on future evictions, the betting favorite would have been found among the many union activists. In one two-year stretch, Kennecott destroyed 175 homes of union supporters it fired and blacklisted.[88]

Kennecott generated "significant profits" through the exploitation of labor, not from the pockets of consumers. With the fixed labor costs that the mine negotiated with the union, the price of energy dictated the mine's production schedule and the firm's margins. If the price of electricity rose by a fraction of a penny, Kennecott shut down all production while it waited for the price to drop. Men sat in idling trucks waiting for the utility of their labor to reappear. When energy prices spiked, and union negotiations grew contentious, Kennecott laid off its workers or closed the mine indefinitely. Those who kept their jobs made higher wages under a union. But to work at the mine meant living in a company town, where nearly every penny received in wages eventually made its way back to Kennecott in the form of rent or food. The more profit the workers generated, the more aggressive Kennecott became. The union objected when Kennecott erected observation posts around the mine staffed by armed guards. "Certainly, the company does not think of us as prisoners," the union wrote to the general manager.[89]

◄▪▪▪▪▪►

What a thing to work for a wage, to labor in the production of great wealth, and to grow poorer because of it. But here was something altogether different. Miners estranged not only from the things they built with their hands or took from the earth—Kennecott claimed everything from the ore in the pit to the pews in the church—but also from the lives they built away from the mine. They dug Kennecott's pit and it eventually doubled as their grave. Karl Marx wrote of the alienation and estrangement that wage work produces. Wage labor converts the worker into a commodity no different to the mining company than the trucks or trains they used to mine the copper. "The devaluation of the world of men is in direct proportion to the increasing value of the world of things." The wage labor of the mine workers enriched Kennecott at the expense of their own bodies and futures. "Through estranged, alienated labor," Marx wrote, "the worker produces the relationship to this labor of a man alien to labor and *standing outside it*."

Easy for Marx to say. A runaway train car never severed his legs. He never slowly poisoned himself driving a truck for Kennecott. He was never evicted from his home in Santa Rita, where workers eventually found themselves without a job, a home, or anything to even *stand outside of*. The mine workers made the mine and then Kennecott's mine unmade them. After every home had fallen to the bulldozers, those born in Santa Rita came to call themselves the "people born in space," former residents of a town annihilated by and converted into capital. Nothing remained of the world they built and once inhabited. Kennecott accumulated great wealth through the

Louis Casuse poses in their Santa Rita home in 1957. Courtesy of Ursula Casuse-Carrillo.

slow and total destruction of every social and natural relation that made life possible. The official close to this period came in 1965 when Kennecott announced the end of Santa Rita in the April edition of *Chinorama*. "Pit Expansion will Need Santa Rita Townsite," read the headline. And thereafter only copper, capital, and hostility remained.

◀■■■■▶

After Erika's birth they all moved briefly to a larger house in Booth Hill, but it didn't last long and wasn't much of an improvement. Booth Hill was better than a tent, but it meant living with wall-rattling explosions, swirling dirt and dust, and the looming certainty of eviction. Louis and Lillian had a bedroom, Larry and Donald shared a second, and Erika and Nijoni, who arrived in 1957, shared a third. Dust covered everything. Snails crawled along the bathroom walls. Lillian woke up at night and found cockroaches crawling on her children. She lost her childhood to war and now her adulthood to a copper company. Increasingly, she turned to Larry for the day-to-day tasks of child raising. He cooked meals, gave baths, and helped with homework. He got the kids ready for school and made sure they made it home safe. His siblings looked to him as a parent. When Lillian cleaned the house, she locked everyone in their rooms all afternoon. If they complained, she

Lillian stands in the Gila River in an early 1960s photo while Larry and Erika swim in the water below her. Courtesy of Ursula Casuse-Carrillo.

told them, they'd just make a mess of the place.[90] Larry fiercely protected his brothers and sisters, but he too was a child. He forgot to put a diaper on Nijoni once when he left her in her crib alone. Three-year-old Erika found the mess and told Lillian who, in a rage, scooped up the feces that covered the sheets and the crib and shoved it in Larry's mouth as a punishment.[91] Shortly after Nijoni arrived, Louis came home to find an eviction notice. The mine had finally reached their home, so they moved out of Santa Rita and into a public housing development in the nearby town of Bayard, a few miles west of the pit. Lillian was twenty-five years old. Copper had finally swallowed her home, just as war had swallowed her childhood.

◄▪▪▪▪▪►

The children of Mexican and Spanish-speaking mine workers in Santa Rita had it as tough as their parents. The children of wealthy parents bullied the children of working parents. The children of English-speaking miners bullied the children of Spanish-speaking miners. Each took it out on the other in Santa Rita and then Bayard, where they fought with rocks on playgrounds and with fists in arroyos. This was group-based conflict, but none claimed the Casuse kids. They were on their own and had only Larry for protection. By the late 1950s, there were more than five hundred school-age children in the Santa Rita area, and few of them accepted the Casuse kids.[92] Larry fought off the kids who picked on his brothers and sisters. He defended them against ruthless teasing on every trip to and from school. The English-speaking kids thought they were Mexican, and the Spanish-speaking kids teased them, shouting "Indio, Indio" whenever they passed.[93] Other kids found their speech patterns weird, peppered by oddly pronounced words that made them easy targets. Both Louis and Lillian spoke English as a second language, and each with a different accent. Larry and his siblings grew up learning to pronounce words based on their parents' speech patterns—they pronounced "comb" as "koom."[94] The other kids could be cruel.

Lillian became a US citizen in May of 1961 when she was twenty-six years old. By then they'd been living in their cramped apartment, officially known as "Housing Project, Bayard, New Mexico," for a few years. Lillian had entirely ceded everyday parenting to Larry by this time. But life in Bayard, at times, brought them together. Louis convinced Lillian, raised Protestant, to attend Catholic church services with him on Sundays, and so most weekends after church they'd drive to a secluded spot along the Gila River for a picnic. Louis watched from a shady spot on the bank as the kids climbed trees, scrambled up and down boulders, and swam in the river. Lillian took long naps in the shade of Cottonwood and Willow trees and listened to Johnny Cash on her portable record player. When they didn't picnic along the Gila, Louis took the kids on long walks along the railroad tracks near their house in Bayard, collecting tin cans.[95]

The children loved Sundays on the Gila, but otherwise life in Bayard mirrored life in Santa Rita. Larry made a few friends, mostly from chess club in school, but otherwise he remained on guard and quiet around other kids. When not cooking or cleaning at home, he read by himself—so much in fact that he eventually got a job at the library. Life in Bayard was difficult for Erika as well, who attended elementary school with white and Hispanic kids who bullied her. They pushed her in the hallway, pulled her hair, and taunted her with "dirty Indian" chants. She hid in the bathroom during lunch to escape. After school, she often walked to a butcher shop where she collected waste bones, which she used to lure a pack of feral dogs into an arroyo near her home. They passed the afternoon together, the dogs chewing on bones and Erika doing backflips. The Casuses had their own dog for a time, but Louis killed it with a pitchfork after it misbehaved.[96] Sometimes,

(Top, left) Larry, Donald, Lillian, and Erika (left to right) picnic in the Gila in the late 1950s. Courtesy of Ursula Casuse-Carrillo.

(Top, right) Lillian poses in her Santa Rita kitchen with Larry (left), Donald (far right), Erika (in Lillian's lap), with newborn Nijoni lying on the kitchen table. Courtesy of Ursula Casuse-Carrillo.

(Bottom, left) The Casuse family sharing a meal in the basement of their Santa Rita church. The children (from left to right) are Donald, Erika, Ursula, Larry, and Nijoni. Courtesy of Ursula Casuse-Carrillo.

during a lull in the teasing, she'd ask the white girls on the playground if she could play Barbie dolls with them, but they never let her. "They loved hurting my feelings, but I got tougher," she said. I didn't need friends, and I didn't need a mom, she told herself. "God is my parent." But Larry was her parent if anyone was. They'd hike through arroyos together. If she fell into a cactus, he pulled her out. They'd walk to the playground together. If red ants attacked, Larry rescued her. When bullies teased her on their walk to or from school, Larry fought them off. As she got older, she helped Larry cook and clean. She played teacher with her younger siblings in abandoned apartments using broken shards of drywall as chalk. They saw less and less of their mom, who left them alone, and often without food in the house. Occasionally a neighbor invited them over to eat tortillas.[97] Lillian gave birth to Daschija, her sixth child, in 1964.

Larry pushes his bike in front of their Bayard, New Mexico, home while his brothers and sisters crowd around him. Courtesy of Ursula Casuse-Carrillo.

Erika remembers a dream from this period. She wakes up in a comfortable bed in a room without cockroaches full of nice furniture. The room disorients her, and she doesn't know where she is. She crawls out from under warm soft covers and steps with bare feet onto a thick, soft carpet. I don't feel cold drafts, she thinks to herself. Where am I? She nervously makes her way out of the room and into a dark, quiet hallway that takes her to a large living room full of more beautiful furniture. Years later, when she was in her early twenties, she mentioned the dream to her mother for the first time. "I wonder what it means?" she asked out loud, not expecting an answer. Lillian looked at her with surprise. "You don't remember?" she asked. "That's not a dream, that was our neighbor's house," she told her. It was the house of a nice couple, she explained. They had money but no kids of their own. "They asked me if they could adopt you," she told Erika. "You were so cute, and we were so poor. I sent you over for a weekend," she said, "to see if maybe it would work out."

Ursula remembers her mother taking her to a big, gray house in Silver City. She remembers the three steps that led from the sidewalk to the front door. She remembers entering the house and walking up more stairs to a landing above the entryway. From there, she remembers looking out a window onto the street where she saw her mother walking back down the steps, leaving her. Ursula never asked Lillian about the memory because she understood why her mother took her there. Years later, though, as her mother lay dying, a flood of hard memories returned. She sat by her mother's deathbed and they talked about some of them, including a memory she had of a man who took her into a garage when she was a girl in Bayard. "I told you not to go near that man," her mother said.

Daschija fell out of a moving car when she was a toddler. The window was open and she crawled up the armrest of the door from the back seat and fell out onto a gravel road. Louis and Lillian rushed her to a hospital in El Paso. When the kids came home from school, their neighbors, who they'd never met before, told them what had happened and invited them to wait at their house until their parents retuned from the hospital. Erika remembers how nice their house was. They don't use cardboard boxes as furniture, she thought. Everyone has their own mattress, she marveled. The doctors shaved one side of Daschija's head and sewed stitches in a circle around where they'd implanted a metal plate.[98]

Louis rolled the family car while driving drunk in Silver City once. Lillian said she'd leave him if he didn't stop drinking, so he stopped and never drank again; but it didn't save their marriage. Lillian got a job working as a waitress in a restaurant in Silver City. Her shift started when Louis's ended so they rarely saw each other. She used the money from her paycheck on nice clothes for herself. She made friends among her coworkers, none of whom understood why she was with Louis. "Why did you marry that Indian?" they would ask her, but she never had an answer. How would she have known? It wasn't like she fell in love and got married. A war came, and then an occupation, and then her family traded her away for their safety, and maybe for hers. She didn't experience a childhood, she survived the destruction of her world. War and occupation expelled her from a life she might have had, like the dynamite that blew up Santa Rita. She came home less and less. Louis worked more and more. Her children spent days without food or parents in the house.[99] "I can't do anything," she told Erika once. "I have a third-grade education. I'm at the end of the line. The end of the line."[100]

◄▪▪▪▪▪►

How does someone learn to be a parent—or learn to just live in the world—when they never had a childhood? And what did Lillian do with the knowledge that she *might* have had a childhood but didn't because the people who were supposed to protect her sacrificed her instead—sacrificed her so that they could escape their own suffering? When this thought came to her, did she wonder if she was doing the same thing to her own children? Did it haunt her like it haunted Ursula?

A deep and unshakable sense of unease, something like doom, settled inside Ursula when they lived in Bayard. It invaded and occupied her childhood. She has no memory of a time before it. She gave up picturing a future free from it. This changed, though, after many hard years, around the time she turned twenty-six—the same age Lillian had been when she stopped being a parent—when she decided that "maybe there's nothing wrong with me." It was a choice only in the way that survival is a choice. She had to first give herself permission to think this. Maybe the poverty and the violence and the death and all that's landed on me and everything bad about

Lillian wears her work clothes and poses in the early 1960s in front of their Bayard home. Courtesy of Ursula Casuse-Carrillo.

this world wasn't my fault. "Maybe it's not me. Maybe wrong things were done to me, and I've suffered because of those things." She decided that this would be true because her life depended on it, and it saved her.[101] And she hoped that maybe her mother had this thought too. Ursula decided to focus on other memories, moments of tenderness. "I'd go in the bathroom when she took baths and ask and listen. Then I got in the tub after her and we'd talk until she was ready."[102] Memories like those grew to eclipse the ones she wanted to forget.

Lillian gave birth to Joseph, her last child, in 1967. Soon after, she started an affair with a regular customer at the restaurant where she worked.[103] Mine-Mill union workers walked off the job in July 1967 in solidarity with other striking locals and didn't come back to work until March 1968. The contract that ended the strike included wage increases and even backpay for truck drivers, but Louis got none of it. He tried to live off strike pay at first but couldn't make it work, so he took a job driving a truck at a copper mine in Arizona and never returned to Santa Rita. Lillian took the kids to Gallup, where they lived in a haunted house a few blocks from the mayor's office.

Man Camp

"These streets never were useful for anything but crying."
—**Simon Ortiz**, "Time to Kill in Gallup"

Gallup, self-proclaimed "Indian Capital of the World," a machine carefully calibrated to kill or incarcerate Navajos. The Casuses rented an old house on Aztec Street not far from the county courthouse, and Lillian found a waitressing job at the Holiday Inn. Louis took a job driving a truck at a mine in Arizona and lived in his car. He worked double shifts most days and could usually come home only twice a month. Larry spent most of his time reading at the public library or in an old backyard shed that he fixed up for himself. He read voraciously there, mostly science fiction and Greek philosophy. He started learning German. He built his own stereo out of parts he found discarded in alleys or dumpsters. He played chess on a magnetic board, composed music, and started painting apocalyptic portraits of America in decay. Crumbling courthouses, cities on fire, the Statue of Liberty with severed arms sinking into polluted water.

The war still haunted Louis. Years earlier, army doctors had given him medication for shell shock, but he threw the drugs away. He didn't want their help. He felt no pride about being made to kill people in war. He'd fought in Europe only because he'd starved at home, not out of any patriotic duty. The only good thing that came out of it was Lillian, yet he found himself estranged from her now, working double shifts a state away and sleeping alone in the back of an old station wagon. He gave each paycheck to Lillian for food and expenses in Gallup and kept only enough for gas and a daily sandwich or two. Lillian spent most of the money on herself. Larry and Erika, de facto parents, began raiding their mother's wardrobe and pawning her clothes to buy food. Lillian put a lock on her closet door. When Louis came home, he'd find the electricity cut off, the windows covered in blankets, no food in the kitchen. He spent those weekends looking for the kids and mending their clothes. He sewed a secret pocket into his coat and shoplifted meat from the grocery store. "It's not good to steal," he told Ursula, "but we got to." Lillian stole things too. "My dad stole food for us," Ursula explained, "and my mom stole hair spray for herself." Larry too. He got a job at a motel and took the carpet from the entryway so he could cover the exposed nails on the floor where the little ones played with found toys. He swiped a TV from the high school and took lawn chairs from neighbors' front porches. When he saw a delivery driver unloading boxes into a convenience store on his way home once, he swiped as many boxes as he could carry when the driver wasn't looking. They lived off Butterfinger candy bars for a month.

The three youngest children slept together in their mother's bed when she wasn't home. Eight-year-old Ursula slept in the middle with her brother Joseph, just starting to walk, on one side, and her four-year-old sister Daschija on the other. As they lay in bed at night in their mother's dark bedroom, they often heard footsteps on the ceiling above them. Some nights they heard knocking from inside the locked closet door, as if someone was trying to escape. Erika slept on the top of a bunk bed, and one morning she woke to find thread everywhere, wrapped around everything. It covered the furniture, hung from the bunk beds, encircled the light fixtures, and wound around the door handle. Their shoes formed a pile in the middle of the room. Erika sat up in bed and watched as one of the shoes started moving. Ursula woke to Erika's screaming and they both watched, wild eyed, as a shoe walked itself around the room. Their blankets suddenly flew off their beds as if pulled by an invisible string. Erika jumped out of bed and walked to the center of the room where she loudly declared that she had no fear of any ghosts even though they were all terrified.

They decided the footsteps they heard most nights were those of a little boy and they named him Billy. "Good night, Billy," Ursula would say before bed. Once, while lying in bed, Erika saw a woman's face peak up at her from over the end of the bed. The ghost woman wore a coat and fourteen-year-old Erika remembered how warm it looked. Ursula decided that the woman with the warm coat watched over them and cared for them. When they moved from the house years later, Ursula invited the ghost to join them. "You were the only one who looked after us," she said to the empty house. "If you want to, I hope you'll come with us."

Lillian grew tired of being poor and, though still married to Louis, started dating a car dealer named W. C. Morehal. Her children called him Shine. He called them "dirty Indians." She made friends with people who had memberships at the country club. She grew more and more impatient with the kids. When Lillian got mad at Erika, she'd send her to live with Louis in Arizona during the week. Erika would sit alone all day in the station wagon waiting for her dad to finish a double shift. She passed the time saying the rosary and eating small sandwiches. After work they'd drive to a secret spot Louis found where they could sleep for the night in the back of the car. Erika didn't mind. She liked the quiet time alone and the nights with just her dad. Lillian used humiliation as a punishment with Larry. She made him wear a dress to school once after he talked back to her. Another time she forced him to stand on a street corner in his underwear when he didn't finish a chore.

There was some structure to their lives when Louis was home. He'd have all of them pray with him each night. They'd gather in a circle on their knees, holding hands and reciting the rosary. It could take hours. Larry passed out once and fell on his face. Mostly though, the kids were on their own. On Saturdays the owners of the many Indian bars in town would wedge open their doors and let people spill out of the packed bars onto the sidewalks. Larry and Donald dodged the drunk men and women on the crowded sidewalks when they walked downtown. According to New Mexico state law, the Liquor Board could only approve one liquor license per every two thousand people in a given city. Gallup had thirty-nine liquor licenses in a town of fifteen thousand people, thirty-two more than the law allowed.[1] And the bars were among the few businesses Navajo people could enter. Signs hung from the doors of some stores in Gallup: "No dogs, niggers or Indians allowed."

Larry and Donald hated the bars. They threw smoke bombs into the open doorways and then ran down alleyways to escape from angry bar owners. Larry started carrying a briefcase so that he'd have somewhere to stash all the Polaroids he took—black-and-white photos of men passed out in alleys or arroyos. Snapshots of overcrowded liquor stores and bars. Portraits of anti-Indianism on display.

When they lived in Santa Rita and Bayard, Louis would bring the kids to ceremonies on the Navajo Nation. When they moved to Gallup, Larry spent more and more time visiting elders he'd met on those trips. Ursula said he wanted to "learn how to be an Indian." He didn't speak Navajo and he had no traditional clothing, so he made do with what he had. He fashioned his own breechcloth cloak out of scrap fabric and wore it to school on days the Indian Club met. His brothers and sisters found this strange, but they revered him and so never thought of teasing him. Among the children only Larry thought of himself as Navajo. Lillian had always taught them they weren't Native, and she tried this with Larry too. "You're not an Indian," she snapped at him once, but he was having none of it. "Yes, I am," he said.

◀••••••▶

In November 1968, just after Larry started high school, the general manager of the Navajo Tribal Utility Authority, Cletus "Mac" Eddy, heard a call on the scanner about a pedestrian hit by an automobile near the Navajo Inn on

Larry Casuse's high school yearbook photo. Courtesy of Ursula Casuse-Carrillo.

Highway 264. Eddy knew that stretch of highway well. His job took him back and forth between Window Rock, the Navajo Nation capital in Arizona, and Gallup, New Mexico. The highway passed the Navajo Inn and "it is a common experience," he wrote, "to dodge intoxicated persons on the highway" near the Navajo Inn, which at that time was the most profitable bar and liquor store in the state of New Mexico. The Navajo Inn was a squat, single-story, cinder block building more than twenty-five miles northwest of Gallup and a few hundred yards from the Navajo Nation border. When Eddy arrived at the accident, he found multiple people "lying partially on the highway east of Window Rock." He and an Arizona patrolman drove by the Navajo Inn and saw people everywhere "passed out from too much liquor." They walked into the bar to look for a phone and instead "found a scene much worse than I have ever observed in my life, which includes three years in the US Army and two years of war in the Pacific."[2] Nearly three dozen people crowded the small bar with even more spilling out onto the highway. Two men lay passed out on the floor and Eddy watched "others walking over them." Among the thirty people were eight girls. They stood under a No Minors Allowed sign while older men surrounded them, ogling and touching them. Eddy thought the girls all looked younger than fifteen, some maybe as young as twelve. He was so horrified that he wrote the governor demanding something be done. "It seems inconceivable," he wrote, "that persons with any conscience at all, can continue to provide sales to persons who are obviously intoxicated and to condone the other actions as were witnessed."

Everyone knew about the Navajo Inn. Larry took pictures of it. Others wrote petitions about it, demanding its closure. In one petition dozens of people demanded that the governor close the bar and have its liquor license "forever canceled and revoked." They'd had enough of the "many deaths at or near the Navajo Inn." Drunk drivers "kill themselves and their passengers, or innocent pedestrians and motorists who happen to be in the area." People walking along Highway 264 after leaving the Navajo Inn "are struck and killed by passing cars." Some people, "after being served in the Navajo Inn, wander off into the cold night air and die of exposure."[3] Gallup police and McKinley County Sheriff's deputies called the frozen dead they found in arroyos and alleys and behind the Navajo Inn "popsicles." Edmund Kahn, a Navajo Nation lawyer, wrote to New Mexico's governor, David

Cargo, and the Liquor Control Bureau about the Navajo Inn on nearly a weekly basis throughout the late 1960s. He'd send clippings with headlines like "Unidentified Man is Found" above text that described bodies found in ditches near the Navajo Inn that "appeared to have been beaten" to death.[4]

In August 1972, a group of adjacent landowners and residents filed a class action lawsuit against the owners of the Navajo Inn claiming that it constituted a nuisance that led to the deaths of scores of people in the past decade. Emmett Garcia, the mayor of Gallup and co-owner of the Navajo Inn, denied every claim in the suit, and he and his co-owners' lawyers submitted a series of interrogatories with the court demanding from the plaintiffs the names of those found dead in or near the Navajo Inn. If Garcia's lawyers thought the interrogatories would call the plaintiffs' bluff, they were wrong. In their response, the plaintiffs included lists of the dead. Zun Chee Slinkey, a sixty-eight-year-old sheep herder and plaintiff to the suit, listed John Hubby and Mike Maloney, killed by cars on the road in front of the Navajo Inn. He offered a longer list if the court required it. Gloria Ann Cisco, who lived a half mile from the Navajo Inn, provided a list that included George Slinkey, who was bludgeoned to death outside the Navajo Inn in 1964, and Sarah Williams, John Tsosie, and Melvin Damon, who were all killed by cars in front of the bar in 1972. Annie Wayne was found dead in the parking lot in 1970. Everyone, it seemed, had their own list of the dead at or near the Navajo Inn.

The misery and suffering that came to Navajo people in Gallup appeared so extreme and inexplicable and such an outlier to other examples of alcohol use or abuse that Navajo drinking in Gallup drew attention from all corners. By the time Larry started taking Polaroids of the misery in Gallup, there were already hundreds of published medical and public health studies on the so-called mystery of Indian drinking. An entire industry of magazine and newspaper reporting chronicled the extreme suffering in Gallup. The National Institute on Alcoholism and Alcohol Abuse reported that McKinley County had the highest composite index of alcohol-related mortality of all United States counties for the 1975–1977 period.[5] Even the novelist and essayist Calvin Trillin wrote about it in the pages of the *New Yorker*. "There is something horrifying," he wrote in a 1971 essay titled "Drunken Indian," "about the look of Navajo drinking in

Gallup—something that makes it less like big-city skid-row drinking than like a medieval epidemic." The Navajo Inn figured prominently in his piece. "Someone who goes in to buy a six-pack of beer in the middle of a Saturday afternoon is likely to have to skirt the bodies of six or eight Navajos who have passed out in front of the door." If they drive to the Navajo Inn from the Navajo Nation, they'll travel a highway so littered with empty liquor bottles "that its shoulders glisten in the sunlight." And if they attempt the lethal drive home that night, they'll dodge the pedestrians who "loom suddenly out of the darkness into their headlight beams—a drunk on his way home who decides to stagger to the other side of the road."[6]

So many researchers, academics, reporters, and policymakers wrote about Gallup and the so-called problem of Indian drinking in these years that it became its own genre of writing—a merging of mystery and horror in which only victims could be found. In the years prior to the 1970s, most looked for causes to the misery in Navajo biology. Trillin was quick to point out that "nobody has ever found any evidence to support the old notion that Indians have a physiological inability to drink—some vulnerable gene or some special chemical in the blood that mixes explosively with alcohol," but this didn't stop people from looking. Even Trillin, who mocked the stereotype of the "drunken Indian," was at a loss to explain the misery. He found something profoundly inexplicable about Navajo drinking in Gallup. He took for granted the idea that Indian drinking existed as some kind of unique, distinctive characteristic of Native life. Though he rejected the genetic explanation, he kept his gaze on Navajos when considering alternative possibilities. "Navajos have a special way of drinking," he wrote. Perhaps its cultural. They drink in groups and "nobody in the group passes up his turn unless he is prepared to undergo a full evening of ridicule." Navajos must lack taboos around drunkenness, he speculated. After all, "Navajos don't like to interfere in other people's lives." He argued, however, that there were no conclusions to draw. "When it comes to explaining why Indians drink so much, there are research findings to support or refute practically any theory."

It's not clear if Trillin knew he was writing in the long settler-colonial tradition of white men preoccupied with the so-called problem of Indian drinking. From the very beginning of European conquest and settlement in the New World, colonial authorities obsessed over the question of alcohol and Indians. In the late seventeenth century, various English colonies throughout what is now the United States prohibited the sale of alcohol to Native peoples. The Connecticut colony declared an alcohol prohibition in 1645.[7] In 1832 the US Congress passed a general law that prohibited the sale of liquor to "any and all American Indians."[8] Congress eventually expanded its prohibition to include the sale, transportation, and possession of alcohol on any Indian reservation and then expanded the prohibition even further in 1854 when Congress banned the sale of alcohol to Native people in surrounding bordertowns. This prohibition was not lifted until 1933.[9] During New Mexico's territorial period, the Pueblo Indian Agency fixated on alcohol. Its many agents, as if by some strange compulsion, collected all the data they could find on alcohol and Indians. They recorded, in particular, patterns of liquor sales and consumption among the Pueblo Indians. Canada's 1876 Indian Act made the consumption of alcohol illegal to anyone who followed "the Indian mode of life" and included punishments of hard labor for anyone violating the act. This was a law, like all settler law, designed to redefine Native life in the interests of settler society. The primary goal of settler society is the elimination of the Native. Colonial laws that limited alcohol for Indigenous peoples served this end because the only way an Indigenous person could legally possess or drink alcohol in Canada was if they first rejected their Indianness.[10] As the legal scholar Mariana Valverde wrote, liquor laws defined Indigenous "racial status as much as, and perhaps more effectively than, they governed drinking."[11] In the United States, all Native reservations were declared dry, and most remain dry today, a bizarre legal geography in which the only legal place to drink is off the reservation, in public, where it is illegal to drink. The law forced drinkers into alleys, drunk people into cars, and pedestrians out onto cold, dark, remote highways, where they were as likely to be killed or arrested as make it home safely. The arrests came in enormous numbers, which helped cement the idea that Native drinking was somehow, and profoundly, different than non-Native drinking. "We are totally administered," said National Indian Youth Council Vice President Bill Pensoneau to a congressional subcommittee in 1969. There was nothing Navajo people could do that wasn't prohibited, administered, controlled, mediated, or manipulated by white society. "The only time we are free is when we are drunk," he said. "We can experience nothing directly but death."[12]

◄ ▪ ▪ ▪ ▪ ▪ ►

Nearly all epidemiological and public health studies on Indian drinking ignore the social, legal, and political context in which drinking happens. Instead of settler law, police, and the predatory liquor trade, researchers looked for answers in various imaginary pathologies among Native peoples. The same year Trillin published his essay in the *New Yorker*, a group of scientists published an essay in the *Canadian Medical Association Journal* claiming to have found a biological difference in the way Native people and white people metabolize alcohol.[13] This would be the last, notorious published claim of a physiological explanation in a medical journal. Most scholars and public health officials by then had abandoned the biophysical explanation and looked instead at Navajo culture and tradition. Something found among the Navajo, they were convinced, would explain the misery. After all, the mortality rate for cirrhosis of the liver in McKinley County in 1975 was more than twice the national average. The alcohol-induced mortality rate was nearly ten times higher, and mortality from all alcohol-related causes was nearly four times the national average.[14] And new studies always seemed to follow. A series of studies in the late 1980s reinforced the idea of a mysterious Navajo drinking problem. Navajos suffered from alcoholism at a rate twenty times higher than the US average.[15] Perhaps this pattern of Navajo drinking, according to the cultural explanation that developed during these years, can be understood as a living legacy of colonial domination. Instead of peering into genes and blood, they peered into Navajo culture and traditions. Hypotheses abounded. Maybe it's a coping mechanism, or an intergenerational trauma response. A 1974 study on Navajo drinking claimed that "levels of social pathology tend to be high [among North American Indians] and that the high levels are the direct result of social disintegration produced by conquest and acculturation."[16] This disintegration thesis transformed Indigenous culture into "a kind of index through which a social pathology, often described as deviancy, is charted as a kind of effect of colonialism, an effect with, apparently, biophysiological manifestations." Colonialism existed only in the past, in this version, and it so warped Indigenous communities and culture that Indigenous peoples in the present were left helpless, condemned to "possess a mysterious incapacity for modern life."[17] A 1988 survey of Navajo respondents found that nearly 70 percent of Navajos surveyed believed that the problem was based on a "physical weakness to alcohol that non-Indians do not have."[18]

Larry's photos, however, offered a different explanation. Colonialism was not history, it was the present. It was the everyday lived experience of Navajo people in Gallup, and it could be found in his photos. Pictures full of bars and liquor stores and pawn shops, none of which were owned by Navajo people. There were cops in Larry's photos and they were arresting Navajo men and women. There were bar owners and pawn shop operators with investment-backed expectations in the profits that came from Navajo misery. If anyone asked Larry, he would have told them that Indian drinking is different in Gallup because Gallup is different. Gallup called itself the "Indian Capital of the World." Larry and many other young Navajo activists called it the "Exploitation Capital of the World." Twice a month, a team of eighteen-wheel tractor trailers from California delivered thousands of bottles of brandy-fortified wine to the scores of bars and liquor stores in town. Garden Deluxe was among the most popular brands. Here it was once again, like the scalp contracts in Gran Apachería, a profit motive attached to cruelty and misery. They called it "Garden Death" on the reservation. Annual revenue from alcohol sales in Gallup exceeded the combined revenue of finance, insurance, and real estate.[19]

The owners of the Navajo Inn had deep political connections, which they used to defend their practices and profits. These businessmen knew about the deaths and suffering, and what they knew about it was that Navajo suffering didn't threaten Gallup commerce, it buoyed it. Larry would have pointed out that Navajo misery in Gallup was not an aberration or product of past colonial conquest. Navajo immiseration produced the conditions that made the Gallup economy possible in the first place. They sold bad alcohol, but they also sold bad loans and bad pawn terms. Little had changed in Gallup in the years between Louis's youth and Larry's. Navajos were still "denied access to all but the most unsanitary and undesirable eating, lodging, and restroom facilities" in Gallup.[20] Auto and truck dealers,

like liquor stores, surrounded the reservation. They refused to honor war-
ranties, refused to disclose interest rates, required that buyers sign blank
sales contracts, sold fake "required" insurance policies. Some dealers took
Navajo rugs or jewelry as a down payment in the form of a loan but refused
to return items when people paid off the note and attempted to retrieve
them.[21] Gallup was a machine carefully calibrated to produce suffering, and
with suffering came profit.

Robert Bergman, the chief of the Indian Health Service's mental health
program in the late 1960s and early 1970s, spent a career telling anyone who
would listen that Indian drinking was no different than any other kind of
drinking. Few were listening. It was the alcohol industry and reservation
prohibition that established the patterns that Trillin found medieval. It
"fostered the hurried gulping of alcohol to avoid being caught and arrested.
As one Navajo man said, 'I was put in jail once for having half a pint of
whiskey in my pocket.'"[22]

Instead of genes or culture, Bergman pointed to bordertown commerce and settler law. He explained that the percentage of Navajos who suffered from alcohol abuse was no higher than the percentage of non-Native
alcoholics, but the law forced Navajo drinking into spaces where it came to
be perceived as a pathology. Public drunkenness on the reservation came
with a five-day jail sentence, but possession of alcohol on the reservation
came with a sentence of sixty days in jail and a $180 fine.[23] As Bergman ex-
plained it, "the safest way to bring home a fifth of whiskey was in the stomach." Navajos who had too much to drink at a bar often drove home along
Highway 264. As a result, and as if by design, the highway that passed the
Navajo Inn recorded the highest fatality rate from traffic accidents on any
highway in the entire state. In a two-year period in the late 1960s, twenty
people were killed and ninety-one injured along a sixteen-mile stretch of
the road. Many of those killed were found within a one-mile stretch of the
Navajo Inn. Nearly forty people died of alcohol-related accidents in one
three-year period in the 1970s. This was law and its enforcement, not pathology, and it was lethal.

Gallup looked more like the concentration camps that Louis patrolled
in Salzburg than the "Indian Capital of the World" touted by the Gallup
Chamber of Commerce. Just shy of 80,000 people lived on the Navajo

Nation in 1960. Between 1958 and 1960, Navajo police arrested just under 25,000 people on alcohol-related charges.[24] By the time Larry graduated from high school in 1971, Navajo police were making 500–700 arrests per month on various liquor violations on the reservation. The year before they left Bayard for Gallup, Gallup built the largest drunk tank in the United States—4,800 square feet—and thereafter, each night, sent its cops out onto the streets to fill it with Navajos, drunk or not. In the poem "Grants to Gallup, New Mexico," Acoma Pueblo poet Simon Ortiz writes that the cops "wear riot helmets, 357 magnums and smirks, you better not be Indian."[25] In 1979, Gallup cops arrested 26,000 people, more than 90 percent of whom were Navajo.[26]

If people didn't die in auto accidents, they died alone in ditches and alleys and parking lots. More than 170 Navajo men and women died from "exposure" between 1958 to 1967, a catchall term that came to describe the cause of death of almost any Native person mysteriously found dead in Gallup.[27] But there was nothing mysterious about it. Drunk drivers ran them over. Sober drivers killed drunk pedestrians. Vigilantes beat them to death in what was called "Indian rolling," a blood sport that often included mutilation. Their bodies would be found in arroyos and alleyways, and since autopsies were rare many of the dead were said to have died of "exposure." Larry took pictures of all of this. He joined petitions, solicited elected officials, and proposed solutions. There was too much money to be made, though, so they refused. And besides, they were always quick to point out, it wasn't as if the problem was Gallup's alone. Even on the reservation, misery took its toll. But the misery on the reservation was also a function of profiteering by non-Natives. Anyone interested in locating the origins of Gallup's anti-Indian political economy could find it on the reservation too, where traders first learned how to weaponize credit. Larry learned this lesson after his parents divorced in 1972 and he spent his summers at Mexican Springs on the reservation.

◀━━━━▶

Louis and Lillian divorced the same year Larry graduated from high school. Larry moved to Albuquerque to enroll in classes at the University of New

Mexico (UNM), where he majored in political science with plans to go to law school. Lillian found a house in Gallup. Other than Erika and Donald, everyone else moved with Louis to Mexican Springs on the reservation. Larry returned to Mexican Springs the summer after his first year in college. Lillian helped him buy a two-door Plymouth so he could get a job washing dishes at a restaurant in Ya-ta-hey.

In his first year at UNM, he joined the KIVA Club, a Native-led student group, where he met other young, Native students. He returned to Gallup in the summer of 1972 and joined a summer youth program put on by a group called Southwestern Indian Development (SID) that was held at the Gallup Indian Community Center. It changed the course of his life. He found Native mentors and met other young Navajo activists and organizers and learned about life on the reservation, where the problems he thought unique to Gallup were just as common, particularly among the many trading posts.

If Southwestern Indian Development is remembered for anything, it is the research it conducted on the trading-post economy. There was little difference between the trading posts of the late 1800s and the ones Larry found when he moved to Mexican Springs. When his father grew up on the reservation, Navajo men and women relied on trading posts to sell wool or lamb, buy food, get mail, pump gas, send a telegraph, use a phone, or even find a job. There were only around a dozen or so trading posts scattered throughout the 25,000-square-mile reservation at that time. By the 1970s, there were nearly 150 trading posts operating under licenses issued by the Bureau of Indian Affairs (BIA), not the Navajo Nation. As in Louis's youth, they held a monopoly on all wholesale, retail, pawn, and credit business on the reservation. Other than a few Navajo-owned cooperatives, trading posts owned by non-Native traders dominated economic life on the reservation. This domination was partly a product of a vast, and largely roadless, reservation. In Louis's youth, up until the 1970s, personal vehicles were rare. Even with a car or truck, travel was difficult. There were few roads, and even fewer paved roads. And every road was often impassable in winter. Living in some of the more remote areas of the reservation was like being marooned on a deserted island. Some trading posts were fifty or even more than a hundred miles from another post. These factors locked people into the nearest trading post and, as Larry learned, traders developed retail, credit, and lending practices that further trapped people in endless cycles of debt.

Southwestern Indian Development was among the first Native-led groups to confront the trading-post economy. In the late 1960s, SID developed a summer program that offered young, Native college-age students an opportunity to examine bordertown violence and economic exploitation. In the summer of 1969, nine community college students took part in the SID summer program directed by SID leaders Charley John and Peterson Zah. The team of student-researchers, which included Gloria Hale-Showalter, Larry Foster, Lorene Ferguson, Michael Benson, Gloria Benson, and GloJean Todacheene, fanned out across the central and eastern part of the reservation to conduct a study of the trading-post economy that would result in a report they called *Traders on the Navajo Reservation: A Report on the Economic Bondage of the Navajo People.*

All summer long, they inspected stores, interviewed traders, and talked to Navajo customers. They analyzed credit agreements and pawn practices, and they compared prices among the posts. They interviewed lawyers, social workers, tribal and BIA officials. "Anglos, billing themselves as Indian experts, for the past century got together and decided Indian policy," they wrote in the foreword.[28] Their report would examine the most enduring legacy of this colonial Indian policy: the trading-post economy, an economy they called a "powerful Anglo intrusion." Their study concluded that the lucrative non-Native-owned trading posts all engaged in deceptive, abusive, and often illegal practices designed to convert Navajos into "prisoners."[29] Their findings infuriated the students, and so they decided to present them to the Navajo Trading Post Committee, but the committee wouldn't even read their report. "They looked at these young people," Peterson Zah would say years later, "and they said that these are just young, radical, college-educated kids."[30] The students then took their findings to an official at the Bureau of Indian Affairs who "brushed that aside and in so many words told the students that they didn't have any basis to make these kinds of charges and complaints."[31] Frustrated, the students contacted the Federal Trade Commission, which agreed to hold a formal investigation by the US Federal Trade Commission (FTC) in 1971. The FTC subpoenaed the BIA area director and tribal officials. Many expected the FTC would blunt or possibly even contradict SID's findings, but the FTC's investigation, and its 1973 report, confirmed everything the students said. The trading-post industry, according to the FTC, was an industry based on "formidable and abusive trade practices" by traders with enormously profitable stores where, by virtue of BIA regulations and licenses, Navajos were literally "compelled to shop."[32]

When Larry first moved to Mexican Springs, he might have found the trading posts familiar. They operated more like the company stores of his youth in Santa Rita than the cash businesses in Gallup where he went to high school. Most traders refused to take cash payment for goods and instead extended credit based on an individual customer's anticipated annual income. Customers would then purchase goods on credit at the post throughout the year and then reconcile the debt at the end of the year when they brought in their wool or lamb to sell. This locked consumers into one store. "Since a trading post will generally extend credit only if it is assured of gaining control over the Navajo's check, the customer can establish an account at only one trading facility."[33] They couldn't shop elsewhere for better prices or find better buyers for wool or lamb. They had no choice but to accept the trader's price—both for the goods they bought throughout the year and the products they sold at the end of the year. Most traders marked up everything they sold, sometimes by as much as 125 percent over wholesale prices.

By the time Larry moved to Mexican Springs, the entire trading-post economy was in the midst of a restructuring. When Louis left for war, the majority share of household income on the Navajo reservation still came from stock raising. By the time Larry moved to Mexican Springs, however, decades of BIA-forced grazing reductions had transformed the economy. Nearly every reservation household owned a truck, and more than 90 percent relied on allotment checks, retirement income, or other government payments, instead of lamb and wool sales.[34] Traders now competed with bordertown grocers, merchants, and pawnbrokers. But traders had a built-in advantage. Each trader was also a banker and an employment agent for the railroads and the firefighting jobs. Trading posts were the only place to make a phone call, find gas for the truck, and send and receive mail. Traders manipulated these roles, particularly the role of postmaster, as a way to outcompete their new bordertown competitors. Since income was based on government checks, traders no longer extended credit based on estimated, annual, agricultural income. Instead, they just opened the mail to find out how much each government check provided, and on what day of the month it arrived.[35] With this information, traders revised their credit business. Out went the long-term credit arrangements based on un-predictable annual wool and lamb sales, in came high-interest, short-term credit terms based on the *exact* monthly household income a customer received from a government check. If you received a one-hundred-dollar check each month, the trader forced you to sign the check over to him, and then extended you a one-hundred-dollar credit for the month. The arrangement, however, came with an undisclosed interest rate, which meant you could never pay off your debt because the trader manipulated the credit into the red each month, which was the whole point. The FTC called this tactic "credit saturation" whereby the interest that accrued on a line of credit always exceeded monthly income, no matter what or how much you purchased. Even if a customer spent less than their monthly check, they were still trapped in perpetual debt because traders only re-funded money in store script.[36] The result of credit saturation, as a lawyer who represented Navajo consumers explained, was "a state of economic bondage."[37] By the time Larry moved to Mexican Springs, trading-post sales were based almost entirely—more than 90 percent—on this high-in-terest, short-term form of credit.[38]

The students from SID and investigators from the FTC heard stories from customers about traders withholding their checks in the mail until they agreed to credit terms they were not allowed to know in advance. "If the Navajo insists on obtaining his check, he may be confronted with threats of withdrawn credit" from the only store within a day's drive.[39] Some trad-ers made reluctant Navajos sign over their checks for store credit by force.[40] Both SID and the FTC struggled to find terms to describe these new credit relations. They called it extortion, debt peonage, credit saturation, and eco-nomic bondage. According to SID and the FTC, the trading-post indus-try duped, cheated, and gouged their customers on the way to over twenty million dollars in annual revenues, with individual posts ranging in sales volume from $100,000 to more than $500,000 per year.[41]

The FTC used the word "unconscionable" to describe nearly every part of the trading-post business. Substandard goods sold at "unconscionable" prices, purchased with credit at "unconscionable interest rates" that led to "unconscionable windfalls" in trading-post profits. The young Navajo SID researchers found rotten meat and moldy vegetables measured for sale on rigged scales.[42] They found cats curled up on meat counters, dogs relieving themselves on bags of flour stacked on the floor. They found fly-covered vegetables and goats wandering aisles. Sale items were routinely displayed out of reach to customers in a bullpen behind counters where most goods were unavailable for inspection. Sour milk sold at prices "consistently and excessively high throughout the reservation."[43] Navajos waited in long lines for hours to buy just the simplest item. Living on the reservation was like living in occupied Salzburg after the war, but without the black market.

It was almost impossible for Navajos to protect or defend themselves from traders. Some traders kept fraudulent books and added to credit balances arbitrarily. Despite a law that required receipts for all trading-post transactions, few traders complied. At the end of the month, if a trader said a customer still owed money, a customer had no receipts against which to compare to the trader's fake or inflated charges on their credit account.[44] The SID researchers found Navajo customers often fearful to complain about this. How would they get their check? Some were unaware they could refuse trader demands to sign over their check. Traders bullied some and convinced others that they were "doing them a favor by allowing them a trade slip or a few dollars cash whenever their welfare check comes in."[45] Some traders threatened violence when the questions started.

Traders extended these practices to every exchange in order to "manipulate all monetary transactions."[46] Traders, having converted Navajo income into debt, also manipulated the squeeze this debt relation placed on Navajo household income in order to generate even more revenue through their pawn business. With their income forcibly converted into trading-post credit, and thus debt, some Navajos regularly pawned their possessions to get the cash they needed to service their ever-growing trading-post debt just to have the "opportunity" to buy food. But traders had designed their credit arrangements in order to produce this circumstance. They trapped customers in debt, forced them to pawn goods in order to service that debt, and then refused to allow customers to redeem pawned items unless all "unrelated" credit accounts were discharged. This was true even if all payments had been made before the pawn redemption date. The FTC called this "pawn hostaging," and it was ingeniously evil. It went something like this: a trader tells a customer in the middle of the month that they've used their entire line of credit. There's nothing left of their check, they have no buying power at all, with the interest still accruing on their account. They're in the negative and getting deeper. The customer, with no other options, pawns a treasured family heirloom with the trader, who is of course also a pawn dealer. The customer uses the pawn payment, which comes to them not in cash but in the form of another line of credit, to buy the food and supplies they and their family need. The customer plans to use their next monthly check to pay back the pawn loan and redeem their family heirloom. This isn't ideal. They'll have to tighten their belt next month because they need part of their income to redeem their pawned item. They'll have to live on a reduced income for the month, but at least they won't lose their treasured family heirloom. On the first of the month, when their check arrives, they find the trap the trader set for them. The pawn agreement includes a stipulation, usually a secret provision, that prohibits the customer from discharging their pawn debt until after first discharging their credit debt. They can't use their allotment check, in other words, to pay off their pawn loan until after they pay off their other debt.

The phrase the researchers used to describe this, "pawn hostaging," perfectly describes the practice. Customers pay a ransom, but some traders never intend to return the pawned item.[47] Even if a customer somehow found the money and made each hostage payment before a pawn redemption date, traders just declared an item lost and refused to reimburse or replace it.[48] One woman found her "lost" pawned jewelry around the neck of a relative. Another found her "lost" pawn sitting on a shelf in a private walk-in storage room.[49] The Bureau of Indian Affairs made all of this possible. The BIA licensed traders, but no BIA agent ever took action on any of the many complaints lodged against the traders. They didn't even inspect the stores.[50] And none of these practices violated a single term of the traders' agreement with the BIA, because the BIA "never bothered to write the regulations for traders" in the first place.[51]

Until SID revealed the full scale and scope of trading-post credit practices, Navajos were on their own dealing with traders, a merchant class that planted hidden traps all along the escape route out of debt peonage. The best escape route out of debt required avoiding trading posts entirely, which meant regular trips into Gallup. But even the ability to make this choice was itself a trap. You needed a truck to make Gallup an alternative to the trading post, but this meant buying a truck from one of the car dealers in Gallup. Few Navajos had the down payment to get a loan for a truck good enough to survive the rough roads and long travel on the Navajo Nation. It was illegal for a dealer to give a customer a second loan to use as a down payment, but they did it anyway because they knew it meant they could repossess the truck. A lawyer named Al Taradash, who worked with DNA People's Legal Services (Dinébe'iiná Náhiiłna be Agha'diit'ahii), a legal aid office that provided free legal services to low-income Navajos, defended dozens of Navajos in civil and criminal cases. "I had a client who kept meticulous records. Based upon what he showed me, he paid off the truck and should've had a title. Instead, his car had been repossessed." The dealer just repossessed the truck after the customer made all the payments for the second loan because he assumed the man hadn't been keeping records and couldn't prove anything.

Regular travel into Gallup meant dealing with police and judges, which was like risking being sold down the river every weekend. "The long-time superior court judge in Holbrooke, Arizona, would sentence Navajo guys to the maximum jail time for public drunkenness. During the day they'd rent them out to work at the Mormon church to repair and paint." The Magdalena magistrate "would arrest Navajo men on public drunkenness and then rent them out to white ranchers."[52]

No one could avoid Gallup entirely. When their children were sick or needed a checkup, they had to travel into town for the Gallup Indian Medical Center, where doctors conducted human trials on Navajo children. They rarely sought consent from parents to do this, worried that it would just "confuse the parents." Moreover, since the Indian Health Service (IHS) was "acting as legal guardian for the children while they attended the boarding schools . . . consent was not required." While medical researchers were conducting medical tests on Navajo children, doctors with the IHS were conducting forced sterilizations on Navajo women. In the first three years after a 1973 federal court–ordered moratorium on sterilizations, IHS doctors sterilized more than three thousand Native women between the ages of fifteen and forty-four.[53]

◄•••••►

Many of the same people who started Southwestern Indian Development also founded a group called Indians Against Exploitation (IAE). Nancy Pioche, a Navajo woman from Farmington, directed the SID summer program the summer of 1972, the year Larry joined. She brought Larry to the Gallup Indian Community Center and introduced him to activists there. The IAE, just like SID, used the center for its offices. It would be his introduction to Navajo political organizing. He began spending most of his time there. "He was always the first to show up at meetings, doing all the chores no one wanted, emptying trash, running the ditto machine, being the first to distribute leaflets."[54] He joined the IAE coordinating committee and this, combined with his experience at SID and the many years he'd spent educating himself about Gallup's alcohol industry, radicalized him. It wasn't just alcohol, and it wasn't just Gallup. The bar owners, art and pawn traders, liquor distributors, and restauranteurs were also the city councilors and the county commissioners and the local judges. They worked in the law offices, held seats on all the commissions, and ran all the civic organizations. The Gallup-McKinley County Chamber of Commerce used "Yeis," the Navajo word for deities or holy ones, as the name for its "goodwill ambassador group." Local white business owners would wear traditional Navajo clothes, call themselves "Yeis" and play Indian in Santa Fe while lobbying for more money from the state legislature to lure tourists to Gallup.

The Indian Communicty Center had become a hub of Navajo activism. Larry, overnight, found himself among an entire generation of young, committed Navajos. Around this time, in 1972, Emmett Garcia created the Gallup Interagency Alcoholism Coordinating Committee in order to apply for federal funds for an alcohol treatment center in Gallup. He put himself in charge of the committee. The long-time director of the Indian Community Center, Herbert Blatchford, couldn't hide his contempt.

"The city uses the Indian's name to secure federal funds," but past efforts have proven that Gallup "is incapable of handling an alcoholism program." They only arrest, incarcerate, and scapegoat Navajos, and all for profit. Blatchford noted that Garcia came from a long line of traders and profiteers. It had been Garcia's father, Ernest, an Indian trader from Mexican Springs, of all places, who'd started the Navajo Inn, and Garcia continued the family tradition. "You have come here only to take something from us," Blatchford told Garcia.[55] Garcia hated the Indian Community Center, that "hot bed" of Indian militancy, as he called it. Since he was being accused of taking things, he took Blatchford's job. Pauline Sice, a Creek woman who'd grown up in Gallup, replaced Blatchford, but she continued to let SID and the IAE use the center for organizing and training. Larry met other young Navajo activists who worked there, like Michael Benson and Mitch Fowler, who recruited him to the campaign to shut down the Gallup Inter-Tribal Ceremonial.

◄■■■■■►

The Gallup Inter-Tribal Ceremonial infuriated young Navajo organizers and activists, who began staging protests against the ceremonial in 1969. They despised its commercialization of Navajo culture and tradition. They detested the fact that the sacred Navajo winter dance, Yei Bi Chei, was performed in the summer and for tourists. They hated the ceremonial association, a Chamber of Commerce–controlled, quasi-state agency that had long ignored Navajo interests and had blocked Native involvement in planning for the ceremonial. Of the twelve board members of the ceremonial association, eleven were white, male business owners in Gallup.[56] Over the years, the ceremonial had grown into the largest tourist event in New Mexico, drawing thousands of tourists each year and generating millions of dollars in revenue, all of which lined the pockets of the same people who profited from liquor sales and Indian trading, and the "white-owned hotels, and the white-owned restaurants."[57] At their first protest, in 1969, a small group of young activists leafleted and held a silent vigil. Police responded by arresting the nineteen-year-old Benson and his sister Elva. In 1970, the protest expanded to include American Indian Movement (AIM) activists who'd been part of the occupation of Alcatraz. They came to Gallup and, along with Indians Against Exploitation (IAE), picketed and briefly occupied the ceremonial offices. The FBI monitored the protests and local agents sent briefs and reports to Washington about young Navajo "militants" throwing a Molotov cocktail at the Chamber of Commerce building in Gallup and painting the words "Honkie Ceremonial" in red across the doors and walls of the National Guard Armory.[58]

The ceremonial remained IAE's primary target in 1972 when Larry joined the coordinating committee. The previous year's protest, in August 1971, had been a "silent, almost funereal march," and some members of IAE had grown frustrated with their lack of success in ending the event.[59] Fowler called an IAE meeting in early August to plan that year's protest. They invited Phil Loretto, who'd been part of a successful campaign to shut down the Flagstaff Pow Wow the previous year. A small group sat around a table at the Indian Community Center, discussing a possible petition, a march, and what they should include in their press release. Larry had other ideas. "There's only one entrance into the Ceremonial," he pointed out. "What if we position ourselves on the hill above the entrance and light car tires on fire and roll them down toward the entrance. Others could call in bomb threats at the same time." Loretto suggested they act provocatively, but they needed to be careful. "They'll just shoot us," he said. They decided to issue a warning instead. They used a statement they'd used first in 1969 on leaflets. Larry printed hundreds of them on the mimeograph machine. "When our Grandfathers had guns," it began, "there were no ceremonials controlled by white people and our culture was not a commodity."

They held a press conference mostly in Navajo, which included long speeches by medicine men on the sacrilege of holding the Yei Bi Chei dance. They planned a silent protest outside the gates of the ceremonial. An IAE member named John Redhouse, a young Navajo activist from Farmington, wrote out a series of demands. In the preamble to their demands, Redhouse referenced a study that "concluded that over 72 percent of all Gallup's business transactions and trade activities was done with local Indians," which Redhouse thought was too conservative. He revised it up to 80 percent to account for the total control Gallup held over Navajo commerce. "The only reason Gallup exists," Redhouse explained, "is because of local Indian trade and commerce."[60] The ceremonial, according to IAE, was a celebration of their economic domination. Larry and John Redhouse met with Emmett Garcia in his mayor's office and gave him their list of demands. "Leaning back in his oversized chair, the arrogant mayor," according to Redhouse, "refused to consider" any of them. These "are rather late and rather ridiculous," he said, dismissing them.[61] They met next with the ceremonial director, who also refused their demands. The ceremonial, under the control of white businessmen, was a "a model of white efficiency," he explained, which "would suffer in the hands of the Indians. Have you ever seen an Indian-run fair" he told a reporter.[62] The mayor convinced the governor to place the National Guard on standby. Local merchants asked the district attorney under what conditions they could shoot people. He cautioned them to "keep their shots low."[63]

Suddenly, Larry's burning tire idea didn't seem so extreme. While an official protest played out at the ceremonial site, with leafleteers, a silent protest march, and speakers with a bullhorn at the entrance to the ceremonial, a separate more militant action took place—"a secret underground guerilla resistance movement quietly went into action. A direct action here and a direct hit there—some reported, some not—took place during the next four 'frenzied' days and nights and in the end, the shock troops of IAE and AIM had succeeded in physically preventing the scheduled performance of the Navajo Yei-Bi-Chei dance."[64]

Larry felt energized by the protest. The following week he would return to Albuquerque to start his sophomore year at UNM, and he planned to link his activism in Gallup to his work in Albuquerque with the KIVA Club. He'd grown close with Phil and Darlene Loretto. He spent as much time with them at their cabin in Window Rock as he did at the Indian Community Center. He was there the night of August 19, 1972, talking with Phil and Darlene about their plans for the fall semester. The day before, lawyers representing six plaintiffs filed a class action lawsuit against the Navajo Inn. It was a good night.

Sometime after 2:00 a.m., Larry left Window Rock to drive home to Mexican Springs. He may have been thinking about the lawsuit and IAE's planned campaign against Garcia as he drove. Along a sharp curve in the road between Gallup and Gamerco, out of the dark, as if conjured there, a woman wearing torn clothes appeared in the road. He swerved the Plymouth to avoid her and slammed his brakes, but the force of the car threw her from the road. When he came to a skidding stop, Larry leaped from the car and found her—he would learn later that she was a young Navajo woman named Doris Brown—near a culvert, unconscious, her clothes and shoes scattered everywhere around her. He couldn't tell if she was breathing. He saw a light on in a house nearby, so he picked her up and placed her in the back of his car and drove toward the house. He knocked and a woman answered, but she wouldn't let him in and wouldn't let him use the phone.[65] The woman told him that a cop lived in Gamerco, and he should find that house. Larry took off and decided to take a shortcut to Gamerco—every second counted—so he veered off the road directly through the Gamerco wash, but his wheels sank into the soft sand. He was forced to abandon his car with Brown in it. He ran to the house of the cop the woman told him about. It was 5:00 a.m. by then and Oscar Frietze, a New Mexico state patrolman, answered the door. Larry told him he'd hit a woman on the road. He told the cop that maybe she'd been attacked and was running from her assailants when he hit her. Maybe that explained her clothes. Larry ran back to the car while Frietze called for an ambulance. When Larry returned to the car, another patrolman, Darnell Austin, was already there. Larry explained to Austin that he'd tried to flag down a car but gave up when no one stopped, and he put Brown in the back seat before driving to find help. Frietze arrived, and he and Austin found Brown in the back of Larry's car—the "alleged death car" as the *Gallup Independent* would call it in an editorial that ran days after the accident. Austin said he found an empty beer can on the floor of the back seat. He said Larry refused a sobriety test. He arrested him for possession of alcohol as a minor, for driving while intoxicated, and for leaving the scene of the accident involving a death. Months later, after a conviction, after a reversal, after new lawyers, after a new trial, after a hung jury, after the prospect of another trial, Larry would ask his attorney why they were doing this to him. "There's no way the DA's gonna let a Navajo kid *not* go to jail."[66]

This was Gallup, self-proclaimed "Indian Capital of the World," a machine carefully calibrated to kill or incarcerate Navajos.

Larry Casuse, March 1, 1973

"This town wants blood, Indian blood."
—Victor Cutnose

Wednesday, February 28, 1973

Larry meets Phil and Darlene Loretto at the Gallup Indian Community Center early in the morning. He'd come back to Gallup the previous Sunday, exhausted. The death of Doris Brown six months earlier still haunted him, his friends would later say. They would explain to the many reporters who would ask that he "felt moral guilt" for killing her.[1] He'd grown convinced that he'd be convicted and eventually sent to jail. Those closest to him said he'd come to see as failures what others saw as successes. They'd shut down the Yei Bei Che dance but not the hated ceremonial. In the months that followed the ceremonial, through the long, cold winter, more people died outside the Navajo Inn and more people died along Highway 264. Larry had killed one of those people and so instead of Garcia facing justice it would be Larry who would stand before a judge and jury.

Larry asks Phil and Darlene if they'll drive him back to Albuquerque. He's attending a conference, he says. He plans to meet someone with proof about Garcia and his organization, he tells them. "What organization?" asks Phil. "I have a plan," Larry says. "I'll meet you back here tomorrow morning."

They make the two-hour drive east to Albuquerque and when they arrive they stop first at the KIVA Club office on the UNM campus. Larry had become the president of the KIVA Club at the start of the academic year in August, just weeks after the death of Doris Brown. He'd transformed the campus group that semester from one that held an annual campus pow-wow and operated like any other campus student group to a hub of Native activism. The KIVA Club became "increasingly active in native issues both on and off campus."[2] He'd spent the fall semester attending meetings with university administrators in which he complained about the depiction of Native people and culture in textbooks and in exhibits at the anthropology museum. He began sending aggressive letters to shopkeepers on KIVA Club letterhead demanding apologies for their use of offensive Native imagery in advertisements and displays. These weren't polite requests. To one he wrote, we "will work to put you and your likes in your place, which really would be nowhere."[3]

They're driving Phil and Darlene's tiny car and they stop on campus where Larry runs into the KIVA Club campus office on Las Lomas to get his checkbook. Then Phil and Darlene drop him off at the house west of downtown that he rents with three roommates. Larry glances at his checkbook register. He has $63.39 in his account. Like everyone he knows, he is broke.

They'd raised money the previous December for KIVA Club by selling luminarias in their neighborhoods and on campus, but the money had run out. During summer and fall, they'd raised money for IAE by selling "Know Your Rights" pamphlets at fairs and conferences. "I'd met with the Justice Department," Loretto explained, "and they gave me this booklet called 'Know Your Rights.' I asked if I could have six thousand of them. They said, 'Are you kidding?' Everywhere we went, we sold them for one dollar so that we could pay for our gas at fairs, meetings, everywhere." They'd put nearly seventy thousand miles on Phil and Darlene's Volkswagen since the summer, driving to and from "Albuquerque, Gallup, Flagstaff, Farmington, Shiprock, all over. We were trying to find as many Native American functions so we could get in front of people and talk. Colleges, chapter houses, meetings with school boards."[4]

Though they'd raised a lot of money, all of it went to IAE or the KIVA Club. Larry had a job over the summer, but not during the semester. He had classes, the KIVA Club, and IAE. On top of that he'd been making trips back and forth to Gallup to see his brothers and sisters, to meet with his lawyer, and to appear in court. He'd been arraigned on September 14 the previous year, but the semester had started by then so he couldn't go. He had class and he'd totaled his car in the accident that killed Brown. His Navajo Legal Aid attorneys entered a not guilty plea on his behalf. The judge set the trial date for November 3, 1972.

He'd borrowed a car that previous Sunday, February 25, to drive back to Gallup. John Redhouse rode with Larry for part of the ride. "I had run out of operating money and was broke," Redhouse recalled. Larry stopped along the interstate to let Redhouse out. Larry continued on to Gallup while Redhouse hitchhiked north to Farmington. They'd just met the previous summer but had grown close in the many months they'd spent organizing marches, collecting signatures for petitions, traveling to conferences and fairs, and meeting with tribal officials. They were an odd couple. Larry, short and stocky, wore steel-rimmed glasses and a rolled, red bandanna around his head; Redhouse, tall and lanky, kept a thin mustache and goatee and often wore a black suit—the preacher suit, Loretto called it—and carried a briefcase. They said goodbye along the interstate and never saw each other again.

After dropping Larry off, Phil and Darlene head back to Gallup. Larry finds Robert Nakaidinae in the apartment. Robert, a young Navajo artist from Fort Defiance, first met Larry the previous summer in Gallup during the ceremonial protests. He'd just graduated from art school in Los Angeles and had come to New Mexico to visit his brother in Santo Domingo. "I had all my equipment with me, and I was planning on traveling around to paint," but Robert had car problems so plans changed. He lingered in New Mexico, and eventually he stopped by the KIVA Club to say hello to friends because he "was only associating with Indians at the time." He found Larry there. "I stayed at his place" the entire month of February, he would explain later, where they spent most evenings together talking late into the night. "There were a lot of things going on in the southwest that weren't right for Indian people, and he talked to me about what he'd tried to do. The different petitions and marches he headed and how nothing really came from that. To me, I kind of felt that he was frustrated by it, by what was being done. Nothing was being done the way he wanted it. We just . . . from there we just talked, not of marching or petitioning, by that time he'd already tried all that. There was nothing else that could be done. To me, there's a lot of people who do a lot of talking about doing this or doing that. A lot of Indian people and Chicanos and low-class white people, a lot of people who talk about doing things in a violent manner, but it's all talk."[5]

Robert and Larry leave the house just west of downtown to catch the last day of the National Congress of American Indians' annual American Indian Development Conference held that year in Albuquerque. This was how Larry spent much of his time then, attending conferences, meetings with Native leaders, marching in protests, attending fairs and school events.

In late September of the previous year, almost exactly a month after the death of Doris Brown, Larry joined four other members of the KIVA Club and IAE, including Phil, Darlene, and John Redhouse at the state fair in Albuquerque, where they "set up and manned an information booth at the entrance of the fair's Indian Village."[6] They gave speeches, talked to vendors, and collected signatures from fairgoers on a petition opposing the Gallup ceremonial's planned move to Church Rock. This was just days after his arraignment and Larry didn't talk much. He stayed quiet and kept to the background. This continued the following weekend at the Northern Navajo Nation Fair in Shiprock. His friends would say later that he seemed constantly worried, preoccupied with the looming trial in November.

That October, a caravan of American Indian Movement activists drove through Gallup and Albuquerque as part of the Trail of Broken Treaties trip to Washington, DC. They came in cars and trucks and buses. The KIVA Club, IAE, and the National Indian Youth Council offered them food, supplies, and other support.

Also in October, for some reason, Larry's lawyers waived his right to a jury trial. Maybe they feared an all-white Gallup jury. The judge rescheduled the trial for December 20.

In early November, with the trial more than a month away, Larry went to Seattle with other members of IAE and the KIVA Club to a National Indian Education Association conference. When they returned, they planned an (Un)thanksgiving march against the ceremonial. They issued a press release. "It is time that the Indian stopped the whiteman's holiday!" As they marched, Larry covered stop signs with paper bags on which he'd written, "Thanks for Nothing." The march began with nearly three hundred people at the Indian Village in Church Rock, a proposed permanent ceremonial site. They headed south and west along Route 66 with drums and signs bound for the Gallup offices of the ceremonial, where they planned speeches and a rally, and then on to the Indian Community Center for a feast of mutton stew and fry bread. Motorists shouted anti-Indian epithets at them as they marched. A state cop arrested Diane Beyal, a fourteen-year-old Navajo girl, for handing out leaflets to passersby. Mitch Fowler intervened and the cop arrested him too. After the arrests, the marchers, furious, spontaneously changed the route and marched directly to the Gallup police station. They stood outside shouting at the building and at the cops inside. They demanded the release of their friends. Larry spoke to the press the next day, telling them that "We were armed only with a drum, signs, and our minds against the police force armed with shotguns, pistols, and billy clubs."

Larry and Robert spend all afternoon at the conference in Albuquerque. When it adjourns for the day, they return to Larry's house. There is much to talk about and planning to be done. The Wounded Knee standoff had just started the day before. Hundreds of armed Oglala Lakota AIM members took the Pine Ridge Indian Reservation town of Wounded Knee by force. They'd had enough of the corruption and the violence of the tribal president's private goons. They'd had enough of broken treaties and grinding poverty. They took hostages. They fought the FBI and the other ninety-some cops surrounding them with guns. Larry and Robert agree: this is different. This isn't talk. It's nothing like the conference they'd just left. "Those were our elected leaders," Robert says. "A lot of them were drinking. They weren't doing anything about the problems except talking about them. They used it as a social gathering, we saw nothing coming out of it." Larry shares Robert's frustration. He paces the room. What should we do?

Larry had begun dating a Lakota woman that semester. She worked as a nurse at the Gallup Indian Medical Center. From her he'd learned about the forced sterilization of Native women and girls and the medical tests and operations that doctors conduct on Native children without consent. The tribes and the courts couldn't stop the IHS doctors from any of it. A month earlier, on January 28, 1973, Robert's brother, Michael Upshaw, took up arms with Victor and John Cutnose, two Cheyenne brothers living in Gallup, along with Woody Foster, a young Navajo man from Fort Defiance. They stormed the Gallup Indian Medical Center with guns, knives, firecrackers, and a fake suitcase bomb. During their seven-hour occupation of the hospital, they demanded the dismissal of hospital staff, including doctors, they deemed "disrespectful" to Native people. Larry, who was in Albuquerque when the standoff began, raced back to Gallup. He arrived in the morning after the four men had surrendered to police. He told the press that IAE and the KIVA Club stand with AIM. "If this brands us as militants or radicals," he said, "so be it."[7]

Larry and Robert are tired of talk that leads nowhere. They'd just listened to it all day at the conference. What alternative is there? We could kidnap the president of UNM, one of them says out loud. Or maybe the governor of New Mexico, says the other. No, they decide. If it's anybody, it's got to be Emmett Garcia.

March 1, 1973

Robert isn't certain this is an actual plan, so it surprises him when he wakes up in the morning and finds Larry still pacing the family room. Larry seems calmer than the previous day, as if he'd resolved something during the long night. He tells Robert it's time to leave. They have to make a quick stop, Larry says, and then onto campus, where they plan to find a ride to Gallup.

Few of Larry's friends in KIVA Club or IAE shared his growing frustration. They weren't new to this. They'd spent years organizing against the ceremonial, and they expected a long fight. They had the support of tribal leaders. "We were going to All Indian Pueblo Council. So, we weren't stepping on anyone's feet. We'd always consult the all-Indian council in Santo Domingo," Loretto remembers. John Redhouse and Larry had been meeting with Navajo leaders, who also opposed the ceremonial. Larry thought of his IAE friends as insurgents and their work as radical, even revolutionary, but the reaction they got disappointed him. The newspapers often depicted them as naive. Elected officials in Gallup and Santa Fe often patronized them. Some treated them as reactionaries or even conservatives. A commitment to Native assimilation so structured establishment politics at this time that nearly every non-Native official saw IAE's defense of Native traditions and Native sovereignty as regressive, some even called it racist.

Few non-Native people understood the profound break that IAE's politics represented from previous generations. The young organizers in IAE didn't equate the white world with progress. When they spoke, they didn't speak to non-Natives. They weren't interested in crafting their message to meet non-Native expectations. Calvin Trillin, who'd returned to Gallup to cover the 1972 ceremonial for the *New Yorker*, misunderstood IAE like all the rest. He wrote an essay in which he depicted them as principled but naive and a bit confused. Trillin, the Yale graduate, painted them as elitist in a subtly dismissive way. "A list of Navajos attending decent colleges," he wrote, "could have almost served as the membership list of the anticeremonial organization, called Indians Against Exploitation."[8] These were naive outsiders, he was claiming. The celebrated writer from New York was calling IAE out of touch. Trillin sat among a crowd of reporters at a press conference that IAE held prior to the ceremonial, frustrated that the IAE activists didn't seem to care about reaching him or the other reporters. They think nothing, he wrote, of "stopping a press conference to furnish a lengthy translation to the one older man in the room who speaks only Navajo." Trillin had come all the way from New York with his pen and pad and expected attention, but IAE organizers ignored him at the press conference. They spent their time instead talking to an elderly Navajo man. Even their bumper stickers were in Navajo, Trillin wrote. He expected to find "young militants threatening to disrupt the town" but instead found young Navajo and Pueblo activists completely disinterested in him and all the other reporters, yet thoughtful and respectful to their elders. They would turn their bullhorns and press conferences over to "Navajo medicine men corroborating, with long speeches in Navajo, the claim that the Ceremonial was committing a sacrilege." All of it baffled Trillin. But he was paid to understand things, so he decided that if he didn't understand their politics they must not understand them either. They're just confused about this, he concluded. He watched as tourists wandered away from their protests because "somebody decided to speak in Navajo." Perhaps he expected a progressive version of assimilationist politics; the kind most non-Native liberals supported. Perhaps he expected to find young activists making familiar demands for equality and development. Instead, he found activists who looked past him and made no room for him. They knew something

Trillin never would. What good had come to Native people, after all, by appealing to non-Native political leaders for solutions? They weren't trustworthy. Larry had been born in Santa Rita, where Mexican soldiers and American mercenaries violated a treaty with the Apache before anyone even had a chance to get up from their seat. What good had recognition provided? Who had assimilation benefited? But things were different, IAE reminded everyone in their leaflets, "when our Grandfathers had guns."

It's late morning. Larry and Robert leave the house on foot. They walk to the American Bank of Commerce on Third and Central where Larry writes a check for $63.39 and closes his account. They head to campus. It's later than Larry planned.

After the previous year's ceremonial protests, IAE turned its attention to Emmett Garcia. After the ceremonial, Garcia appointed himself chair of the Gallup Interagency Alcoholism Coordinating Committee. The city that runs on alcohol, and the mayor that profits from it most, wanted millions of dollars to build and run an alcohol treatment facility for Navajos? Redhouse called it "part of a larger hypocrisy which was killing Indian people" in Gallup.[9] They spent early December collecting signatures on a petition to remove Garcia from the post. Larry finished the semester and returned to Gallup. His trial began on December 20, 1972.

Standing trial in Gallup's second-floor McKinley county courtroom is like being prosecuted in the middle of a carefully curated diorama of anti-Indianism. Floor-to-ceiling murals cover each wall, depicting settlers and cavalry officers competing to subdue Navajos rendered in caricature as passive or on the warpath. The last time Larry had found himself there had been the previous year when his parents had divorced. Now, a year later, he sat next to Ellis French, his Navajo Legal Aid lawyer, as they watched Joe Rich, the assistant district attorney, call a parade of witnesses against him. Oscar Frietze, a state cop, testified first. He said that Larry woke him at his Gamerco house at 5:00 a.m. Larry told Frietze that he'd struck a girl on the highway. He thought maybe the girl had been raped or was fleeing somebody or something and had run into the road in front of him because of it. "I was told by Casuse," he testified, "that he thought the girl had been run over twice."[10] Inexplicably, Larry's attorney had no questions. Rich then showed the judge gruesome photos of Brown. Pictures of her blood-covered, half-clothed body, shots of her lying next to a culvert, clothes scattered around her. Again, Larry's lawyer had nothing to say, made no objection. Darnell Austin, another state cop, testified next. He was on duty that morning and got a call at 5:00 a.m. about a pedestrian fatality on the access road to Gamerco. He told the judge he went to the site of the accident but found nothing. He spotted a car a mile away stuck in a wash. "The car was backed into an arroyo," he told the judge, "and could not be moved under its own power." He found the body of Doris Brown in the back seat. Casuse showed up, back from Frietze's house, and found Austin next to the car. Austin told the judge that Casuse had explained to him at the time that he'd tried to flag someone down on the road but no one had stopped, so he placed Brown in the back seat and drove for help. Austin didn't believe him. He testified that Casuse didn't render aid to Brown as the law required. He testified that he didn't believe Casuse drove his car into soft sand while frantically looking for help. He testified that he believed Casuse drove into the wash while looking for somewhere to dispose of the body. The prosecution rested its case. For the defense, French presented none. He called no witnesses. Larry never took the stand, didn't say a word in his defense. Instead, French called all the evidence circumstantial and asked the judge to dismiss the charges. The judge acquitted Larry of two lesser charges but convicted him on the most serious one: leaving the scene of an accident involving death or personal injury. He scheduled the sentencing for January 4.

Larry left the court stunned but somehow kept it together enough to buy Christmas presents for his brothers and sisters that afternoon. He went to his mom's house on Green Street on the east side of Gallup, where they all planned to celebrate Christmas together. He met John Redhouse there a few days later, and they talked about the petition to remove Garcia from the alcohol committee and then watched the Oakland Raiders lose to the Pittsburgh Steelers. On Christmas morning, after presents, Larry wrestled on the floor in front of the tree with a giggling Ursula. Lillian sat on the couch dour faced and watched them. "What are you trying to do, Larry?" she said. "What do you mean?" he asked, but he knew what she meant. His name was constantly in the paper and his mom disapproved of his activism and his politics. "The Indians are going to kill you," she said. "You're going to end up dead."

That night Larry stayed up late with Erika, who'd come back from Albuquerque for Christmas. They drank soda and smoked pot and he told her about a recurring dream he'd been having. He's surrounded by police, he told her. The cops are everywhere. It's loud and bright; all sirens and flashing lights. Suddenly one of the cops grabs him and cuffs his arms behind his back and throws him in a paddy wagon where it's dark and silent; he thinks he's alone. He hears some rustling. His eyes start to adjust to the darkness just as a faint light appears. Somebody has kindled a small campfire on the floor of the paddy wagon. As the light from the fire grows brighter, Larry sees that he's not alone. He's not even in the paddy wagon anymore. He's sitting around a fire and around him are row after row of relatives and elders, all with painted faces turned down, their bodies huddling around and toward the fire. He looks up, over the fire, and one of his relatives looks up directly at him, catching his eye. The man smiles at him and says, "You're going to be OK."

Larry's dreams may be reassuring but life had become a nightmare. He needed a new lawyer. Each Monday in the early 1970s, Navajo men and women crowded into the small waiting room of the DNA People's Legal Services office in Window Rock. The same people who started Southwestern Indian Development started DNA too. They didn't trust the Navajo Legal Aid lawyers, as Larry would learn. They started their own free legal service on the reservation in 1967. They pieced together an office in Window Rock from the discarded parts of other buildings. A hogan for an entryway grafted onto part of an old trailer connected to walls and ceilings made with used adobes and found timber. People came on Mondays because "things happened over the weekend" in Gallup.[11] They came for many reasons. Some looked for a lawyer to represent a son arrested in Gallup. Others came looking for a lawyer to sue a car dealer who'd repossessed their car, or for help dealing with a pawnbroker who'd "lost" their pawn. Some sought help finding a daughter who'd gone missing. A man from Chinle once came on a Monday and told Al Taradash, one of the DNA attorneys, that his wife had just given birth in a hospital. He said he hadn't understood all the requests for insurance by the people at the hospital. "Why do they want my car insurance?" he thought at the time. After the birth, someone came into their room and gave him a bill that he couldn't afford to pay.

When he told them he didn't have the money, they told him his wife and daughter couldn't leave. He went home, he told Taradash, and sold some sheep and then came back two days later with the money, but they told him that the money only covered the two days that he'd been gone. There's another option, they told him. Sign away your custody and we'll erase your debt. Don't worry, they told him, we'll find a good home for the baby. This was the "Chinle Mormon adoption scheme," as Taradash called it. He and another DNA lawyer, Richard Collins, met Larry in a DNA waiting room on a Monday after his conviction. Larry fired his other lawyer and hired DNA instead. Taradash and Collins entered their appearance for Larry the day of the sentencing, January 4, 1973. They petitioned the court for a new trial, and the judge gave them ten days to file a motion. In it they argued in polite legalese that Larry's lawyers had been incompetent. They'd never consulted him. His Navajo Legal Aid lawyer, Ellis French, was not much of a lawyer at all, it seemed, and gave no aid. French prepared no defense, offered no evidence, and cross-examined no witnesses. The same judge who convicted Larry in December granted their January motion for a new trail. He vacated the conviction and scheduled the new trial for Valentine's Day, February 14, 1973.

Larry returned to school for the spring semester and moved into a rented house west of downtown. A week later New Mexico's governor, Bruce King, appointed Emmett Garcia to the board of regents at the University of New Mexico. The nomination infuriated Larry. It was bad enough Garcia was mayor of the City of Exploitation.[12] It was inexcusable that he'd spent a lifetime profiting from Navajo misery through his owner-ship of the Navajo Inn. It was true to form that he defended the ceremonial. It was beyond hypocritical that he'd named himself the director of the al-cohol treatment committee. And for all that, he would be rewarded. Garcia profits from Navajo misery and the white world thanks him for it. And Larry's probably going to jail.

Larry and Robert finally make it to campus. It's early in the afternoon. They need to find a car to get to Gallup, so they walk to a student parking lot on the corner of Girard and Central. It's a gravel lot and there aren't any painted lines marking out the parking spots, so students just park anywhere they want and, as a result, the cars are packed in tight. Larry and Robert find a spot from where they can see the entire lot and crouch between two cars. They watch as a man with a backpack holding a pair of cowboy boots walks toward them. Just as the man arrives at his car and places his boots on the ground to get his keys, Larry stands up and pulls out a pearl-handled .32 Colt automatic pistol. "I didn't know Larry had that," Robert says to himself. The man looks up. Larry points his gun at him. "Don't move."

Delbert Rudy holds out the keys to his Chevy Nova and says, "Take it," but Larry says they're taking him with them. Robert puts the knife he's holding back in his bag and takes out handcuffs. They put Rudy in the back seat and cover him with a blanket. Larry drives to a gas station, then onto the highway, then west for Gallup.

At least it isn't February anymore, that terrible month. It had begun with the governor's nomination of Garcia to the board of regents and all the organizing to oppose it. Then Larry had to travel back to Gallup for his trial on Valentine's Day. On their way into court, Taradash saw Rich, the assistant district attorney and former FBI agent, talking loudly with a witness in the vestibule outside the courtroom. It was the woman to whose house Larry first went looking for help after the accident. "Was Rich coaching his witness?" Taradash wondered? He'd worked in Gallup long enough to know this was bad. He didn't have a good feeling. He knew firsthand that Gallup cops lied in court. He knew from experience that local prosecutors solicited perjured testimony; he'd seen it over and over again. The district attorney relentlessly prosecuted Navajos for even the most trivial offenses. Anti-Indianism permeated both Gallup and the law. Taradash hoped for a hung jury. The trial lasted two days. Larry testified on the second day, breaking down on the stand. His attorneys aggressively cross-examined witnesses, objected to all the hearsay, and pointed out the circumstantial nature of the evidence, all of it. They submitted actual evidence—evidence that Larry had in fact offered aid, as the law required. But this was Gallup, Taradash knew. The jury was composed of people with names like Mamie Houston and David Smith and Marietta Fairchild. They all voted to convict, along with eight others. There was, however, a Navajo woman on the jury, a woman named Marianita Tallbird, and she voted to acquit. She refused to change her vote and finally the judge was forced to declare a mistrial. Before Larry could ask his attorneys what came next, Rich, on his way out

A 1973 photo, used by local newspapers, of Larry testifying in Santa Fe against the appointment of Emmett Garcia as a University of New Mexico regent. Courtesy of Special Collections/Center for Southwest Research (UNM Libraries).

of the courtroom, told Larry that they planned to prosecute him all over again, a third time. "Why are they doing this to me?" Larry asked Taradash. "Because you're Navajo," he told him. The *Gallup Independent* published a picture of Larry standing outside the courtroom next to his lawyer and Phil Loretto. In the photo, Larry, in his red bandanna, looks chiseled out of rock, like the Kneeling Nun come to life. The court initially scheduled a third trail for February 27, but later changed it to late April.

After the trial, on February 20, Larry traveled to Santa Fe to testify against Garcia's appointment to the UNM Board of Regents before the New Mexico Senate Rules Committee. The KIVA Club and IAE rallied outside the Roundhouse, the building that housed the capitol, but only a few went into the meeting, Larry among them. He brought his briefcase full of photos and their petition opposing the nomination. The only person abusing alcohol in Gallup, Larry told them, is Garcia. "Does he not abuse alcohol? Does he not abuse it by selling it to intoxicated persons who often end up in jail or in a morgue from overexposure?" He and another IAE member, Larry Emerson, had developed their own decolonial theory based on conversations with medicine men and Navajo elders. An evil had descended over the land, they concluded, that "began to outweigh the good." This evil arrived when "the whiteman had come." They "brought disease, raped our women, killed our brothers—the animals, murdered our elders, leveled out the vast forests, polluted our rivers, filled our air with chemicals, called us savage, pagans, Indians. The Indian movement was born. It was born because we must once again regain the balance of good and evil." The committee thanked Larry for his testimony and then voted unanimously to approve Garcia's nomination.

The next day, the UNM Student Senate passed a resolution opposing Garcia's appointment. Larry spoke before the vote. "We must ask Emmett Garcia if he can claim to be a human being. Are you a human being? Are you a murderer?"[13] After the vote, they brought out a rag doll that someone had fashioned in the image of Garcia and the students burned Garcia in effigy on the tile floor. "We're worth the dirty tile," one student senator said.

Two days after that, on February 23, the board of regents met on the UNM campus. Larry pushed past the crowd and the other regents and read a statement. People like Garcia "have condoned the murder of our people," he said. He condemned Garcia and demanded they remove him from the board, and then he left. After the meeting, as Garcia was walking to his car, he found a coffin with his name on it in front of the student union building.

They're almost to Gallup. Robert is quiet in the car. He's a little shocked this is all happening. He didn't think they'd actually do it, and he definitely didn't think they'd do it today. Larry, however, is calm and focused. They park in a lot behind city hall. Robert takes the handcuffs off Delbert. They need them for Garcia. They no longer care about Rudy, who turns and runs while Larry and Robert walk to the back entrance of city hall. Robert carries a small homemade explosive with him, "some kind of ball that they'd put gunpower in," that Larry made the night before.

They walk past the waiting room, knock on the mayor's office door, and Pete Derizotis, Gallup's alcoholism coordinator, answers. "You'll have to wait, Larry," he says. "The mayor's in a meeting." Garcia, behind the door, is expecting reporters, so he yells, "Let 'em in," but Larry is already in. He pushes past Derizotis and pulls out his gun. "Stand back, or I'll kill you," he says to Garcia, who is coming out from behind his desk. "Don't do it, Larry," Garcia pleads. Larry keeps the gun pointed at Garcia as he walks around the desk and comes up behind him. Garcia won't stop talking. "Shut up," Larry says, "I don't want to talk to you." A code compliance officer in another room hears loud voices coming from the mayor's office and barges in. Larry turns his head to look when the door opens and Garcia grabs for the gun. They struggle. The gun misfires. Just then the police chief, Manuel Gonzales, bursts into the office, but Robert is waiting for him and demands the gun from his holster. "I'm not giving you a loaded gun," Gonzales says. Robert doesn't care what the police chief wants or doesn't want, and he tells him he better not unload it. But Gonzales ignores him and empties the bullets from his gun onto the floor before Robert can snatch the gun from his hands. He also takes the cartridge belt from the cop's waist.

Robert then cuffs Garcia while Larry keeps his gun pointed at his head. They walk him out of his office, past city employees who stand and watch. After they leave, Gonzales calls the police station from the mayor's office and orders an alert to all units. Larry pushes Garcia out onto the street in front of them. Robert isn't sure where they're going, so he holds the bomb and the chief's gun and follows behind while Larry walks Garcia down the street. Derizotis and four other city employees follow behind at a distance. A cop in a cruiser hears the alert on the radio and also follows Larry and Robert, who walk in the middle of the street. Larry turns onto Route 66. A feeling comes over Garcia. At that moment, he would say later, "I knew I wasn't going to die." The three of them walk past Ivan Stearns, who'd just closed his sporting goods store. Stearns sees the guns and the cops and watches as Larry breaks the glass on the front door of his store with a kick and reaches in and unlocks the door. Once inside, Robert starts barricading the entrance while Larry, still leading Garcia, heads to the back of the store where he starts grabbing rifles and shotguns. He gives one to Robert. Outside the store, three cops holding long rifles take up positions on a nearby roof. Four more stand behind cars in front of Stearns's. Seven others hide in the alley behind the store. Two with what eyewitnesses call sniper rifles crouch beside their cruisers down the street. Gonzales stands in the middle of the road directing traffic.

Robert places his pistol down and reaches for the shotgun Larry holds out to him, but before he can grab it Garcia kicks him in the chest, pushes him, and runs for the door. Robert grabs the shotgun and shoots wildly at Garcia. The glass shatters and the door frame splinters from the buckshot just as Garcia launches himself through it all. He comes flying through the plate class window "as though thrown out" and lands on his face on the sidewalk.[14] Gonzales grabs him and drags him to the side.

Larry comes to the front of the store holding a rifle "not leveled to shoot" when Gonzales shouts "fire" and suddenly the store is engulfed in tear gas, bullets raining down on them.[15] Gonzales shouts again: "Get back. They'll come out shooting." But only police are shooting. Every cop on the scene "started shooting" into the store.[16] For minutes that seemed like hours, they fired into the store, emptying clips, reloading, and firing more. People scatter on the street. Lillian, who doesn't know Larry is even in Gallup, hears the gunfire while waiting in line across the street at the welfare office.

Tear gas starts billowing out of the store. Larry and Robert can hardly see, much less talk. They're coughing from the gas, trying to find their way to safety at the back of the store when suddenly a shot hits Larry below his ribs, knocking him to the ground. Robert turns toward Larry, who's now crawling on the floor, just as another bullet tears into Larry's hip.

They finally find cover in the back of the store and Robert checks Larry's body, finding two bullet wounds. He tells him they should surrender, but Larry says no, he doesn't want to be saved. So, Robert lays beside him, watching him weaken, watching his breathing slow down. Finally, Larry holds out his pistol and asks Robert to shoot him. "I didn't want to shoot him," Robert would say later. "By then there were lots of shots coming in, and the tear gas came in and he finally passed out." Robert starts tossing guns and rifles away from Larry, throwing them toward the front of the store and out the broken door, except "for the .32 he had. Everything else was on the sidewalk."[17] Robert stays crouched down, hiding from the bullets, and makes his way to front of the store. He needs to get Larry out of there, so he stands up in the middle of a barrage of gunfire and walks straight out of the store toward the shooting. "Casuse is hurt," he yells, just as two cops grab him and drag him into a police car.

Gonzales and two other officers rush past Robert and into the store. One carries a shotgun with him. They emerge dragging Larry's body behind them, out onto the sidewalk. Gonzales will claim later that he found Larry dead from a self-inflicted shotgun wound under his chin. The next day the district attorney will tell the press that an autopsy confirms this. The coroner finds powder burns on Larry's chin, consistent with a self-inflicted gunshot wound. Ivan Stearns tells the press that he kept a 20-gauge and 12-gauge shotgun, and a .30-30 Winchester rifle in stock, but the store had no .30-caliber shells, and Larry and Robert didn't use one of the shotguns because they were trying "to use the wrong ammunition."[18] The only working shotgun was the one held by the cop who ran into the store with Gonzales after Robert left.

Someone runs into the welfare office and yells, "That Larry Casuse finally got what he deserved!" Lillian, frantic, tries to leave but a social worker won't let her, and instead restrains her. Two women put her in a room and keep her away from the street. You don't want to see that, they tell her.

Phil Loretto is at the Indian Community Center waiting for Larry to come back from Albuquerque when someone runs in and yells, "They just shot Larry, they just shot Larry!" Phil just starts running. He runs from the Indian Community Center across the railroad tracks, and he gets to the sporting goods store in time to see the cops dragging Larry's body out of it.

A red-headed cop sees Phil coming and yells, "God damn you motherfuck-ing Indians," and throws a punch, but Phil ducks and instead of punching Phil the cop's hand slams into a brick wall. "You're going in too, Loretto," another cop says as they arrest him. "Riot control," the cop says. Phil is booked and eventually placed in a cell next to Robert. "What happened?" he asks him. "They shot him," Robert says. "I heard he committed suicide," Phil tells him. "No," says Robert, "they shot him."

Ursula, Joe, and Daschija are playing on a neighbor's teeter-totter across the alley from their mom's place on Green Street, chewing on cherry candy. They eat all the candy they have, and Ursula asks Daschija to go get more. She runs into the house and finds the phone ringing. "Larry's been shot," a voice tells her on the other end.

Nijoni is playing pool with friends at a billiard hall when someone tells her that her brother's been shot. She drops the cue and runs out the door. When she gets to Stearns's she sees Larry's body on the sidewalk. "That's my brother," she yells. She sees a blanket in a truck parked nearby, grabs it, and covers Larry. They tell her she can't stay, she has to go.

With Nijoni gone, the cops, like scalp hunters, take trophies. They cradle their rifles and shotguns on their hips and pose over Larry's body, some with serious looks, others smiling broadly. A photographer from the *Gallup Independent* takes their picture over and over again. Trophies of dead Indians. Like the presidios and churches that ran Apache scalps up flag poles 150 years earlier, a framed photo of Larry's body surrounded by his killers will hang above the bar at the Fraternal Order of Police for years while off-duty cops get drunk looking at it.

Erika is driving downtown to meet Nijoni at the pool hall when she hears sirens. An ambulance passes and she sees someone covered in an Indian blanket through the window. She parks near city hall and gets out, no idea what's going on. She sees her sister Nijoni walking toward her, cry-ing. "What's wrong?" she asks. "What happened?" "They killed Larry?"

The two run back to the car and drive to the hospital, where a doctor asks if they're family and if so can they identify the body. They're brought into a room where they see Larry under a blood-soaked blanket. Erika can't bring herself to look, so Nijoni does it. "Yes," she says. "That's my brother." As they're leaving, a doctor gives Erika a box of Larry's belongings. It holds his glasses, a ring, and a notebook. The hospital sends Larry's body to the mortuary. Erika wears Larry's ring. Ursula, who drops out of school after police kill her brother, starts wearing Larry's steel-rimmed glasses. She will spend the next decade being harassed by cops because she's the sister of Larry Casuse. And the cops will spend the next decade being harassed by Ursula, who eventually forces them to take that damn photo off the wall above the cop bar.

Larry's brother Donald works at a supermarket in Gallup delivering meat to restaurants in a refrigerated truck. He works with Garcia's son, Ernie. Donald's on a delivery that afternoon, driving down to Route 66, when he comes to a police roadblock—chaos downtown, people everywhere. He turns around but can't find a way to make his delivery, so he gives up and goes back to the grocery store. His boss sees him pull up and comes rushing out of the store hollering "Give me your apron. Your brother's been shot!"

Donald jumps in his own car and drives back downtown, still chaos, still people everywhere, sirens going off, cops on every corner, it seems. He gets around the police blockades by driving the wrong way on one-way streets. People are yelling at him. He still can't get downtown. He thinks, there's only one mortuary in town, so I'll go there. He bangs on the big back door of Rollie's Mortuary, yelling, "Who killed my brother?" The chief of police or someone like that opens the door, but he's not sure. It's all a blur. Donald pushes past, still yelling. "Who killed my brother?" He sees Larry in the huge back room of the mortuary, laying in his own blood on a table. All his clothes still on, dead. The police chief is yelling at Donald. "You can't be here. Get out of here."

Al Taradash is in the library at the DNA office preparing for Larry's retrial when he hears on the radio that Larry and Robert kidnapped the mayor. He jumps in his car and races toward Gallup but hits a roadblock. Word spreads at UNM. Dozens of students crowd around a radio at the KIVA Club office listening for updates.

Lillian finally leaves the welfare office. Someone there tells her that Larry's body is at Rollie's Mortuary. When she gets there, she finds police guarding the door. They refuse her entry. She's numb. She drives back to her house on Green Street where Ursula, Dashija, and Joe wait. She sits down, doesn't know what to say or what to do. Erika, Donald, and Nijoni return. Everyone's talking, the little ones are crying, Lillian is silent. She has the feeling there's something she should be doing but "there was nothing I could do . . . he was gone."[19]

◼▶ ◀◼

Phil Loretto, draped in a blanket and holding his son, marches in the Albuquerque protest that followed the police killing of Larry Casuse. Courtesy of Special Collections/Center for Southwest Research (UNM Libraries), 000-954(4)-0008.

Louis was out of town the day the police killed his son. He arrived home the next day, and they began making funeral arrangements. The city agreed to demands by IAE that all bars in Gallup be closed for Larry's funeral on Monday, March 5, 1973. The day before the funeral, more than five hundred people marched from the Indian Community Center to Rollie's Mortuary, where Larry's body was laid out. On Monday, hundreds of Gallup High School students walked out of class, while hundreds more packed the small Tohatchi Catholic church at 2:00 p.m. for Larry's funeral. They decided to bury Larry in a small cemetery in Mexican Springs not far from where Louis lived on the reservation. They picked out a plot, and Louis dug Larry's grave by hand, just like the foxholes he'd dug in the Hürtgenwald. He wouldn't let anyone help him do it. After the service, so many cars clogged the narrow dirt road that led to the small cemetery—more than four hundred by some estimates—that the hearse couldn't make it through. They took the casket out and put it in the back of a pickup truck, and Larry's friends slowly drove his body around the cars and past three thousand mourners. It began to snow as they lowered his body into the earth.

■■▶ ◀■■

Emmett Garcia bought out the other two co-owners of the Navajo Inn and promised to close the bar, but he lost his reelection bid for mayor on April 3 and changed his mind. Robert sat in jail until that same day, April 3, 1973, when his friends finally raised enough money to bail him out. The state charged him with attempted murder, kidnapping, aggravated battery, aggravated assault, assault with intent to commit murder, and burglary. The court set his jury trial for November 12, 1973. In October, Robert's lawyer filed a motion to quash the jury panel. Of sixty-six potential jurors, fifty-four were white. None were Native. "Indian people," according to Robert's lawyer, "have been systematically excluded and subsequently underrepresented" on the panel. When the judge rejected the motion, Robert faced the prospect of an all-white jury and a life in prison.

The state offered a plea bargain. The state would drop the charges if Robert pleaded guilty to false imprisonment and aggravated battery. As they considered the offer, Emmett Garcia contacted Robert's lawyer and said he'd write a letter to the judge asking for clemency in sentencing, but first Robert would have to meet with him and answer his questions. What choice did Robert have? He met with Garcia, and they talked for just under an hour. Garcia wanted to know who shot him. "When I went through that door, you could have shot me. Am I right?" Robert was hesitant to say anything. Garcia pressed him but Robert told him he couldn't say for sure. It's not like "I got the gun and pointed it at you and shot," he tells Garcia. "That's not what happened," he says. "I didn't try to shoot you. I tried to pull the gun away. I saw pieces flying by the door. I thought that's where the shot went."

Garcia spent most of the interview lecturing Robert. He asked him why they didn't just come talk to him. We could have worked it out, he told him. He wanted to know if Larry really killed himself. "While I was in jail," Robert says. "I thought about it a lot. I figured maybe he did it, until I read the autopsy report." It doesn't jibe with the facts, Robert tells him. He only had that .32 pistol, which wouldn't make that large an entry wound under his chin. The police claim he used a shotgun, but Robert knows there weren't any shotguns near Larry. The police had the only shotguns at that point. "I'm pretty sure the police did it," he tells Garcia.

Robert took the deal and pleaded guilty. He sat beside his lawyer in an empty courtroom in mid-November 1973 waiting for the judge to sentence him to prison. Delbert Rudy walked into the courtroom. "The day that they were going to have the trial, I had to go down to the courthouse." Someone, Rudy doesn't remember who, told him they needed him to come to the courthouse and positively identify Robert. "There were two people in the courtroom, sitting at a table, it was where the defendant would sit. And I assumed it was a police officer or his lawyer, and this short guy with long, dark hair and a ponytail and a suit. And then I walked out, and he says, 'Did you recognize anyone in there?' And I said, 'Well it's been six months. The guy at the table is in a suit, he's all cleaned up, his hair's all slicked back, I'm assuming that's Nakaidinae.' The guy says, 'OK.'" He goes in the room and then comes out and says, "We've reached a plea deal."

Emmett Garcia read his letter in court asking for clemency for Robert but the judge gave Robert two concurrent prison terms, ordering him incarcerated for one to five years for the false imprisonment charge and two to ten years for the aggravated battery charge. He suspended five years from the sentence and remanded Robert to the New Mexico State Penitentiary in Santa Fe. The Navajo Nation requested a different prison, and in January 1974, Robert was transferred to the Los Lunas Correctional Center, south of Albuquerque, where he remained until he was paroled in June.

Robert made art and music while in prison, and in November of that year, he performed a set at the Native American Folk Music Festival held near Window Rock, Arizona, in a lineup that advertised Buffy Sainte-Marie as its headliner. Among the songs Robert played, there was one about Larry that he'd written while sitting in jail waiting to be bailed out. In the festival, he played a slightly revised version of the song he first played for Garcia at the end of their hour-long interview before his sentencing. "Do you want to hear it?" the lawyer asked Garcia, as the interview was ending. "Yes," Garcia said, "of course." The audio recording is good, and the sound of Robert pulling his guitar out of its case is clear. As he does it, a man who hadn't yet spoken on the recording suddenly shouts, "What is the name of it, Robert?" But Robert ignores the question and starts tuning his guitar. His lawyer speaks: "Do you have a name, a name for it?" he asks. "No," Robert says softly, "not really." That's how the whole interview went. Garcia would ask a question, and then Robert would offer a short nonanswer. For an hour, Garcia fished for admissions of guilt and remorse, but Robert never said the things Garcia wanted to hear. Garcia insisted Robert was trying to kill him in the sporting goods store. "No, I didn't mean to shoot you," he told him. Garcia insisted Larry killed himself at the back of the store. "No," Robert said, "Larry couldn't have killed himself." That was how it went. Garcia did most of the talking, in a lecturing kind of way. But now they've asked Robert to sing a song.

The song has no title and no beginning. Robert starts tuning the guitar as soon as it's out of the case, and there's no obvious point at which the tuning of the guitar ends and the song begins. The chords just seem to assemble themselves into a song on their own. Robert plays slowly at first, fingerstyle, a beautiful and quiet melody. He disappears into the song. The fingerstyle overture continues for nearly half a minute until Robert clears his throat and then, as if readying himself for something, abandons the fingerstyle for a hard, insistent strumming pattern. The song shifts into something else, something not just *about* Larry Casuse but *of* him.[20] He wrote the song in jail, alone, with no guitar. Here it is:

[Song from a Gallup Jail]

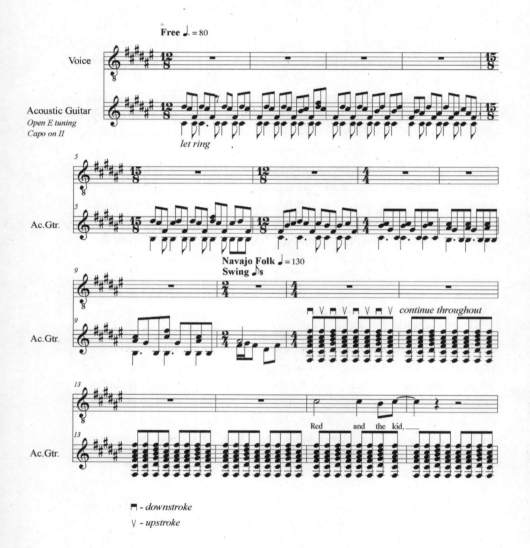

◻ - *downstroke*

∨ - *upstroke*

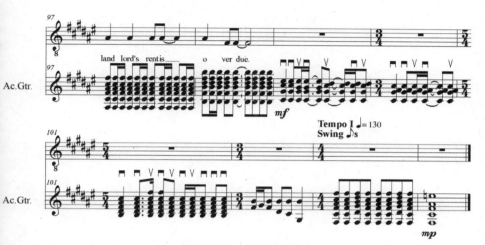

Music/Lyrics - Robert Nakaidinae
Transcribed/Arranged - Aaron Eldred

Acknowledgments

I would like to thank Larry Casuse's brothers and sisters, particularly Ursula, Erika, and Donald. They shared their time and their stories and trusted I would do something meaningful with those. I hope they're not too disappointed.

It's a small miracle Delbert Rudy let me interview him. He'd never given an interview to anyone about the day Larry and Robert hijacked his car and took him by gunpoint to Gallup. In fact, he'd never even told his family about that day. Thank you, Delbert.

Many thanks to the librarians and archivists at the many archives I visited. The Benson Latin American Collection at the University of Texas at Austin and the library on the campus of the University of Texas at El Paso offered original and microfilm copies of Mexican newspapers, the records of the Janos Presidio, and the letters to, from, and about Juan José Compá. Grants from the Center for Regional Studies and the Research Allocation Committee at the University of New Mexico funded these trips to the archives. And many thanks to Lean Sweeney, who did the bulk of the translations.

Documents and photos related to the Santa Rita copper mine are scattered throughout New Mexico and Colorado, and finding them required the help of Ashley Smith at the Silver City Museum, Andrea Jaquez at the Miller Library archives on the campus of Western New Mexico University, and the kind librarians in the "Treasure Room" at the Silver City Public Library.

Years ago, someone told Terry Humble, a retired Santa Rita copper miner living in Bayard, New Mexico, that Kennecott was dumping company records in the landfill. He raced over and rescued boxes of records that included rosters, internal company memos, and reports related to all kinds of things, including the hiring of Navajo men in the 1940s. He saved those, indexed them, and wrote amazing books of his own about the mine. And he was kind enough to let me spend an afternoon in his living room years ago looking through his private archive. There's no story here without his generosity.

The bulk of the records related to the International Union of Mine, Mill and Smelter Workers (IUMMSW) are found in the archives at the University of Colorado Boulder. Many thanks to Jennifer Sanchez and David Hays. The personal records of one IUMMSW official can be found at the Center for Southwest Research in Zimmerman Library on the campus of the University of New Mexico, which is a five-minute walk from my campus office. I've spent a lot of time over the years looking through collections at that archive, including records related to Jesus Arviso, the KIVA Club, Robert Nakaidinae, and more. Many thanks to Nancy Brown-Martinez, Cindy Abel Morris, Jennifer Eggleston, and Samuel Sisneros.

Shortly before it shut down because of COVID-19, I spent a week at the National Archives and Records Administration in College Park, Maryland, in mid-March 2020 working through collections related to the Bureau of Indian Affairs, the US Army's 1st Infantry Division, and the postwar records of the United States Forces in Austria. Finding anything in that enormous archive would have been impossible if not for the help of an army of archivists who seemed to know the material in the collections by heart.

I first learned about Larry Casuse while working through microfilm collections at the New Mexico State Records Center and Archive. Budget cuts over the years have hollowed that place out, and shame on New Mexico for that. But despite the cuts, the librarians and archivists who remain there continue to work under difficult conditions and make that library and archive a special place.

A Lannan Foundation Residency Fellowship gave me a month in Marfa, Texas, to write. They know what they're doing at the Lannan Foundation, and they, and I, have Martha Jessop, Sarah Knopp, Douglas Humble, and Ray Freese to thank for it.

I'm not naming names, but there are an awful lot of presses out there that think they're doing an author a favor when they publish their book.

Haymarket ain't one of them. Anthony Arnove's enthusiasm for this book meant a lot. Trevor Perri's careful editorial work made a real difference in the text. Many thanks to Nisha Bolsey, John McDonald, Rory Fanning, and Eric Kerl.

Thank you and much love to Toni Kuehn, Willa Correia-Kuehn, and Harper Correia-Kuehn, particularly for listening to me tell stories about Larry and Louis and Lillian over the years. I hope I didn't ruin the book for them.

Many thanks to Aaron Eldred for transcribing Robert Nakaidinae's song and for producing the sheet music that ends the book.

I have good friends I've talked to about this book over the years. Thanks to Lorena Oropeza, who might be the first person to whom I ever told that I was writing a book about Larry Casuse. Andy Doolen's a terrific writer and a great friend and someone I frequently called up when I felt like something needed to be worked through and talked out. Thanks to Tyler Wall, with whom I've spent a lot of time over the years writing things that took me away from this book, which gave me the time and occasional distance I needed to write this as well as I possibly could. Thanks to John Hintz, who came through in the clutch.

John Redhouse was there at the very beginning of all of this, much earlier than me. John's an intellectual giant as far as I'm concerned, and it was only after he'd read a draft of this manuscript and told me that he liked it that I finally exhaled.

Thanks to Melanie Yazzie for writing the foreword. Larry matters today to so many young Navajo scholars, students, and organizers because of the work of Melanie, Nick Estes, and their comrades in The Red Nation, whose Albuquerque office they call The Larry Casuse Freedom Center.

My colleague Jennifer Nez Denetdale is the first Navajo woman ever to receive a PhD in history. She remembers Larry, went to his funeral, and told me years ago that she was "so glad you're writing this book, David, although I wish a Navajo writer would've done it a long time ago." I knew exactly what she meant, and I never disagreed.

It was that thought—who am I to write this?—that made this such a difficult book to write. It's quite a terrifying responsibility to tell the story of a family. To represent them. To take their words and the events of their lives and assemble them into a narrative and by doing so risk reducing those lives, narrowing them somehow into a story with a beginning and a definite end. If it's no good, it's my fault. But if it's good at all, to be honest, I've got Ursula Casuse-Carrillo to thank for it. If this book is *for* anyone, it is for her.

Notes

Delbert Rudy

1. All quotes attributed to Delbert Rudy are based on a personal interview conducted in Tyler, TX, September 14, 2013.
2. By "T.A. raid," he means the 1967 Tierra Amarilla courthouse raid in northern New Mexico by a group called La Alianza Federal de Mercedes. See David Correia, *Properties of Violence: Law and Land Grant Struggle in Northern New Mexico* (Athens: University of Georgia Press, 2013).
3. Bill Donovan, "Friends Blame Recent Troubles," *Gallup Independent*, March 2, 1973.

Their Evil Is Mighty

1. Author's interview with Donald Casuse, Gallup, NM, January 16, 2014.
2. Bill Donovan, "Friends Blame Recent Troubles," *Gallup Independent*, March 2, 1973.
3. Calvin Trillin, "You Always Turn Your Head," *New Yorker*, May 12, 1973.
4. KIVA Club statement, KIVA Club File, MSS 780 BC, University of New Mexico, Center for Southwest Research.
5. Author's interview with Phil Loretto, San Pedro, NM, August 19, 2014.
6. Larry Casuse, "The People's Movement," John Redhouse Collection, MSS 780 BC, Box 2, Folder 13, "Larry Casuse," University of New Mexico, Center for Southwest Research.

Blood Contracts

1. William B. Griffen, "The Compás: A Chiricahua Apache Family of the Late 18th and Early 19th Centuries," *American Indian Quarterly* 7, no. 2 (1983): 37.

185

2. August 4, 1836, Compa, F38, S1, Presidio de San Felipe y Santiago de Janos Records, Benson Latin American Collection, LLILAS Benson Latin American Studies and Collections, The University of Texas at Austin.

3. July 23, 1836, F38, S1, Benson Latin American Collection, General Libraries, University of Texas at Austin.

4. April 25, 1833, Compá0000, RJ25, University of Texas at El Paso Library.

5. See also, Lance R. Blyth, *Chiricahua and Janos: Communities of Violence in the Southwestern Borderlands, 1680–1880* (Lincoln: University Nebraska Press, 2012), 126.

6. May 7, 1833, Compá0000, RJ25, University of Texas at El Paso Library.

7. May 1, 1833, Compá0000, RJ25, University of Texas at El Paso Library.

8. June 4, 1835, Compá, F37, S1 Benson Latin American Collection, General Libraries, University of Texas at Austin.

9. Mark Santiago, *The Jar of Severed Hands: Spanish Deportation of Apache Prisoners of War, 1770–1810* (Norman: University of Oklahoma Press, 2014), 60.

10. Santiago, *The Jar of Severed Hands*, 64.

11. Santiago, *The Jar of Severed Hands*, 79.

12. See the discussion of Spanish and Mexican property laws and conventions in David Correia, *Properties of Violence: Law and Land Grant Struggle in Northern New Mexico* (Athens: University of Georgia Press, 2013).

13. Silver City Public Library Archive, Silver City–Grant County Chamber of Commerce, *A History of the Santa Rita Mine* (December 2004).

14. William B. Griffen, *Apaches at War and Peace: The Janos Presidio, 1750–1858* (Norman: University of Oklahoma Press, 1998), 88.

15. Ralph A. Smith, *Borderlander: The Life of James Kirker, 1793–1852* (Norman: University of Oklahoma Press, 1999), 32.

16. Griffen, "The Compás: A Chiricahua Apache Family of the Late 18th and Early 19th Centuries," 33.

17. University of Texas at El Paso, MF491 Archivo de Ayuntamiento de Chihuahua, R154 1803–1828, Petition for Francisco Manuel Elguea.

18. Christopher J. Huggard and Terrence M. Humble, *Santa Rita del Cobre: A Copper Mining Community in New Mexico* (Boulder: University Press of Colorado, 2012), 13.

19. As cited in Huggard and Humble, *Santa Rita del Cobre*, 14.

20. Smith, *Borderlander*, 32.

21. Sam Bean, quoted in Smith, *Borderlander*, 33.

22. March 12, 1825, RJ17, University of Texas at El Paso Archive. William B. Griffen, *Utmost Good Faith: Patterns of Apache-Mexican Hostilities in*

Northern Chihuahua Border Warfare, 1821–1848 (Albuquerque: University of New Mexico Press, 1988), 5.

23. See "Apaches Go To War," in Griffen, *Utmost Good Faith.*
24. April 22, 1835, RJ28, University of Texas at El Paso Library.
25. May 7, 1833, RJ25, University of Texas at El Paso Library.
26. July 9, 1835, F37, S1, Benson Latin American Collection, General Libraries, University of Texas at Austin.
27. May 17, 1832, RJ24, and January 22, 1832, RJ25, University of Texas at El Paso Library.
28. Smith, *Borderlander,* 38.
29. January 22, 1832, RJ25, University of Texas at El Paso Library.
30. March 24, 1833, RJ25, University of Texas at El Paso Library.
31. April 25, 1833, RJ25, University of Texas at El Paso Library.
32. Griffin, *Apaches at War and Peace,* 144.
33. November 4, 1834, *El Fanal de Chihuahua,* University of Texas at El Paso Library.
34. March 9, 1836, José Calvo, F38, S1, Benson Latin American Collection, General Libraries, University of Texas at Austin.
35. March 10, 1836, F38, S1, Benson Latin American Collection, General Libraries, University of Texas at Austin; April 8, 1836, RJ27, University of Texas at El Paso Library.
36. April 4, 1836, F38, S1, Benson Latin American Collection, General Libraries, University of Texas at Austin.
37. July 4, 1836, José Calvo, F38, S1, and August 4, 1836, F38, S1, Benson Latin American Collection, General Libraries, University of Texas at Austin.
38. July 23, 1836, F38, S1, Benson Latin American Collection, General Libraries, University of Texas at Austin.
39. June 21, 1836, F38, S2, Borrador No 55 and, February, 10, 1836, F38, S2, Borrador No. 8, Benson Latin American Collection, General Libraries, University of Texas at Austin.
40. See Griffin, *Apaches at War and Peace,* 168–69; June 21, 1836, F38, S2, Borrador No. 55, Benson Latin American Collection, General Libraries, University of Texas at Austin.
41. June 21, 1836, F38, S2, Borrador No. 55, Benson Latin American Collection, General Libraries, University of Texas at Austin.
42. October 28, 1836, RJ27, University of Texas at El Paso Library.
43. *El Noticioso del Chihuahua,* May 24, 1838, University of Texas at El Paso Library.
44. *El Noticioso del Chihuahua,* May 24, 1838, University of Texas at El Paso Library.

45. Smith, *Borderlander*, 49; *El Fanal de Chihuahua*, October 21, 1834, University of Texas at El Paso Library.

46. Griffen, *Utmost Good Faith*, 6.

47. Anastasia M. Griffin, "Georg Friederici's 'Scalping and Similar Warfare Customs in America,' with a Critical Introduction" (MA thesis, University of Colorado Boulder, 2008), 99.

48. Nathaniel Knowles, "The Torture of Captives by the Indians of Eastern North America," *Proceedings of the American Philosophical Society* 82, no. 2 (1940): 154.

49. Gabriel Nadeau, "Indian Scalping: Technique in Different Tribes," Paper presented at the 17th annual meeting of the American Association of the History of Medicine, AC, NJ, May 4–6, 1941, reprinted in George Friederici, Gabriel Nadeau, and Nathaniel Knowles, *Scalping and Torture: Warfare Practices Among the North American Indians* (Ontario, CA: Iroqrafts, 1983), 18.

50. Knowles, "The Torture of Captives by the Indian of Eastern North America," 36.

51. James Axtell and William C. Sturtevant, "The Unkindest Cut, or Who Invented Scalping," *The William and Mary Quarterly: A Magazine of Early American History* 37, no. 3 (1980): 461.

52. Nadeau, "Indian Scalping," 22.

53. Nadeau, "Indian Scalping," 26.

54. Nadeau, "Indian Scalping," 26.

55. Nadeau, "Indian Scalping," 27.

56. Ralph A. Smith, "'Long' Webster and the 'Vile Industry of Selling Scalps,'" *West Texas Historical Association Yearbook* (Lubbock, TX: West Texas Historical Association, 1961), 100.

57. Smith, "'Long' Webster," 101.

58. Vine Deloria, *Custer Died for Your Sins: An Indian Manifesto* (Norman: University of Oklahoma Press, 1969), 7.

59. Griffin, "Georg Friederici's 'Scalping and Similar Warfare Customs in America,'" 52.

60. Ray Brandes, "Don Santiago Kirker, King of the Scalp Hunters," *The Smoke Signal* 6 (1962): 3.

61. Smith, "'Long' Webster and the 'Vile Industry of Selling Scalps,'" 102.

62. Deloria, *Custer Died for Your Sins*, 6–7.

63. Axtell and Sturtevant, "The Unkindest Cut," 455.

64. Axtell and Sturtevant, "The Unkindest Cut," 455.

65. Axtell and Sturtevant, "The Unkindest Cut," 470.

66. Axtell and Sturtevant, "The Unkindest Cut," 455.

67. Knowles, "The Torture of Captives," 38.
68. Griffin, "Georg Friederici's 'Scalping and Similar Warfare Customs in America,'" 65.
69. Knowles, "The Torture of Captives," 163.
70. Knowles, "The Torture of Captives," 154.
71. Wolf D. Bueschgen and D. Troy Case, "Evidence of Prehistoric Scalping at Vosberg, Central Arizona," *International Journal of Osteoarchaeology* 6, no. 3 (1996): 230–48.
72. Griffin, "Georg Friederici's 'Scalping and Similar Warfare Customs in America,'" 139.
73. Griffin, "Georg Friederici's 'Scalping and Similar Warfare Customs in America,'" 35.
74. Griffen, *Utmost Good Faith*, 39 note 27.
75. Griffen, *Utmost Good Faith*, 38 note 26.
76. March 12, 1825, RJ17, University of Texas at El Paso Archive.
77. Edwin R. Sweeney, *Cochise: Chiricahua Apache Chief* (Norman: University of Oklahoma Press, 2012), 32.
78. *El Noticioso de Chihuahua*, May 5, 1837, University of Texas at El Paso Library.
79. Jacob Piatt Dunn, *Massacres of the Mountains: A History of the Indian Wars of the Far West* (United Kingdom: S. Low, Marston, Searle & Rivington, 1886), 305.
80. Huggard and Humble, *Santa Rita del Cobre*, 23.
81. Griffen, *Utmost Good Faith*, 54.
82. April 3, 1849, *El Faro de Chihuahua*, University of Texas at El Paso Library.
83. August 6, 1837, Letter signed by Pedro Olivares and Angel Trias, *El Noticioso de Chihuahua*, University of Texas at El Paso Library.
84. Smith, *Borderlander*, 71.
85. See Karl Marx, *Capital*, vol. 1, *A Critique of Political Economy* (New York: Penguin Classics, 1992), chap. 21.
86. Marx, *Capital*, chap. 21.
87. Griffen, *Apaches at War and Peace*, 124.
88. July 24, 1849, "Contratos de Sangre," *El Faro*, University of Texas at El Paso Library.
89. June 21, 1838, "Occurrence of Barbarous Indians," *El Noticioso de Chihuahua*, University of Texas at El Paso Library.
90. Marx, *Capital*, 176.
91. September 22, 1849, "Contratos de Sangre," *El Faro*, University of Texas at El Paso Library.

92. September 4, 1849, "Contratos de Sangre," *El Faro*, University of Texas at El Paso Library.

93. September 25, 1849, "Barbarous Indians," *El Faro*, University of Texas at El Paso Library; Smith, *Borderlander*, 130, 223.

94. October 6, 1849, "Barbarous Indians," *El Faro*, University of Texas at El Paso Library.

95. Smith, *Borderlander*, 103; November 13, 1849, "Barbarous Indians." *El Faro*, University of Texas at El Paso Library.

96. November 29, 1849, "Barbarous Indians." *El Faro*, University of Texas at El Paso Library.

97. Marx, *Capital*, 926.

The Story of the Boy Who Was Traded for a Horse

1. Based on the many stories and oral histories of Jesus Arviso, some collected by Tom Ration and held at the American Indian Oral History Collection, University of New Mexico Library, Center for Southwest Research. These were told by Mary Barbone of Smith Lake, NM, in October 1968 (MSS 314, BC Tape 566); Bob Manuelito, Tohatchi, NM, February 1969 (MSS 314, BC Tape 341); and Rex Becenti Jr., Tohatchi, NM, December 1969 (MSS 314, BC Tape 365). The story is recorded also by Virginia Hoffman in *Navajo Biographies*, vol. 1 (Phoenix: Navajo Curriculum Center Press, 1974); David M. Brugge in his "Appendix B: Jesus Arviso," from his book *Navajos in the Catholic Church Records of New Mexico, 1694–1875* (Tsaile, AZ: Navajo Community College Press, 1985); and Robert A. Roessel Jr. in his "Navajo History, 1850–1923," *Handbook of North American Indians* vol. 10, *Southwest*, ed. Alfonso Ortiz (Washington, DC: Smithsonian Institution Scholarly Press, 1983): 506–23.

Blood for Soil

1. Harold L. James, "The History of Fort Wingate," *New Mexico Geological Society Guidebook, Eighteenth Field Conference, Defiance- Zuni-Mt. Taylor Region*, ed. Frederick D. Trauger (Socorro, NM: New Mexico Geological Society, 1967), 158.

2. David S. Jones, *Rationalizing Epidemics* (Cambridge, MA: Harvard University Press, 2004), 4, 18.

3. Jones, *Rationalizing Epidemics*, 195.

4. US Department of the Interior, "Historic Properties Report: Fort Wingate Depot Activity, New Mexico" (July 1984), 15–16.

5. "Press Release: War Department, Bureau of Public Relations, Procurement Information Branch, 3 December 1941," NARA II, College Park, MD, RG407, Records of the Adjutant General's Office 1917, Legislative and Policy Precedent Files, 1943–75, nos. 110–12, Box 14, Folder "204–58, Indians 110 (1–99)."

6. Author's interview with Ursula Casuse-Carrillo, Gallup, NM, June 12, 2013.

7. John Collier, "The Indian in a Wartime Nation," *The Annals of the American Academy of Political and Social Science* 223, no. 1 (1942): 29; Jeré Franco, "Loyal and Heroic Service: The Navajos and World War II," *The Journal of Arizona History* 27, no. 4 (1986): 403–4.

8. Alison R. Bernstein, *American Indians and World War II: Toward a New Era in Indian Affairs* (Norman: University of Oklahoma Press, 1999), 23.

9. Donald L. Parman, "J.C. Morgan: Navajo Apostle of Assimilation," *Prologue: The Journal of the National Archives* 4, no. 2 (1972): 83–98.

10. Bernstein, *American Indians and World War II*, 34. Despite Morgan's claim of a patriotic loyalty among the Diné to the United States, and a torrent of celebratory press accounts in the early 1940s lauding Native peoples for their enthusiastic support for the war effort, resistance to the draft was widespread. In Arizona and New Mexico, the Hopi and Zuni "sought deferment from the military service as conscientious objectors," and the Six Nations Iroquois refused to submit to either US or Canadian authorities. See R. Scott Sheffield and Noah Riseman, *Indigenous Peoples and the Second World War: The Politics, Experiences and Legacies of War in the US, Canada, Australia and New Zealand* (Cambridge: Cambridge University Press, 2018), 206–9.

11. Bernstein, *American Indians and World War II*, 43.

12. Franco, "Loyal and Heroic Service," 393.

13 "Selective Service in Wartime: Second Report of the Director of the Selective Service, 1941–42," (Washington, DC: US Government Publishing Office, 1943), 287.

14. Report of John Collier, Commissioner of Indian Affairs, *Annual Report of the Secretary of the Interior*, 1944 (Washington, DC: US Government Publishing Office, 1944), 237.

15. Memo from Col. James Banville, AGD Chief, Strength Accounting Branch, "Request for Number of American Indians Who Served, WW II (XTN-1185), NARA II, College Park, MD, RG407, Records of the Adjutant General's Office, 1917, Legislative and Policy Precedent Files, 1943–1975, Nos. 110–12, Box 14, Folder 204–58: "Indians 110 (1–99).

16. His discharge papers list no date for his enlistment, which suggests, despite his age, that Louis may have been drafted, rather than enlisted, into the

army. His military records were destroyed in a 1973 fire at the National Archives in St. Louis.

17. Bernstein, *American Indians and World War II*, 43.

18. Franco, "Loyal and Heroic Service," 395.

19. Kenneth William Townsend, *World War II and the American Indian* (Albuquerque: University of New Mexico Press, 2000), 87.

20. Keats Begay and Broderick H. Johnson, eds., *Navajos and WW II* (Tsaile, AZ: Navajo Community College Press, 1977), 66.

21. Tom Holm, "Fighting a White Man's War: The Extent and Legacy of American Indian Participation in World War II," *The Journal of Ethnic Studies* 9, no. 2 (1981): 70.

22. Bernstein, *American Indians and World War II*, 40–41; Holm, "Fighting a White Man's War," 71.

23. As quoted in Holm, "Fighting a White Man's War," 71.

24. See The WWII 300th Combat Engineers (website), accessed September 8, 2021, http://www.300thcombatengineersinwwii.com/europe.html.

25. See 1944 World War II Troop Ship Crossings (website), accessed October 5, 2020, https://www.skylighters.org/troopships/1944.html; "Enlisted Record and Report of Separation" for Louis Casuse (author's files); Steve Harding, *Gray Ghost: The R.M.S. Queen Mary at War* (Missoula: Pictorial Histories Publishing, 1982), 79.

26. Jörg Friedrich, *The Fire: The Bombing of Germany, 1940–1945* (New York: Columbia University Press, 2006), 15.

27. Friedrich, *The Fire*, 17, 208–10.

28. Friedrich, *the Fire*, 9.

29. Friedrich, *The Fire*, 208.

30. Friedrich, *The Fire*, 210.

31. 301-INF(18)7-0.3, 1st Infantry Division, After Action Reports, Nov–Dec 1944, 3, 1st Infantry Division Museum Archives.

32. 301-INF(18)7-0.3, 1st Infantry Division, After Action Reports, Nov–Dec 1944, 3, 1st Infantry Division Museum Archives.

33. Courier, The Office of Strategic Services, p. 39. From "Studies in Intelligence," Folder 2, Series: Second Release of Subject Files Under the Nazi War Crimes and Japanese Imperial Government Disclosure Acts, ca. 1981–ca. 2003, Record Group 263: Records of the Central Intelligence Agency, 1894–2002, College Park, MD, NARA.

34. Kenneth McMillin, *The Battle of the Huertgen Forest: Why?* (Carlisle Barracks, PA: Army War College, 2001), 4.

35. Gerald Astor, *The Bloody Forest: Battle for the Hurtgen, September 1944–January 1945* (Novato, CA: Presidio Press, 2000), 9; Malcolm Marshall,

ed., *Proud Americans: Men of the 32nd Field Artillery Battalion in Action, World War II, as Part of the 18th Regimental Combat Team, First US Infantry Division* (self pub., 1996), 247.

36. H. R. Knickerbocker, et al., *Danger Forward: The Story of the Fist Division in World War II* (Washington, DC: Society of the First Division, 1947), 299.

37. Judith Sumner, *Plants Go to War: A Botanical History of World War II* (Jefferson, NC: McFarland, 2019), 232.

38. Sumner, *Plants Go to War*, 232.

39. Charles B. MacDonald, *Battle of the Hurtgen Forest* (Philadelphia: University of Pennsylvania Press, 2002), 53.

40. Friedrich, *The Fire*, 124.

41. "Danger Forward," 301-0 1st Infantry Division History, August 14, 1942–May 8, 1945, 1st Infantry Division Museum and Research Center, Wheaton, IL, 288.

42. Astor, *The Bloody Forest*, 23; Allen N. Towne, *Doctor Danger Forward: A World War II Memoir of a Combat Medical Aidman, First Infantry Division* (Jefferson, NC: MacFarland, 1999), 147.

43. John Brinckerhoff Jackson, *Discovering the Vernacular Landscape* (New Haven: Yale University Press, 1986), 135.

44. Jackson, *Discovering the Vernacular Landscape*, 136.

45. "Danger Forward," 301-0 1st Infantry Division History, August 14, 1942–May 8, 1945, 1st Infantry Division Museum and Research Center, Wheaton, IL, 295.

46. Jackson, *Discovering the Vernacular Landscape*, 135, 152.

47. McMillin, *Battle of the Hurtgen Forest: Why?*, 9.

48. "Danger Forward," 301-0 1st Infantry Division History, August 14, 1942–May 8, 1945, 1st Infantry Division Museum and Research Center, Wheaton, IL, 301.

49. Jackson, *Discovering the Vernacular Landscape*, 157.

50. Towne, *Doctor Danger Forward*, 146.

51. Charles Whiting, *The Battle of Hurtgen Forest* (Boston: Da Capo Press, 2000), 119.

52. See Robert Sterling Rush, *Hell in Hurtgen Forest: The Ordeal and Triumph of an American Infantry Regiment* (Lawrence: University Press of Kansas, 2001), 329.

53. Rush, *Hell in Hurtgen Forest*, 341.

54. "Danger Forward," 301-0 1st Infantry Division History, August 14, 1942–May 8, 1945, 1st Infantry Division Museum and Research Center, Wheaton, IL, 286.

55. 301-INF(18)-1.2, 18th Infantry S–1 Journal, 1st Infantry Division Museum Archives, 192.

56. Towne, *Doctor Danger Forward*, 151.

57. "Danger Forward," 301-0 1st Infantry Division History, August 14, 1942–May 8, 1945, 1st Infantry Division Museum and Research Center, Wheaton, IL, 291.

58. Robert W. Baumer and Mark Reardon, *American Iliad: The History of the 18th Infantry Regiment in World War II* (Bedford, PA: Aberjona Press, 2004), 300.

59. Towne, *Doctor Danger Forward*, 146.

60. Broderick Johnson, ed., *Navajos and World War II* (Tsaile, AZ: Navajo Community College Press, 1977), 71.

61. 301-INF(18)-1.2, 18th Infantry S-I Journal, 1st Infantry Division Museum Archives, 195.

62. Friedrich, *The Fire*, 122–23.

63. Friedrich, *The Fire,* 124.

64. 301-INF(18)-1.2, 18th Infantry S-I Journal, 1st Infantry Division Museum Archives, 196.

65. "Bloody Hamich, Part 3," 16th Regiment Infantry Historical Society (website), accessed February 10, 2020, https://www.16thinfantry.com/unit-history/bloody-hamich-part-3/; Baumer and Reardon, *American Illiad*, 301.

66. November 17, 1515 hours, 301-INF(18)-1.2, 18th Infantry S-I Journal, 1st Infantry Division Museum Archives, 196.

67. November 17, 310-ART-0.3, A/A Report, First Infantry Division, 1st Infantry Division Museum Archives, 43.

68. November 17, 310-ART-0.3, A/A Report, First Infantry Division, 1st Infantry Division Museum Archives, 44.

69. "Danger Forward," 301-0 1st Infantry Division History, August 14, 1942–May 8, 1945, 1st Infantry Division Museum and Research Center, Wheaton, IL, 287.

70. November 18, 1200 hours, 301-INF(18)-1.2, 18th Infantry S-I Journal, 1st Infantry Division Museum Archives, 198.

71. 301-3 (22325) G-3 Report of Operations, 1st Infantry Division, European Campaign, Jun 44–Dec 44, 382.

72. "Danger Forward," 301-0 1st Infantry Division History, August 14, 1942–May 8, 1945, 1st Infantry Division Museum and Research Center, Wheaton, IL, 309.

73. Jonathan A. Beall, "'The Street Was One Place We Could Not Go': The American Army and Urban Combat in World War II Europe" (PhD diss., Texas A&M University, 2014), 274; Baumer and Reardon, *American*

Illiad, 301; 301-INF(18)-1.2: G-1 Journal and File, 1 Jun 44 – 31 May 45, Collection: "Historical Records of the First Infantry Division and Its Organic Elements," WWII RRMRC Digital Collection, 201.

74. 301-INF(18)7-0.3, 1st Infantry Division, After Action Reports, Nov–Dec 1944, 3, 1st Infantry Division Museum Archives.

75. Knickerbocker, *Danger Forward*, 290.

76. Beall, "The Street Was One Place We Could Not Go," 273.

77. Knickerbocker, *Danger Forward*, 296.

78. 301-INF(18)-1.2: G-1 Journal and File, 1 Jun 44 – 31 May 45, Collection: "Historical Records of the First Infantry Division and Its Organic Elements" WWII RRMRC Digital Collection, 201.

79. Whiting, *Battle of Hurtgen Forest*, 118.

80. Towne, *Doctor Danger Forward*, 148; 3b journal, 200; Baumer and Reardon, *American Illiad*, 301.

81. Marshall, "Proud Americans," 299.

82. 301-INF(18)-1.2: G-1 Journal and File, 1 Jun 44 – 31 May 45, Collection: "Historical Records of the First Infantry Division and Its Organic Elements," WWII RRMRC Digital Collection, 207.

83. 301-INF(18)-1.2: G-1 Journal and File, 1 Jun 44 – 31 May 45, Collection: "Historical Records of the First Infantry Division and Its Organic Elements," WWII RRMRC Digital Collection, 202–4.

84. Knickerbocker, *Danger Forward*, 288.

85. 301-INF(18)7-0.3, 1st Infantry Division, After Action Reports, Nov–Dec 1944, 4, 1st Infantry Division Museum Archives.

86. Knickerbocker, *Danger Forward*, 300.

87. 301-INF(18)-1.2: G-1 Journal and File, 1 Jun 44 – 31 May 45, Collection: "Historical Records of the First Infantry Division and Its Organic Elements," WWII RRMRC Digital Collection, 206.

88. Towne, *Doctor Danger Forward*, 150.

89. Whiting, *Battle of Hurtgen Forest*, 118.

90. Whiting, *Battle of Hurtgen Forest*, xi; Charles Glass, *The Deserters: A Hidden History of World War II* (New York: Penguin, 2014), xv. There are a dozen or more careful historical studies of the Hurtgen battle, but not one examines the question of combat desertion. When the topic is addressed, it is limited to the question of German deserters. Infantry soldiers, however, in memoirs or in oral histories, discuss it freely, and rarely do they make moral judgements on the men who fled from the slaughter in the woods.

91. Towne, *Doctor Danger Forward*, 147.

92. 301-INF(18)7-0.3, 1st Infantry Division, After Action Reports, Nov–Dec 1944, 4, 1st Infantry Division Museum Archives.

93. Beall, "'The Street Was One Place We Could Not Go,'" 274.
94. November 21, 310-ART-0.3, A/A Report, and 301-INF(18)7-0.3, 1st Infantry Division, After Action Reports, Nov–Dec 1944, 4, First Infantry Division, 1st Infantry Division Museum Archives, 46.
95. 301-INF(18)7-0.3, 1st Infantry Division, After Action Reports, Nov–Dec 1944, 4, 1st Infantry Division Museum Archives.
96. 301-INF(18)-1.2: G-1 Journal and File, 1 Jun 44 – 31 May 45, Collection: "Historical Records of the First Infantry Division and Its Organic Elements," WWII RRMRC Digital Collection, 208.
97. 301-INF(18)-1.2: G-1 Journal and File, 1 Jun 44 – 31 May 45, Collection: "Historical Records of the First Infantry Division and Its Organic Elements," WWII RRMRC Digital Collection, 209; Baumer and Reardon, *American Iliad*, 304.
98. Baumer and Reardon, *American Iliad*, 304.
99. Baumer and Reardon, *American Iliad*, 305.
100. November 22, 310-ART-0.3, A/A Report, First Infantry Division, 1st Infantry Division Museum Archives, 47.
101. 301-INF(18)7-0.3, 1st Infantry Division, After Action Reports, Nov–Dec 1944, 5; Knickerbocker, *Danger Forward*, 307.
102. Towne, *Doctor Danger Forward*, 146.
103. November 20, 310-ART-0.3, A/A Report, First Infantry Division, 1st Infantry Division Museum Archives, 46.
104. 3b journal, 198, 1st Infantry Division Museum Archives.
105. Marshall, *Proud Americans*, 249.
106. Knickerbocker, *Danger Forward*, 292.
107. David R. Higgins, *Roer River Battles: Germany's Stand at the Westwall, 1944–45* (Haverton: Casemate, 2010), 182; Knickerbocker, *Danger Forward*, 292.
108. 301-INF(18)7-0.3, 1st Infantry Division, After Action Reports, Nov–Dec 1944, 5, 1st Infantry Division Museum Archives.
109. Towne, *Doctor Danger Forward*, 152.
110. 301-INF(18)7-0.3, 1st Infantry Division, After Action Reports, Nov–Dec 1944, 8, 1st Infantry Division Museum Archives.
111. 301-INF(18)-1.2, S-1 Journal, 18th Infantry Regiment, 1st Infantry Division, Jun–Dec 1944, 306, 1st Infantry Division Museum Archives.
112. 301-INF(18)7-0.3, 1st Infantry Division, After Action Reports, Nov–Dec 1944, 8, 1st Infantry Division Museum Archives.
113. *Fact Sheet*, Information Section, Analysis Branch, HQ Army Ground Forces, Washington DC, March 1, 1947, held at 1st Infantry Museum, 301-0: *Fact Sheet*, 1917–1946.

114. 301-INF(18)-1.2, S-1 Journal, 18th Infantry Regiment, 1st Infantry Div, Jun–Dec 1944, 306, 1st Infantry Division Museum Archives.
115. 301-INF(18)-1.2, S-1 Journal, 18th Infantry Regiment, 1st Infantry Div, Jun–Dec 1944, 306, 1st Infantry Division Museum Archives.
116. Marshall, *Proud Americans*, 280.
117. Baumer and Reardon, *American Illiad*, 311.
118. 301-INF(18)-1.2, S-1 Journal, 18th Infantry Regiment, 1st Infantry Div, Jun–Dec 1944, 308, 1st Infantry Division Museum Archives.
119. 301-INF(18)-1.2, S-1 Journal, 18th Infantry Regiment, 1st Infantry Div, Jun–Dec 1944, 308, 1st Infantry Division Museum Archives.
120. Baumer and Reardon, *American Illiad*, 312.
121. 301-INF(18)-1.2, S-1 Journal, 18th Infantry Regiment, 1st Infantry Div, Jun–Dec 1944, 308, 1st Infantry Division Museum Archives.
122. 301-INF(18)-1.2, S-1 Journal, 18th Infantry Regiment, 1st Infantry Div, Jun–Dec 1944, 308, 1st Infantry Division Museum Archives.
123. 301-INF(18)-1.2, S-1 Journal, 18th Infantry Regiment, 1st Infantry Div, Jun–Dec 1944, 312, 1st Infantry Division Museum Archives.
124. 301-INF(18)-1.2, S-1 Journal, 18th Infantry Regiment, 1st Infantry Div, Jun–Dec 1944, 1st Infantry Division Museum Archives, 312; Towne, *Doctor Danger Forward*, 156.
125. Baumer and Reardon, *American Illiad*, 313.
126. 301-INF(18)-1.2, S-1 Journal, 18th Infantry Regiment, 1st Infantry Div, Jun–Dec 1944, 314, 1st Infantry Division Museum Archives.
127. 301-INF(18)-1.2, S-1 Journal, 18th Infantry Regiment, 1st Infantry Div, Jun–Dec 1944, 316, 1st Infantry Division Museum Archives.
128. 301-INF(18)-1.2, S-1 Journal, 18th Infantry Regiment, 1st Infantry Div, Jun–Dec 1944, 328, 1st Infantry Division Museum Archives.
129. 301-3, G-3 Ops Rpt, January 2, 8–9, 1st Infantry Division Museum Archives.
130. 301-3, G-3 Operations Report, European Campaign, 1st Infantry Division, January 1 report, 5, 1st Infantry Division Museum Archives.
131. 301-INF-(18)-0.2, History, 1st Infantry Division, Jan–May 1945, 3, 1st Infantry Division Museum Archives.
132. 301-3, G03 Ops Rpt, 10, 1st Infantry Division Museum Archives.
133. 301-3, G03 Ops Rpt, 14, 1st Infantry Division Museum Archives.
134. Marshall, *Proud Americans*, 288.
135. 301-INF(18)-1.2, S-1 Journal, 18th Infantry Regiment, 1st Infantry Div, Jun–Dec 1944, 332, 1st Infantry Division Museum Archives.
136. 301-INF(18)-1.2, S-1 Journal, 18th Infantry Regiment, 1st Infantry Div, Jun–Dec 1944, 333, 1st Infantry Division Museum Archives.

137. 301-INF(18)-1.2, S-1 Journal, 18th Infantry Regiment, 1st Infantry Div, Jun–Dec 1944, 335, 1st Infantry Division Museum Archives.

138. 301-INF(18)-1.2, S-1 Journal, 18th Infantry Regiment, 1st Infantry Div, Jun–Dec 1944, 337, 1st Infantry Division Museum Archives.

139. 301-INF(18)-1.2, S-1 Journal, 18th Infantry Regiment, 1st Infantry Div, Jun–Dec 1944, 339, 1st Infantry Division Museum Archives.

140. 301-INF(18)-1.2, S-1 Journal, 18th Infantry Regiment, 1st Infantry Div, Jun–Dec 1944, 340, 1st Infantry Division Museum Archives.

141. 301-INF(18)-1.2, S-1 Journal, 18th Infantry Regiment, 1st Infantry Div, Jun–Dec 1944, 341, 1st Infantry Division Museum Archives.

142. 301-3, G03 Ops Rpt, 15–16, 1st Infantry Division Museum Archives.

143. 301-INF(18)-1.2, S-1 Journal, 18th Infantry Regiment, 1st Infantry Div, Jun–Dec 1944, 343, 1st Infantry Division Museum Archives.

144. Knickerbocker, *Danger Forward*, 346.

145. Knickerbocker, *Danger Forward*, 347.

146. Baumer and Reardon, *American Illiad*, 317.

147. 301-INF-(18)-0.2, History, 1st Infantry Division, Jan–May 1945, 3, 1st Infantry Division Museum Archives.

148. Marshall, *Proud Americans*, 280.

149. Towne, *Doctor Danger Forward*, 157.

150. 301-3, G-3 Operations Reports, 1st Int Div European Campaign, Jan 45 – Dec 45, 1st Infantry Division Museum Archives, 33.

151. 301-INF-(18)-0.2, History, 1st Infantry Division, Jan–May 45, 3, 1st Infantry Division Museum Archives.

152. Baumer and Reardon, *American Illiad*, 315.

153. 301-3, G03 Ops Rpt, 27; 301-INF(18)7-0.3, 1st Infantry Division, After Action Reports, Nov–Dec 1944, 12, 1st Infantry Division Museum Archives.

154. Baumer and Reardon, *American Illiad*, 316; 301-3, G-3 Operations Reports, 30–31.

155. 301-INF(18)7-0.3, 1st Infantry Division, After Action Reports, Nov–Dec 1944, 13, 1st Infantry Division Museum Archives.

156. Knickerbocker, *Danger Forward*, 347.

157. Author's Interview with Ursula Casuse-Carrillo, August 24, 2021.

158. Knickerbocker, *Danger Forward*, 348.

159. 301-INF(18)7-0.3, 1st Infantry Division, After Action Reports, Nov–Dec 1944, 13, 1st Infantry Division Museum Archives.

160. 301-INF(18)-1.2, S-1 Journal, 18th Infantry Regiment, 1st Infantry Div, Jun–Dec 1944, 352, 1st Infantry Division Museum Archives.

161. 301-INF(18)-1.2, S-1 Journal, 18th Infantry Regiment, 1st Infantry Div, Jun–Dec 1944, 353, 1st Infantry Division Museum Archives.

162. 301-3, G-3 Operations Reports, 36, 1st Infantry Division Museum Archives.
163. 301-INF(18)-0.2: History, 1st Infantry Division, Jan–May 1945, 1st Infantry Division Museum Archives, 2.
164. 301-INF-(18)-0.2, History, 1st Infantry Division, Jan–May 1945, 3, 1st Infantry Division Museum Archives.
165. Astor, *The Bloody Forest*, 9; MacDonald, *The Battle of the Huertgen Forest*, 195.
166. Thomas G. Bradbeer, "General Cota and the Battle of the Hürtgen Forest: A Failure of Battle Command?" *Army History* 75 (2010): 19; MacDonald, *The Battle of the Huertgen Forest*, 196.
167. Author's interview with Ursula Casuse-Carrillo, Gallup, NM, July 23, 2013.
168. Johnson, *Navajos and World War II*, 75.
169. Author's interview with Ursula Casuse-Carrillo, Gallup, NM, June 12, 2013.
170. Author's interview with Donald Casuse, Gallup, NM, January 16, 2014.
171. A fire in 1973 destroyed any records that might have shed light on Louis's capture.
172. This is based on a comparison of his enlistment and discharge records.
173. Johnson, *Navajos and World War II*, 77.
174. Johnson, *Navajos and World War II*, 79.
175. Christoph Rass and Jens Lohmeier, "Transformations: Post-Battle Processes on the Hürtgenwald Battlefield," *Journal of Conflict Archaeology* 6, no. 3 (2011): 190.
176. Rass and Lohmeier, "Transformations," 190–91.
177. Sumner, *Plants Go to War*, 255.
178. How he got from New York to Texas is unclear. Louis's honorable discharge papers include a note that he went AWOL for fourteen days at some point during his service. It's possible this was between landing in New York in April and his official separation at Camp Fannin in Texas in October. It's also possible he walked away from the fight in the Hürtgen like so many other men. There are no records to explain it. He received a smallpox vaccination the following day and was sent to Camp Fannin in Texas, where he was discharged in October of 1945 and given $197.65.
179. Knickerbocker, *Danger Forward*, 315.
180. Towne, *Doctor Danger Forward*, 150.

Child War Bride

1. Louis's army separation papers list his military occupational specialty as "Security Man 2677." This is a "military policeman" according to "TM 12-427 Military Occupational Classification of Enlisted Personnel, 1944."

2. Alexander N. Lassner, "The Invasion of Austria in March 1938: Blitzkrieg or Pfush?" in *The Marshall Plan in Austria*, eds. Günter Bischof, Anton Pelinka, and Dieter Stiefel (New Brunswick: Transaction Publishers, 2000), 447–60.

3. David Walker, "Industrial Location in Turbulent Times: Austria through Anschluss and Occupation," *Journal of Historical Geography* 12, no. 2 (1986): 182.

4. Günter Bischof, *Austria in the First Cold War, 1945–55: The Leverage of the Weak* (New York: Palgrave Macmillan, 1999), 8–9.

5. "The History of the NSDAP in Austria," April 1945, 16, in Box 1, Folder 000.1: "Politics," RG260 Records of the US Occupation HQ, WWII, USFA, USACA Section, Internal Affairs/Displaced Persons Division, Land Salzburg Liaison, General Records, 1945–1950, NARA Archives II, College Park, MD.

6. Bischof, *Austria in the First Cold War*, 8.

7. "The History of the NSDAP in Austria," 16.

8. "The History of the NSDAP in Austria," 25.

9. "The History of the NSDAP in Austria," 23.

10. "The History of the NSDAP in Austria," 27.

11. Richard Germann, "Austrian Soldiers and Generals in World War II," in *New Perspectives on Austrians and World War II*, eds. Günter Bischof, Fritz Plasser, and Barbara Stelzl-Marx (New Brunswick: Transaction Publishers, 2009), 29; Thomas R. Grischany, "Mental Aspects of Austrian Wehrmacht Service," in *New Perspectives on Austrians and World War II*, 46.

12. Rolf Steininger, "12 November 1918 – 12 March 1938: The Road to the Anschluss," in *Austria in the Twentieth Century*, eds. Rolf Steininger, Günter Bischof, and Michael Gehler (New Brunswick: Transaction Publishers, 2002), 85.

13. Bischof, *Austria in the First Cold War*, 12

14. Bischof, *Austria in the First Cold War*, 15.

15. Thomas R. Grischany, "Mental Aspects of Austrian Wehrmacht Service," in Bischoff, Plasser, and Stelzl-Marx, *New Perspectives on Austrians and World War II*, 52.

16. Bischof, *Austria in the First Cold War*, 16.

17. Walker, "Industrial Location in Turbulent Times," 186.

18. Bischof, *Austria in the First Cold War*, 16.

19. Bischof, *Austria in the First Cold War*, 17.

20. Georg Wimmer, Jorg Dept, and Thomas Kupfer, "The Gypsy Camp at Salzburg-Maxglan: 1939–1943," Radiofabrik Salzburg, Cultural Broadcasting Archive, 2009, https://cba.fro.at/13855.

21. Erika Thurner, "Nazi and Postwar Policy against Roma and Sinti in Austria," in Roni Stauber and Raphael Vago, eds., *The Roma—A Minority in Europe: Historical, Political and Social Perspectives* (Budapest: Central European University Press, 2007), 56–58.

22. Thurner, "Nazi and Postwar Policy against Roma and Sinti in Austria," 58.

23. Bischof, *Austria in the First Cold War*, 18.

24. Walker, "Industrial Location in Turbulent Times," 191.

25. Bischof, *Austria in the First Cold War*, 18–20.

26. Donald R. Whitnah and Florentine E. Whitnah, *Salzburg under Siege: U.S. Occupation, 1945–1955* (Wesport, CT: Praeger Publishers, 1991), 13.

27. "Monthly Bulletin of Austrian Statistics, #14, September 1947," RG260 Records of the US Occupation HQ, WWII, USFA, USACA Section, Internal Affairs/Displaced Persons Division, Land Salzburg Liaison, General Records, 1945–1950, Box 4, Folder: "Courts," NARA Archives II, College Park, MD.

28. Donald Robert Whitnah and Edgar L. Erickson, *The American Occupation of Austria: Planning and Early Years* (Westport, CO: Greenwood Press, 1985), 107–17.

29. Whitnah and Erickson, *American Occupation of Austria*, 235.

30. Bischof, *Austria in the First Cold War*, 31.

31. Whitnah and Erickson, *American Occupation of Austria*, 117.

32. Albion Ross, "Terrorism Causes Crisis in Austria," *New York Times*, June 22, 1948.

33. Perry Biddiscombe, "Dangerous Liaisons: The Anti-Fraternization Movement in the U.S. Occupation Zones of Germany and Austria, 1945–1948," *Journal of Social History* 34, no. 3 (2001): 614.

34. Klaus Eisterer, "Austria Under Allied Occupation," in Steininger, Bischof, and Gheier, *Austria in the Twentieth Century*, 193.

35. Eisterer, "Austria Under Allied Occupation," 193.

36. Jeffrey Burds, "Sexual Violence in Europe in World War II, 1939–1945," *Politics & Society* 37, no. 1 (2009): 37.

37. Burds, "Sexual Violence in Europe in World War II," 38–39.

38. Burds, "Sexual Violence in Europe in World War II," 43.

39. Muge Demirkır Unlu, "Rape as a Political Tool and as a Weapon of War," *International Journal on Rule of Law, Transitional Justice and Human Rights* 9, no. 9 (2018): 25.

40. Elisabeth Jean Wood, "Rape as a Practice of War: Toward a Typology of Political Violence," *Politics & Society* 46, no. 4 (2018): 513–37.

41. Kellie Wilson-Buford, *Policing Sex and Marriage in the American Military: The Court-Martial and the Construction of Gender and Sexual Deviance, 1950–2000* (Lincoln: University of Nebraska Press, 2018), 163.

42. Whitnah and Erickson, *American Occupation of Austria*, 217.

43. Whitnah and Whitnah, *Salzburg Under Siege*, 11–12.

44. "Report of Denazification in U.S. Zone of Austria, 19 November 1946," Box 3, Folder: "Denazification: Misc. 1946 July–Dec," RG260, Records of US Occupation HQ, WWII, USFA, USACA Section, Internal Affairs/ Displaced Persons Division, Statistics Branch, General Records, 1945–1950, NARA Archives II, College Park, MD.

45. "HQ USFA 6 April 1948 Staff Study," RG260, Records of the US Occupation HQ, WWII, USFA, USACA Section, Internal Affairs/ Displaced persons Division, Denazification Branch, General Records, 1945–1950, Box 1, Folder: "Denazification Policy," NARA Archives II, College Park, MD.

46. "HQ USFA 6 April 1948 Staff Study," RG260, Records of the US Occupation HQ, WWII, USFA, USACA Section, Internal Affairs/ Displaced persons Division, Denazification Branch, General Records, 1945–1950, Box 1, Folder: "Denazification Policy," NARA Archives II, College Park, MD.

47. "Directive to Commander in Chief of US Forces of Occupation regarding the Military Government of Austria," 24 June, 1945, RG260, Records of US Occupation HQ, WWII, USFA, USACA Section, Internal Affairs/ Displaced Persons Division, Statistics Branch, General Records, 1945–1950, Box 2, Folder 19, NARA, Archives II, College Park, MD.

48. "Directive to Commander in Chief of US Forces of Occupation regarding the Military Government of Austria," RG260, Records of US Occupation HQ, WWII, USFA, USACA Section, Internal Affairs/Displaced Persons Division, Statistics Branch, General Records, 1945–1950, 24 June 1945, Box 2, Folder 19, NARA, Archives II, College Park, MD.

49. *Wiener Zeitung*, 11 October 1947, RG260, Records of US Occupation HQ, WWII, USFA, USACA Section, Internal Affairs/Displaced Persons Division, Statistics Branch, General Records, 1945–50, Box 3, Folder: "Denazification, Misc., 1947 July–Dec," NARA Archives II, College Park, MD; "Registration statistics, 1 April 1948," RG260, Records of US Occupation HQ, WWII, USFA, USACA Section, Internal Affairs/ Displaced Persons Division, Statistics Branch, General Records, 1945–1950, Box 3, Folder: "Denazification, Misc. 1948," NARA Archives II, College Park, MD.

50. "Counter Intelligence Corps, de-nazification section, Land Salzburg Section, 4 February 1947," RG260, Records of the US Occupation HQ, WWII, USFA, USACA Section, Internal affairs/Displaced Persons Division, Denazification Branch, General Records, 1945–1950, Box 1 NARA Archives II, College Park, MD.

51. Bayerisches Hauptstaatsarchiv; München; Abteilung IV Kriegsarchiv. Kriegstammrollen, 1914–1918; Volume: 1932. Kriegstammrolle: 2. Kompanie, Bd. 1, Kriegsstammrollen, 1914–1918. Bavarian State Archives. Department IV, War Archive, Munich; Bavaria, Germany, Lutheran Baptisms, Marriages, and Burials, 1556–1973; Custodian: Zentralarchiv Der Evangelischen Kirche Der Pfalz, Speyer; Film Number: 1632539.

52. Allied Control Council, Directive No. 38: The Arrest and Punishment of War Criminals, Nazis, and Militarists and the Internment, Control, and Surveillance of Potentially Dangerous Germans, October 1946.

53. Jill Lewis, "Dancing on a Tightrope: The Beginning of the Marshall Plan and the Cold War in Austria," in Bischof, Pelinka, and Stiefel, *The Marshall Plan in Austria*, 141.

54. Whitnah and Erickson, *American Occupation of Austria*, 237.

55. Whitnah and Erickson, *American Occupation of Austria*, 180–94.

56. Lewis, "Dancing on a Tightrope," 142.

57. *Salzburger Nachricten*, September 4, 1948, RG260, Records of the US Occupation HQ, WWII, USFA, USACA Section, Internal Affairs/Displaced Persons Division, Land Salzburg Liaison, General Records, 1945–1950, Box 1, Folder 000.75: "Press Clippings," NARA Archives II, College Park, MD.

58. *Demokratisches Volksblatt*, February 21, 1948, RG260, Records of the US Occupation HQ, WWII, USFA, USACA Section, Internal Affairs/Displaced Persons Division, Land Salzburg Liaison, General Records, 1945–1950, Box 1, Folder 000.75: "Press Clippings," NARA Archives II, College Park, MD.

59. "Memorandum: HQ Land Salzburg Area Command," February 25, 1948, RG260, Records of the US Occupation HQ, WWII, USFA, USACA Section, Internal Affairs/Displaced Persons Division, Land Salzburg Liaison, General Records, 1945–1950, Box 2, Folder 004.06: "Labor Disputes and Strikes," NARA Archives II, College Park, MD.

60. *Demokratisches Volksblatt*, January 31, 1948, RG260, Records of the US Occupation HQ, WWII, USFA, USACA Section, Internal Affairs/Displaced Persons Division, Land Salzburg Liaison, General Records, 1945–1950, Box 1, Folder 000.75: "Press Clippings," NARA Archives II, College Park, MD.

61. *Demokratisches Volksblatt*, February 21, 1948, RG260, Records of the US Occupation HQ, WWII, USFA, USACA Section, Internal Affairs/Displaced Persons Division, Land Salzburg Liaison, General Records, 1945–1950, Box 1, Folder 000.75: "Press Clippings," NARA Archives II, College Park, MD.

62. Whitnah and Erickson, *American Occupation of Austria*, 190.

63. Lewis, "Dancing on a Tightrope," 147; Jessica Reinisch, "Introduction: Relief in the Aftermath of War," *Journal of Contemporary History* 43, no. 3 (2008): 371–404.

64. Demokratisches Volksblatt, August 19, 1947, RG260, Records of the US Occupation HQ, WWII, USFA, USACA Section, Internal Affairs/Displaced Persons Division, Land Salzburg Liaison, General Records, 1945–1950, Box 1, Folder 000.75: "Press Clippings," NARA Archives II, College Park, MD.

65. "Memorandum: HQ USFA," July 29, 1947, RG260, Records of the US Occupation HQ, WWII, USFA, USACA Section, Internal Affairs/Displaced Persons Division, Land Salzburg Liaison, General Records, 1945–1950, Box 2, Folder 004.06: "Labor Disputes and Strikes," NARA Archives II, College Park, MD.

66. "Census, General Conditions, labor & Social Conditions," "Memo: Food & Labor," June 17, 1949, RG260, Records of US Occupation HQ, WWII, USFS, USACA Section, Internal Affairs/Displaced Persons Division, Land Salzburg Liaison, General Records, 1945–1950, Box 4, NARA Archives II, College Park, MD.

67. "Memorandum: HQ Military Government Land Salzburg, Austria," August 4, 1947, RG260, Records of the US Occupation HQ, WWII, USFA, USACA Section, Internal Affairs/Displaced Persons Division, Land Salzburg Liaison, General Records, 1945–1950, Box 2, Folder 004.06: "Labor Disputes and Strikes," NARA Archives II, College Park, MD.

68. *Salzburger Tagblatt*, August 19, 1947, RG260, Records of the US Occupation HQ, WWII, USFA, USACA Section, Internal Affairs/Displaced Persons Division, Land Salzburg Liaison, General Records, 1945–1950, Box 1, Folder 000.75: "Press Clippings," NARA Archives II, College Park, MD.

69. *Salzburger Tagblatt*, October 30, 1947, RG260, Records of the US Occupation HQ, WWII, USFA, USACA Section, Internal Affairs/Displaced Persons Division, Land Salzburg Liaison, General Records, 1945–1950, Box 1, Folder 000.75: "Press Clippings," NARA Archives II, College Park, MD.

70. Author's interview with Erika Casuse, Albuquerque, NM, August 14, 2018.

71. Press Clippings. Document: *Demokratisches Volksblatt* (Socialist paper) October 30, 1947, RG260, Records of the US Occupation HQ, WWII,

USFA, USACA Section, Internal Affairs/Displaced Persons Division, Land Salzburg Liaison, General Records, 1945–1950 (A1 2073), Box 1, Folder 000.75, NARA Archives II, College Park, MD.

72. Petra Goedde, *GIs and Germans: Culture, Gender and Foreign Relations, 1945–1949* (New Haven: Yale University Press, 2003), 134.

73. As cited in Goedde, *GIs and Germans*, 134.

74. March 31, 1948, RG260, Records of US Occupation HQ, WWII, USFS, USACA Section, Internal Affairs/Displaced Persons Division, Land Salzburg Liaison, General Records, 1945–1950, Box 4, Folder, "Economics, "Minutes of Conference among Salzburg Police and USFA officials," NARA Archives II, College Park, MD.

75. February 5, 1947, RG40,7 Records of the Adjutant General's Office 1917–, WWII Operations Reports, 1940–1948, First Infantry Division, 301-INF-(16) 0.3 APR 1946 to 301-INF-(16)-0.3 APR 1947, Operations Reports, Sixteenth Infantry Regiment, First Infantry Division, Jan 1947, HQ Sixteenth Infantry Regiment, Office of the Regimental Commander, NARA Archives II, College Park, MD.

76. March 10, 1947, RG407, Records of the Adjutant General's Office 1917–, WWII Operations Reports, 1940–1948, First Infantry Division, 301-INF-(16) 0.3 APR 1946 to 301-INF-(16)-0.3 APR 1947, Box 5236, Folder: Operations Report, Sixteenth Infantry Regiment, First Infantry Division, Feb 1947, Document: Service Company Sixteenth Infantry, NARA Archives II, College Park, MD.

77. RG 260 Records of the US Occupation HQ, WWII, USFA, USACA Section, Internal Affairs/Displaced Persons Division, Land Salzburg Liaison, General Records, 1945–1950 (A1 2073), Box 1, Folder 000.5: "Crimes, Criminals, Offenses, and Domestic Subversive Activities," NARA Archives II, College Park, MD.

78. HQ 1st Battalion, 350th Infantry, September 2, 1948. (With the exchange nearly 1 Austrian Schilling to 20 US dollars.) l RG407, Records of the Adjutant General's Office 1917–, WWII Operations Reports, 1940–1948, Eighty-eighth Infantry Division, 388-INF(350)7-0 to 388-INF(350)7-0.3. Box 10984, Folder: "Operation Reports, Occupation of Austria, 1st Battalion, 350th Infantry Regiment, 88th Infantry Division, July–September 30, 1948," NARA Archives II, College Park, MD.

79. July–September 30, 1948, RG 407 Records of the Adjutant General's Office 1917–, WWII Operations Reports, 1940–1948, Eighty-eighth Infantry Division, 388-INF(350)7-0 to 388-INF(350)7-0.3, Box 10984, Folder: "Operation Reports, Occupation of Austria, 1st Battalion, 350th Infantry

Regiment, 88th Infantry Division, 1 Document: HQ 1st Battalion, 350th Infantry, 2 August 1948," NARA Archives II, College Park, MD.

80. February 5, 1947, RG 407 Records of the Adjutant General's Office 1917–, WWII Operations Reports, 1940–1948, 1st Infantry Division, 301-INF-(16) 0.3 APR 1946 to 301-INF-(16)-0.3 APR 1947, Box 5236, Reports Operations, 16th Infantry Regiment, 1st Infantry Division, Jan 1947, HQ 16th Infantry Regiment, Office of the Regimental Commander, NARA Archives II, College Park, MD.

81. March 31, 1948, RG 260 Records of US Occupation HQ, WWII, USFS, USACA Section, Internal Affairs/Displaced Persons Division, Land Salzburg Liaison, General Records, 1945–1950, Box 4, Folder: "Economics, "Minutes of Conference among Salzburg Police and USFA officials," NARA Archives II, College Park, MD.

82. As cited in Goedde, *GIs and Germans*, 136.

83. Author's interview with Erika Casuse, Albuquerque, NM. July 18, 2013.

84. Author's interview with Ursula Casuse-Carrillo, Mexican Springs, Navajo Nation, January 18, 2014.

85. June 30, 1947, RG 407 Records of the Adjutant General's Office 1917–, WWII Operations Reports, 1940–48, 1st Infantry Division, 301-INF-(16)-0.3 May 1947 to 301-INF-(16)-0.3 Dec 1948, Box 5237, Folder: Report of Operations, 16th Infantry Regiment, 1st Infantry Division, June 1947, Document: Land Salzburg Area Command, Office of the Special Service Officer, NARA Archives II, College Park, MD.

86. May 31, 1949 "Smuggle of Cigarettes," RG260, Records of the US Occupation HQ, WWII, USFA, USACA Section, Internal Affairs/ Displaced Persons Division, Land Salzburg Liaison, General Records, 1945–1950 (A1 2073), Box 1, Folder 000.5: "Crimes, Criminals, Offenses, and Domestic Subversive Activities," Document HQ Zone Command Austria, NARA Archives II, College Park, MD.

87. February 6, 1947, RG407, Records of the Adjutant General's Office 1917–, WWII Operations Reports, 1940–1948, 1st Infantry Division, 301-INF-(16) 0.3 APR 1946 to 301-INF-(16)-0.3 APR 1947, Box 5236, Operations Reports, 16th Infantry Regiment, 1st Infantry Division, Jan 1947, HQ, 1st Battalion, 16th Infantry, NARA Archives II, College Park, MD.

88. Biddiscombe, "Dangerous Liaisons," 622.

89. Biddiscombe, "Dangerous Liaisons," 621.

90. Goedde, *GIs and Germans*, 89.

91. Susan Zeiger, *Entangling Alliances: Foreign War Brides and American Soldiers in the Twentieth Century* (New York: NYU Press, 2010), 3.

92. Elizabeth L. Hillman, "Front and Center: Sexual Violence in U.S. Military Law," *Politics & Society* 37, no. 1 (2009): 103.
93. Burds, "Sexual Violence in Europe in World War II," 60.
94. Biddiscombe, "Dangerous Liaisons," 615.
95. Ellen D. Wu, "It's Time to Center War in U.S. Immigration History," *Modern American History* 2, no. 2 (2019): 215.
96. Biddiscombe, "Dangerous Liaisons," 612.
97. Zeiger, *Entangling Alliances*, 72.
98. Wilson-Buford, *Policing Sex and Marriage in the American Military*, 57.
99. Biddiscombe, "Dangerous Liaisons," 636 note 40.
100. Steininger, Bischof, and Gheier, *Austria in the Twentieth Century*, 194.
101. Goedde, *GIs and Germans*, 90.
102. Zeiger, *Entangling Alliances*, 87.
103. Biddiscombe, "Dangerous Liaisons," 617.

Red Scare

1. Author's interview with Alice Bitsilly, Coyote Canyon, Navajo Nation, January 18, 2014.
2. New York, Passenger Lists, 1820–1957, List of In-Bound Passengers, United States Customs.
3. Author's interview with Terry Humble, Bayard, NM, July 22, 2013.
4. "Track Department Seniority List, January 1, 1952," Box 872, Folder 35, IUMMSW Local 890 Archives, Boulder, Colorado.
5. Petra Goedde, *GIs and Germans: Culture, Gender and Foreign Relations, 1945–1949* (New Haven: Yale University Press, 2003), 100.
6. Author's interview with Alice Bitsilly, Coyote Canyon, Navajo Nation, January 18, 2014.
7. Neal Ackerly, *An Overview of the Historic Characteristics of New Mexico's Mines* (Santa Fe: New Mexico Historic Preservation Division, 1997).
8. *Chinorama*, September 1955, Jack Cargill Collection, J. Cloyd Miller Library Archives, Western New Mexico University, Silver City, New Mexico.
9. Christopher J. Huggard and Terrence M. Humble, *Santa Rita del Cobre: A Copper Mining Community in New Mexico* (Boulder: University Press of Colorado, 2012), 69.
10. Bernard L. Himes, "The General Managers at Chino," Silver City Public Library, "Treasure Room," n.d., 29.

11. "Wage Chronology No. Kennecott Copper Corp., 1942–1950," Jack Cargill Collection, Box 3, Folder 7, Cloyd Miller Library Archives, Western New Mexico University, Silver City, New Mexico.

12. "Wage Chronology No. Kennecott Copper Corp., 1942–1950," Jack Cargill Collection, Box 3, Folder 7, Cloyd Miller Library Archives, Western New Mexico University, Silver City, New Mexico.

13. Research Department, "Position in Industry," IUMMSW Local 890 Archives, Box 870, Folder 7: Kennecott Copper Corporation, University of Colorado Boulder; Himes, "The General Managers at Chino," 23.

14. Bernard L. Himes, "The Unions and the Chino Mine," Silver City Public Library, "Treasure Room," n.d., 5.

15. Huggard and Humble, *Santa Rita del Cobre*, 124.

16. Himes, "The Unions and the Chino Mine," 5.

17. Letter from Horace Moses to W. S. Boyd, July 15, 1943, Personal Archive of Terry Humble, Bayard, New Mexico.

18. "Trackman" wages: $5.36 in 1945; $5.88 in 1946; $7.36 in June 3, 1946; $7.36 on December 31, 1946. Source: Letter from William Goodrich to Horace Moses, January 7, 1947.

19. Horace Moses to Boyd, July 15, 1943, Terry Humble Archive.

20. W. Goodrich to Horace Moses, August 7, 1943, Terry Humble Archive.

21. B. L. Himes to Juan Chacon, November 3, 1955, IUMMSW Local 890 Archives, Box 867, Book 1: Correspondence from Kennecott, University of Colorado Boulder; Himes, "The Unions and the Chino Mine," 6.

22. Terry Humble Archive, 1943.

23. W. Goodrich to Horace Moses, September 6, 1943, Terry Humble Archive.

24. W. Goodrich to Horace Moses, October 6, 1943, Terry Humble Archive.

25. W. Goodrich to Horace Moses, labor statistic report, November 7, 1943; Goodrich to Moses, labor report, December 7, 1943, Terry Humble Archive.

26. Himes, "The General Managers at Chino," 22.

27. W. Goodrich to Horace Moses, February 8, 1944, Terry Humble Archive.

28. Report by W. S. Boyd, July 14, 1944, Terry Humble Archive.

29. W. Goodrich to Horace Moses, August 7, 1944, Terry Humble Archive.

30. Horace Moses to Boyd, September 7, 1943, Terry Humble Archive.

31. Horace Moses to Boyd, January 15, 1945, Terry Humble Archive.

32. Horace Moses to Boyd, December 10, 1944, Terry Humble Archive.

33. W. Goodrich to Horace Moses, January 31, 1946, Terry Humble Archive.

34. W. Goodrich to Horace Moses, January 31, 1946, Terry Humble Archive.

35. W. Goodrich to Horace Moses, January 7, 1947, Terry Humble Archive.

36. IUMMSW Local 890 Archives, Box 870, Folder 2: "Kennecott Copper Corporation Travel Time Data," University of Colorado, Boulder.

37. IUMMSW Local 890 Archives, Box 864, Folder 5: "July 1946 dues roster," University of Colorado Boulder.

38. Himes, "The Unions and the Chino Mine," 3.

39. Himes, "The Unions and the Chino Mine," 4.

40. Himes "The Unions and the Chino Mine," 8.

41. Himes, "The Unions and the Chino Mine," 5.

42. Jack Cargill Collection, Box 1, Folder: "Interviews," J. Cloyd Miller Library Archives, Western New Mexico University, Silver City, New Mexico.

43. Himes, "The Unions and the Chino Mine," 5–8. Managers at the mine would tell an apocryphal story of the general manager, Rone Tempest, who considered unionism a form of terrorism and who, after the National Labor Relations Board finally approved the union at the mine, shot himself in the head.

44. Himes, "The General Managers at Chino."

45. Data based on a review of 1943–1948 wage rates, Terry Humble Archives.

46. "Wage Chronology No. Kennecott Copper Corp., 1942–1950," Jack Cargill Collection, Box 3, Folder 7, Cloyd Miller Library Archives, Western New Mexico University, Silver City, New Mexico.

47. Himes, "The Unions and the Chino Mine," 9.

48. "Euclid Truck Department Seniority List," July 1, 1953, IUMMSW Local 890 Archives, Box 873, Folder 5: "Seniority Lists," University of Colorado Boulder. Louis started in the truck department on March 2, 1953.

49. James J. Lorence, *Palomino: Clinton Jencks and Mexican-American Unionism in the American Southwest* (Urbana: University of Illinois Press, 2013), 62.

50. August 4, 1948, letter from W. H. Goodrich to Employees of Chino Mines Division, IUMMSW Local 890 Archives, Box 870, Folder 7: "Kennecott Copper Corporation," University of Colorado Boulder.

51. July 8, 1948, letter from the union to W. H. Goodrich, Superintendent Chino Mines Division, IUMMSW Local 890 Archives, Box 870, Folder 7: "Kennecott Copper Corporation," University of Colorado Boulder; Himes, "The Unions and the Chino Mine," 10.

52. July 3, 1948, memorandum from W. H. Goodrich to all employees, IUMMSW Local 890 Archives, Box 870, Folder 16: "Kennecott Leaflets," University of Colorado Boulder.

53. IUMMSW Local 890 Archives, UC, Boulder, Box 867, Folder 1, University of Colorado Boulder.

54. n.d., Arthur Flores, IUMMSW Local 890 Archives, Box 867, Folder 1, University of Colorado Boulder.

55. Katherine G. Alken, "'When I Realized How Close Communism was to Kellogg, I was Willing to Devote Day and Night': Anti-Communism, Women, Community Values, and the Bunker Hill Strike of 1960," *Labor History* 36, no. 2 (1995): 166.

56. Alicia Schmidt Camacho, *Migrant Imaginaries: Latino Cultural Politics in the US-Mexico Borderlands* (New York: NYU Press, 2008); Ellen R. Baker, "Salt of the Earth: Women, the Mine, Mill and Smelter Workers' Union, and the Hollywood Blacklist in Grant County, New Mexico, 1941–1953" (PhD diss., University of Wisconsin, Madison, 1999); Lorence, *Palomino*.

57. August 15, 1946, monthly union meeting, IUMMSW Local 890 Archives, Box 864, Local 63 Santa Rita, Chino Mines Division, Kennecott Copper Corporation, Book 2: Roll Book, 1945–1957, University of Colorado Boulder.

58. Based on a comparison of trackmen roster and union member rosters in Box 864, Folder 5, IUMMSW Local 890 Archives, University of Colorado Boulder.

59. October 1945 IUMMSW union dues roster, IUMMSW Local 890 Archives, University of California Boulder, Box 864, Folder 5, University of Colorado Boulder. Nez's name appears on an October 1945 union roster crossed out by pencil below the handwritten word "out."

60. IUMMSW Local 890 Archives, Box 864, University of Colorado Boulder.

61. IUMMSW Local 890 Archives, Box 319, Envelope 21, IUMMSW poster titled "AFL-CIO Insults Indian People of Arizona and New Mexico."

62. July 1946 IUMMSW union dues roster, IUMMSW Local 890 Archives, Box 864, Folder 5, University of Colorado Boulder.

63. 1946 labor report, Terry Humble Archive.

64. Huggard and Humble, *Santa Rita del Cobre*, 228.

65. April 10, 1947 IUMMSW Local 890 Archives, Box 870, Folder 7: "Kennecott Copper Corporation," Research Department, IUMMSW–CIO, University of Colorado Boulder.

66. April 10, 1947, IUMMSW Local 890 Archives, Box 870, Folder 7: "Kennecott Copper Corporation," Research Department, IUMMSW–CIO, University of Colorado Boulder.

67. June 27, 1955, letter from Chacon to IUMMSW President John Clark, IUMMSW Local 890 Archives, Box 867, Folder 1, University of Colorado Boulder.

68. "Kennecott Negotiations—Monday, August 30, 1954," Alfredo Montoya Collection, Box 20, Folder 18, IUMMSW Local 890 Archives: "Kennecott

Copper Corporation, Correspondence, grievances, negotiations, and agreements, 1953–1961," University of New Mexico, Center for Southwest Research.

69. November 25 letter G. J. Ballmer, superintendent of mines, to Arthur Flores, Grievance Committee, IUMMSW Local 890 Archives, Box 867, Book 1: Correspondence from Kennecott, University of Colorado Boulder.
70. Author's interview with Terry Humble, Bayard, NM, July 22, 2013.
71. As quoted in Huggard and Humble, *Santa Rita del Cobre*, 113.
72. *Chinorama*, February 1956. Juan Chacon Collection, Box 1, "Chinorama: 1956–1971," J. Cloyd Miller Library Archives, Western New Mexico University, Silver City, New Mexico.
73. Author's interview with Terry Humble, Bayard, NM, July 22, 2013.
74. Author's interview with W. C. Morehal (Shine), Gallup, NM, July 23, 2013. I spoke to Shine on what would have been Lillian's seventy-eighth birthday. He never mentioned it.
75. *Chinorama*, February 1958; author's interview with former Tyrone mine trucker, El Rito, NM, July 24, 2013.
76. *Chinorama*, February 1958, 11.
77. *Chinorama*, January–February 1964, Juan Chacon Collection, Box 1, J. Cloyd Miller Library Archives, Western New Mexico University, Silver City, NM.
78. Huggard and Humble, *Santa Rita del Cobre*, 165.
79. *Chinorama*, Fall 1968, Juan Chacon Collection, Box 1, J. Cloyd Miller Library Archives, Western New Mexico University, Silver City, NM; Huggard and Humble, *Santa Rita del Cobre*, 166.
80. Author's interview with Donald Casuse, Gallup, NM, January 16, 2014.
81. Author's interview with Alice Bitsilly, Coyote Canyon, Navajo Nation, January 18, 2014.
82. IUMMSW Local 890 Archives, Box 874, Folder 5: "Kennecott Grievances, 1954," University of Colorado Boulder.
83. Author's interview with Ursula Casuse-Carrillo, Gallup, NM, June 12, 2013.
84. "Who's a Tycoon?" *Chinorama*, July 1957.
85 "Who Profits from Profits?" *Chinorama*, January 1958, Jack Cargill Collection, J. Cloyd Miller Library Archives, Western New Mexico University, Silver City, NM.
86. *Chinorama*, February 1959, Jack Cargill Collection Cloyd Miller Archives, J. Cloyd Miller Library Archives, Western New Mexico University, Silver City, NM.
87. Huggard and Humble, *Santa Rita del Cobre*, 147.
88. Huggard and Humble, *Santa Rita del Cobre*, 147.

89. October 9, 1960, IUMMSW Local 890 Archives, Box 869, Folder 5: "Kennecott Copper Corporation Meetings, 1960–1965," University of Colorado, Boulder.
90. Author's interview with Erika Casuse, Albuquerque, NM, August 14, 2018.
91. Author's interview with Erika Casuse, Albuquerque, NM, August 14, 2018.
92. Huggard and Humble, *Santa Rita del Cobre*, 131.
93. Author's interview with Donald Casuse, Gallup, NM, January 16, 2014.
94. Author's interview with Ursula Casuse-Carrillo, Gallup, NM, July 12, 2018.
95. Author's interview with Erika Casuse, Albuquerque, NM, August 14, 2018.
96. Author's interview with Ursula Casuse-Carrillo, Gallup, NM, August 24, 2018.
97. Author's interview with Donald Casuse, Gallup, NM, January 16, 2014.
98. Author's interview with Erika Casuse, Albuquerque, NM, August 14, 2018.
99. Author's interview with Donald Casuse, Gallup, NM, January 16, 2014.
100. Author's interview with Erika Casuse, Albuquerque, NM, August 14, 2018.
101. Author's interview with Ursula Casuse-Carrillo, Gallup, NM, July 12, 2018.
102. Author's interview with Ursula Casuse-Carrillo, Gallup NM, December 18, 2020.
103. Author's interview with Erika Casuse, Albuquerque, NM, August 14, 2018.

Man Camp

1. Scott Beavan, "Gallup: City of Unrest," *Albuquerque Journal*, March 25, 1973, A8.
2. December 5, 1968, letter from Mac Eddy to Governor David F. Cargo, David Cargo Collection, 62:1206L, New Mexico State Records Center and Archives, Santa Fe, NM.
3. Petition, David Cargo Collection, Box 62:1206 (Liquor), New Mexico State Records Center and Archives, Santa Fe, NM.
4. April 2, 1969 letter from Edmund Kahn to Governor David Cargo, David Cargo Collection, 62:1206 (L), New Mexico State Records Center and Archives, Santa Fe, NM.
5. National Institute on Alcoholism and Alcohol Abuse (NIAAA), *US Alcohol 1981 Epidemiological Data Reference Manual 3: County Alcohol Problem Indicators, 1975–77* (Rockville, MD: US Department of Health and Human Services, 1981).
6. Calvin Trillin, "U.S. Journal: Gallup, New Mexico. (Drunken Indians)," *New Yorker*, September 25, 1971, 108.

7.   Philip A. May and Matthew B. Smith. "Some Navajo Indian Opinions about Alcohol Abuse and Prohibition: A Survey and Recommendations for Policy," *Journal of Studies on Alcohol and Drugs* 49, no. 4 (1988): 345.

8.   Jill E. Martin, "'The Greatest Evil': Interpretations of Indian Prohibition Laws, 1832–1953," *Great Plains Quarterly* 23, no. 1 (2003): 35–53.

9.   Lauren L. Fuller, "Alcoholic Beverage Control: Should the Remaining Reservations Repeal Prohibition Under 18 USC 1161," *American Indian Law Review* 3 (1975): 431; see also United States v. Mazurie, 419 U.S. 544 (1975), which held, inter alia, that 18 U.S.C. § 1154—which regulated the introduction of "spiritous liquors" into "Indian Country"—was not unconstitutionally vague. It concluded that Congress had the authority to regulate distribution of alcoholic beverages in "Indian Country" even though the land was held in fee by non-Indians, and, finally, that Congress could delegate authority to regulate alcohol to the reservation's tribal council.

10. Robert A. Campbell, "Making Sober Citizens: The Legacy of Indigenous Alcohol Regulation in Canada, 1777–1985," *Journal of Canadian Studies* 42, no. 1 (2008): 108.

11. Mariana Valverde, *Diseases of the Will: Alcohol and the Dilemmas of Freedom* (Cambridge: Cambridge University Press, 1988), 164.

12. Testimony of William Pensoneau, vice president, National Indian Youth Council, Indian Education Subcommittee Hearings, 90th Congress, 1st and 2nd sess., February 24, 1969.

13. D. Fenna, O. Schaefer, L. Mix, and J. A. Gilbert, "Ethanol Metabolism in Various Racial Groups," *Canadian Medical Association Journal* 105, no. 5 (1971): 472.

14. Bernard H. Ellis Jr., "Mobilizing Communities to Reduce Substance Abuse in Indian Country," in *Healing and Mental Health for Native Americans: Speaking in Red*, eds., Ethan Nebelkopf and Mary Phillips (Lanham, MD: AltaMira Press, 2004), 88.

15. May and Smith, "Some Navajo Indian Opinions about Alcohol Abuse and Prohibition," 325.

16. Jerrold E. Levy and Stephen J. Kunitz, *Indian Drinking: Navajo Practices and Anglo-American Theories* (New York: Wiley, 1974), 97.

17. Sherene Razack, *Dying from Improvement: Inquests and Inquiries into Indigenous Deaths in Custody* (Toronto: University of Toronto Press, 2015), 19.

18. May and Smith, "Some Navajo Indian Opinions about Alcohol Abuse and Prohibition," 328.

19. Paul Brodeur, "Combating Alcohol Abuse in Northwestern New Mexico: Gallup's Fighting Back and Healthy Nations Programs," in *To Improve Health and Health Care: The Robert Wood Johnson Foundation Anthology*,

vol. 6, eds. Stephen L. Isaacs and James R. Knickman (San Francisco: Jossey-Bass Publishers, 2002).

20. President's Committee on Civil Rights, *To Secure These Rights: The Report of the President's Committee on Civil Rights.* (Washington DC: US Government Publishing Office, 1947).

21. Federal Trade Commission (FTC), *The Trading Post System on the Navajo Reservation: Staff Report to the Federal Trade Commission* (Washington DC: US Government Publishing Office, 1947), 33.

22. Frances Ferguson, "Navaho Drinking: Some Tentative Hypotheses," *Human Organization* 27, no. 2 (1968): 163.

23. P. Katel, "Sleeping It Off in Gallup, NM," *Corrections Magazine* 6, no. 4 (1980): 21.

24. Ferguson, "Navaho Drinking," 161.

25. Simon J. Ortiz, *Woven Stone* (Tucson: University of Arizona Press, 1992), 242.

26. See Katel, "Sleeping it Off in Gallup, NM."

27. Scott Beavan, "Gallup: City of Unrest," *Albuquerque Journal*, March 25, 1973.

28. Southwestern Indian Development (SID), *Traders on the Navajo Reservation: A Report on the Economic Bondage of the Navajo People* (Window Rock, AZ: Southwestern Indian Development, 1969), iii.

29. Southwestern Indian Development, *Traders on the Navajo Nation*, iii.

30. "Peterson Zah and Peter Iverson Interview, December 17, 2008" (2012-04590), Labriola National American Indian Data Center. Department of Archives and Special Collections, University Libraries, Arizona State University, Tempe, Arizona.

31. "Peterson Zah and Peter Iverson Interview, December 17, 2008" (2012-04590), Labriola National American Indian Data Center, Department of Archives and Special Collections, University Libraries, Arizona State University, Tempe, Arizona.

32. Federal Trade Commission (FTC), *The Trading Post System on the Navajo Reservation* (Washington DC, US Government Publishing Office, 1973), 3.

33. FTC, *The Trading Post System on the Navajo Reservation*, 13.

34. FTC, *The Trading Post System on the Navajo Reservation*, 8.

35. SID, *Traders on the Navajo Nation*, 10.

36. FTC, *The Trading Post System on the Navajo Reservation*, 20.

37. Author's interview with Al Taradash, Albuquerque, NM, March 30, 2015.

38. FTC, *The Trading Post System on the Navajo Reservation*, 12.

39. FTC, *The Trading Post System on the Navajo Reservation*, 20.

40. FTC, *The Trading Post System on the Navajo Reservation*, 19–20; SID, *Traders on the Navajo Nation*, 11.

41. FTC, *The Trading Post System on the Navajo Reservation*, 3.

42. SID, *Traders on the Navajo Nation*, xx; FTC, *The Trading Post System on the Navajo Reservation*, 17–27.
43. FTC, *The Trading Post System on the Navajo Reservation*, 17.
44. SID, *Traders on the Navajo Nation*, 14.
45. SID, *Traders on the Navajo Nation*, 11.
46. SID, *Traders on the Navajo Nation*, 18.
47. FTC, *The Trading Post System on the Navajo Reservation*, 26.
48. FTC, *The Trading Post System on the Navajo Reservation*, 25.
49. FTC, *The Trading Post System on the Navajo Reservation*, 25.
50. FTC, *The Trading Post System on the Navajo Reservation*, 36.
51. Author's interview with Al Taradash, Albuquerque, March 30, 2015.
52. Author's interview with Al Taradash, Albuquerque, March 30, 2015.
53. Carol Chiago Lujan, "Women Warriors: American Indian Women, Crime, and Alcohol," *Women & Criminal Justice* 7, no. 1 (1996): 17, 18.
54. Gloria Emerson, "Where Two Cultures Cross," *Youth Magazine* 24, no. 11 (November 1973).
55. John Redhouse, "Getting It Out of My System" (unpublished memoir, December 2014), 11.
56. Calvin Trillin, "A Reporter at Large: Tribute," *New Yorker*, August 9, 1972.
57. Trillin, "A Reporter at Large: Tribute."
58. August 21, 1970, Report of SAC, Albuquerque, and August 14, 1970, memo from SAC, Albuquerque to Director, FBI, "The FBI files on the American Indian Movement and Wounded Knee [microform]," Reel 1, File 105-203686, Section 1, 244 and 275.
59. Calvin Trillin, "U.S. Journal: Gallup, NM, You Always Turn Your Head," *New Yorker*, May 12, 1973.
60. Indians Against Exploitation, "Gallup Ceremonial '73: The Issue and Our Recommendations," October 1973.
61. Redhouse, "Getting It Out of My System," 12.
62. Trillin, "A Reporter at Large: Tribute," 34.
63. Trillin, "A Reporter at Large: Tribute," 36.
64. Redhouse, "Getting It Out of My System," 12.
65. Author's interview with Al Taradash, Albuquerque, March 30, 2015.
66. Author's interview with Al Taradash, Albuquerque, March 30, 2015.

Larry Casuse

1. Bill Donovan, "Friends Blame Recent Troubles," *Gallup Independent*, March 2, 1973.

2. John Redhouse, "Getting It Out of My System" (unpublished memoir, December 2014), 9.

3. January 10, 1973, letter from KIVA Club to Gulf Mart, KIVA Club File, John Redhouse Papers, MSS 780 BC, University of New Mexico, Center for Southwest Research.

4. Author's interview with Phil Loretto, San Pedro, NM, August 19, 2014.

5. Audio recording of interview between Robert Nakaidinae and Emmet Garcia, "Kidnapping a Regent," Calvin Horn Collection, UNMA 108, Box 7, Folder 19, University of New Mexico, Center for Southwest Research.

6. Redhouse, "Getting It Out of My System," 12.

7. Staff, "IAE Backs 'PHS Six,'" *Gallup Independent*, January 30, 1973.

8. Calvin Trillin, "A Reporter at Large: Tribute," *New Yorker*, August 6, 1972.

9. Redhouse, "Getting It Out of My System," 16.

10. "Casuse is Guilty of Leaving Death Scene; Freed of Others," *Gallup Independent*, December 21, 1972.

11. Author's interview with Al Taradash, Albuquerque, NM, March 30, 2015.

12. When Larry wrote letters to Gallup, he'd address the envelope to the "City of Exploitation."

13. "Kidnapping a Regent," Calvin Horn Collection, UNMA 108, Box 7, Folder 19, University of New Mexico, Center for Southwest Research.

14. Don Green, "'Get Back; They'll Come Out Shooting,'" *Gallup Independent*, March 2, 1973.

15. Sylvia Ann Abeyta, "Casuse Rated More Talk, Less Shooting," *Gallup Independent*, March 2, 1973.

16. Bonnie Meyer, "Mayor Safe; Abductor Dead," *Gallup Independent*, March 2, 1973.

17. "Kidnapping a Regent."

18. "Merchant Had Close Call," *Gallup Independent*, March 2, 1973.

19. Bonnie Meyer, "Mrs. Casuse Talks About Dead Son," *Gallup Independent*, March 3, 1973.

20. In addition to playing the song during his interview with Emmet Garcia, Nakaidinae played the song in a set he performed on November 25, 1974, at the Native American Folk Festival in Tsaile, Arizona. The second recording included revised lyrics from the interview with Garcia. See James B. Wright Collection of Southwestern Native American and Hispanic Music, Interviews and Literary Programs, 1973–1986, MSS 829 BC, Box 1, CD 74/12F, Part 1, University of New Mexico, Center for Southwest Research.

Index

Page numbers in italics indicate pictures

About Haymarket Books

Haymarket Books is a radical, independent, nonprofit book publisher based in Chicago. Our mission is to publish books that contribute to struggles for social and economic justice. We strive to make our books a vibrant and organic part of social movements and the education and development of a critical, engaged, international left.

We take inspiration and courage from our namesakes, the Haymarket martyrs, who gave their lives fighting for a better world. Their 1886 struggle for the eight-hour day—which gave us May Day, the international workers' holiday—reminds workers around the world that ordinary people can organize and struggle for their own liberation. These struggles continue today across the globe—struggles against oppression, exploitation, poverty, and war.

Since our founding in 2001, Haymarket Books has published more than five hundred titles. Radically independent, we seek to drive a wedge into the risk-averse world of corporate book publishing. Our authors include Noam Chomsky, Arundhati Roy, Rebecca Solnit, Angela Y. Davis, Howard Zinn, Amy Goodman, Wallace Shawn, Mike Davis, Winona LaDuke, Ilan Pappé, Richard Wolff, Dave Zirin, Keeanga-Yamahtta Taylor, Nick Turse, Dahr Jamail, David Barsamian, Elizabeth Laird, Amira Hass, Mark Steel, Avi Lewis, Naomi Klein, and Neil Davidson. We are also the trade publishers of the acclaimed Historical Materialism Book Series and of Dispatch Books.